# Weaving the Strands of Life

# Weaving the Strands of Life

Joanna Kubicka Fenn

Copyright © 2016 Joanna Kubicka Fenn
First Edition

All rights reserved

No part of this book may be reproduced by any means without written permission of the author. The exception would be in the case of brief quotations embodied in the critical articles or reviews and pages where permission is specifically granted by the publisher or author.

Published in the United States by Fennland Press.

ISBN-10: 1544264879   ISBN-13: 978-1544264875

Library of Congress Number

2016962924

Printed in the United States of America

Fennland Press
fennlandpress@jeffnet.org

*To my children and to Donnelly*

*Thank you for your love and support*

*Life weaves upon her brow*
*Everything she does, thinks, and writes.*
*Everything is contained in the weave.*
*Life's shuttle comes and goes.*

Norwegian lullaby, translated by Chris Dahl

"My trade and art is to live."
— Michel de Montaigne, from *Essays, Book II*

## PROLOGUE

A FEW DAYS AGO I HEARD John Prine singing. In one of the songs there was a line: "I built me a castle of memories to have a place to go home to." It is such a magnificent way of describing what old people do. When the present becomes less and less enjoyable, we build these memory castles where we can hide and relive moments of strength, intelligence, passion. There is a danger though; it comes when you lift up the drawbridge.

    I started to think about the castles I build. Yes, I do build them. I am afraid I often embellish their walls, reorganize, beautify the views from their windows. Sweep under the carpet things that are painful, enlarge those that I like to think of as more prevalent. And yet, all my life I've tried to be truthful to myself, not to cling to invented memories. I use the word cling — because it is impossible not to create memories out of stories heard, out of wishful thinking, or fearing truth. The strength of seeing oneself in plain view, the strength of not allowing oneself to build myths about one's actions, or motives for them, was something my father instilled in me quite early.

I tried, I was quite cruel to myself at times, and yet I see that many times I failed. Hence the castles. Those castles are, in my view, very important although rather artificial. We create our comfort with them, that's the whole idea of "to go home to." They become the repositories of memories, of who we were, who we became with the years. After all, the I at ten, fifteen or thirty are still in me at nearly seventy. That's who I am, as opposed to who I would like to be.

Luckily, although I like them, I do not need artificially created castles for enjoyment of the day. My life is absorbing to a high degree. My present is still challenging and satisfying. The foundation laid by my parents is stable enough — I haven't collapsed, I am still standing straight and managing to add to the structure, I am still building me.

Not long ago my older son, Jarek (Yarek), asked me to write about our family, my own past, his childhood of which he has but little memory. I promised him to do it, although what I remember, say about people, happenings, places, beliefs, will be, has to be, very subjective. Even if we try to see something objectively, as is, we cannot do away with our whole past growing process which colors everything. Writing the word "colors," which I used figuratively, I thought of the literal meaning of colors and of how different the colors are if I look at the surroundings with my reddish-brown tinted sunglasses on or without them. So which colors are real? Is there a "real" color? Maybe each of us sees them differently? Just think of optical illusions — don't they show us that we have no true access to reality? And that's about optics only. How about characters of people? How about experiences? There are so many things that happened when my kids were children which they remember totally differently than I do.

I also found that I don't want to write in an orderly time frame. It would be boring for me, and thus most probably for the reader too. And there is another thing — I learned my

English as a child in a British school in Cairo, now I live in the U.S., thus some of the grammatical rules that I use represent a hybrid of British and American influences. I, personally, like it and hope you will too.

I think I might enjoy writing a diary interspersed with memories, some of my poems and short stories when they tie in with my thoughts or daily happenings. This way it will be clearer that it does not pertain to the absolute truth, and that my views have changed over the years. And there is no doubt that they have. Not long ago I found a notebook in which I wrote a diary when I was twelve. Reading it I was astounded how miserable I was at the time. I remember it as a happy time, yet in that diary I wrote only about sadness, about certainty of not being loved, about despair that nobody understood me, about feeling ugly. Then I looked at dates — most of them were weeks apart. I must have written only when feeling unhappy. On good days, I suppose I was too much filled with life, with the joy of living to even think about recording my feelings. Is this true about memory in general? Do we remember only extremes? The great happenings, not the mundane, the regular, the middle of the road. So, can a memoir give a true picture of a person's life? After all quite a big percentage of it usually is humdrum. Well, who cares? After all we love to read fiction, don't we? So let's hope that what I will commit to paper will be interesting enough for readers. If it won't answer my son's need for family history, it will at least give him a picture of his mother's perception of said family and her own attitude towards life.

## JANUARY 2005

The evening is cold, a full moon shines harshly on frost-covered branches. Somewhere a dog is barking fiercely. That is outside. Here in my room it feels like nothing bad can touch me. Ottmar Liebert is playing his guitar and it gives rhythmic construction to the space and time. A wood fire in the stove keeps the room comfortably warm, lights are on, my man is sitting on the same sofa on which I half sit, half lie. He is reading Paul Johnson's *A History of the American People*, totally absorbed in it. Yet when I reached for my pen and this notebook, he lifted his eyes from his book and looked intently, searchingly at me. He likes when I write. He likes when I am active. I think he is afraid of my aging. He is afraid of his own aging. He is afraid of us both aging. We are both afraid of us both aging. Does it sound like an obsession? Hell, no. We are not obsessed, yet, but lately we started to be painfully aware of how much we can lose. It seems this painful awareness is stronger when we are happy. Ironically, the older we get the happier we are. Just look at us — Donnelly has just deeply burped, and it made me feel so tender towards him. In moments like this I know for sure the curvature of time, how it bends around me, envelops me in a cocoon so that everything important in the past, present, and future is right here in me, and the sum of it is overwhelmingly precious.

Before I started writing I was reading Anne Lammot's *Bird by Bird*, a book about writing. It made me think why do I write so rarely. Am I afraid? Is writing like opening a drain? Am I worried I'll drain too much of my inner self away, or am I afraid to see, black on white, all those things that I consider worth sharing? To see that they are really nothing much? To see to what extent I am deluding myself about my life, myself, the people I love?

Now Ottmar's guitar gave way to the "Long Black Veil" by The Chieftains. What a different mood. There is plenty of sadness in Irish music, yet so much life and energy at the same time. I think I'll make myself a cup of tea.

## STILL JANUARY 2005

People often ask me how did it happen that I, a Pole, was born in Egypt. I usually evade answering by saying "oh, it's a long story." But now that I think about it I do realize it is a fascinating story, so let's tell it.

My paternal grandfather, Bohdan Pohoski, born to a family of landowners in eastern Poland in 1880, lost his father when he was thirteen or fourteen. His mother remarried shortly after, but Bohdan disliked her new husband to the point of running away. In those days when boys ran away from home, they usually went to the sea. There was always a need for ships' boys, and as hard as it is to imagine now, captains didn't ask where the candidate came from or even whether they were of age. He sailed for a year or so, and then one day, in Athens, a Greek ship owner visited the captain. As they were talking business over drinks served by young Bohdan, the captain pulled the boy into the conversation and the Greek (I don't even know his name, although I did hear it when I was a child) was so impressed with Bohdan's intelligence that he offered to pay for the education of the boy. As the story has it, not having a son of his own, he wanted to be instrumental in the development of a bright young man. And so it happened.

My grandfather was sent to Paris where in a matter of two or three years he got his baccalaureate, then went to L'Ecole Politechnique and, in due time, graduated with an engineering diploma. His first big job was on the construction of the railroad from Cairo to Khartoum, around fifteen hundred miles. Shortly after starting his job he met a lovely young Polish girl, Zofia Karlinska, who came to Egypt for her health. They fell in love, got married and in due time produced a son. For quite a long time the new family lived part of the time in train carriages, converted to living quarters and moving along the freshly laid rails, and part of the time in a house in Heliopolis, a suburb of Cairo. Before the work was done two more boys were born. One of them, the middle one, was my father, who although he had as an official birthplace Cairo, in reality was born in a small place called Beni Suef. Somewhere between Cairo and Khartoum.

The boys had a nanny — an old Arab man, Mahmood, who told them countless stories. The *Arabian Nights* style, full of djinns, and adventures, and dreams coming true. Tales of camel caravans bringing spices and bolts of cloth from faraway lands, of merchants telling stories about magnificent, rich cities they saw, about seas and ships and brave sailors. And, of course, he told them tales from the Koran. The boys loved historical stories, but the history the old man knew, the only one that was important to him, was the Muslim history. Stories of battles won over the infidels, of great pilgrimages, of wise caliphs and their harems.

My father often reminisced about the tales Mahmood told them. And when I was in my teens, and we lived in Poland, my friends and I loved to listen to him retelling the stories. We would all sit cross-legged in a circle on a big Persian carpet, with a pile of apples in the center for us to munch on. The room was lit by an old Arabic oil lamp and he, like Scheherazade, would interrupt his story in the most interesting place, so that we were impatient for our next evening.

But let's stop digressing. Back to Egypt — my paternal grandmother, a nice, well educated Polish woman, of good family, was a loving mother. She read to her children all the important Polish books so that they were being brought up with a feeling of belonging to that nation. Especially *The Trilogy* by Henryk Sienkiewicz. Polish books were hard to get in Egypt, they read the ones they had so many times that those books became memorized, and memorized so well that even in his fifties my father could compete with his friend Janusz Witomski who could better recite big paragraphs of *Potop* (English title *Deluge* which is part of *The Trilogy*). She also taught them the basics of math, geography (to show her sons that not the whole world was made of a desert), history and French. Because of all that, the boys spoke fluent Polish, Arabic and French from the very beginning. My father even learned to sew and embroider. Well, there must not have been many things to do in the desert.

His childhood was free from want and filled with love, yet in some ways it was pretty harsh — both physically and emotionally. The Sahara is not gentle to anyone. And the children saw the Egyptian workers toiling all day long in the glare of un-pardoning sun, using a handful of water for washing, eating a bowl of beans and going to sleep in the sand. It must have made a lasting impression on the boys. They must have compared their relative comfort to the way the Arabs lived, and they must have asked questions, and who knows what answers they got, but they all grew sensitive to others and never took for granted what they had.

Then there was religion. Their mother, a Catholic like most Poles, taught them about heaven and hell, about sin and about the importance of sacraments like baptism. Those who were not baptized were supposed to go to hell after death. Or was it purgatory for the babies?

I remember, when at thirteen I first started to have doubts about church and its dogmas, my father told me about his first doubts, how after having obediently listened to his mother, he would go outside and look at the workers kneeling on little pieces of material, all facing in the same direction, and praying to their god. He did not understand at first why they prayed to Allah, didn't they know that he couldn't save them? Then as he grew older he just couldn't understand why people were so stupid, why they seemed not to be able to see what he saw quite clearly — that either it didn't matter which god you pray to, as there is only one, no matter what you call him, or that there is no god whatsoever.

Anyway, when my father was fourteen (his older brother fifteen, the younger one thirteen) their father decided that something had to be done about their education. So, following the steps he had taken in his youth, he took the boys to Paris, enrolled them in a school, found a nice family that took boys for boarding, and left them there.

All three of them successfully finished high school. The oldest one Mieszek went on to study finance at the Sorbonne, the youngest Maciek followed in his father's footsteps to the Politechnique, and my father, Henryk Pohoski, decided to go to Poland. He wanted to see the country of his parents' origin, to meet the extended family before he decided what to do with his life. It was 1927, he was eighteen, Poland was in a frenzy of building, modernizing, organizing. For a long time it had been divided into three parts between Russia, Prussia and Austria (1772–1918). Now, newly one and independent again following the First World War, it thrived on the energy that comes with hope, with the feeling of so many possibilities. There were great plans to redo the school system. There was a totally new port city, Gdynia, being built on the shore of the Baltic Sea. There was an enormous need for a strong, modern army and air force. There was as always, historically speaking, a danger coming from the east, Russia and its relatively new successor, the Soviet Union, and from the west, Germany with its need of ever more land.

That might have been enough for a young boy to decide to stay and study at the Military Academy. But, there was also something else that drove him. When introduced to his extended family, he met Ewa (Eva) Pohoska — his second cousin. A few months older than he, a pretty, vivacious student of chemistry at the University of Warsaw, she caught his eye, and soon his heart. The decision became easy. They got engaged, and were engaged for a long time as he was not allowed to marry before graduating from the Academy. There was another problem — second cousins had to ask permission of the Pope for a Catholic wedding. In 1935 they finally did marry. My father who by that time was working for the Chiefs of Staff took a long leave of absence and they went to Egypt so that his new wife and his parents could get to know each other. That is where I was conceived and then born at the end of 1936. I spent my first two years there. By then my grandfather was a director of Egyptian Railroads. He and his wife Zofia lived in a lovely villa in Heliopolis, a suburb of Cairo, so there was plenty of space for my parents and me. I was the first grandchild, doted on by everybody. My uncle Mieszek worked for a French bank Credit Lyonnais in Cairo. The youngest brother of the three, Maciek, worked in Port Said in the administration of the Suez Canal. Compared to what was brewing in Europe this was paradise.

It was 1938, and to those who paid attention it became obvious that war in Europe was unavoidable. The whole family tried to convince my father to stay. They were ready to find him a job, to help in any way needed. But he was a patriot, a responsible officer of the Polish army, there was no doubt in his mind — he had to go back. He did. My mother and I in tow.

Well, so this is the story. *Si non e vero e ben trovato.* (Even if not true, it's well received.) I tried to remember what my father told me at one time or another. Only now I know what I should have asked, now when it is too late. He is gone, everybody who could have known the dates, names, particulars gone. My son Jarek is absolutely right. I have to write so that at least what I remember, or can reconstruct, may be passed on to them, my children and grandchildren. Who knows how far in time such musings will be enjoyed.

The summer of 1939 was gorgeous, my father was very busy at his job and pretty sure that the Germans were getting ready to attack us, my mother was pregnant with a second child so they decided for her and me to go east to her country estate. There was a new manor which had just been built to replace the old one destroyed in the First World War. There was also my maternal grandmother living nearby. What better, safer place for a woman and a child? What better place to await the new one expected in October?

Those months in the country proved to be great for us.

Fresh air, plenty of milk, butter, eggs, fruit, vegetables, all home grown. Servants to do all the hard work. We thrived. I heard many stories about that summer. Most of them are of my stubbornness. One is especially dear to me. I've always thought it was a good prediction of my future character. As I was later told, I was angry at my mother and decided to run away. I was two and a half. I got dressed in a coat, a hat and shoes, and went to the front door. The handle though was too high. This didn't dissuade me. I pulled a chair to the door. Fine, now I could reach the handle, but — the door wouldn't open as the chair was blocking it. According to my mother, I sat there for quite some time thinking and then tried to move the chair's position. It didn't work, the door still didn't open. Then I calmly went to my room and started to play with my toys. This is how I operate to this day. Think, plan, decide, most of the time succeed, but if it proves undoable, I do not get upset, I choose another way to live. That's why I am now in America.

But back to 1939. In Poland we have a saying: "A man shoots, but God carries the bullets." In this case the bullets literally came from an unexpected direction.

The expected did happen. On the first of September 1939 Germany invaded Poland. Even with all the preparations done by Poland, the twenty years from the regaining of independence was too short a time to create a strong army and air force capable of withstanding an attack by the well equipped and trained Wehrmacht. The Poles were losing ground, retreating, trying to regroup to create a stronger barrier in the east of the country. That was when the unexpected happened. A knife thrust in the back. The Soviet Union attacked from the east.

My mother's lands were in eastern Poland. Today it is Ukraine. For hundreds of years that part belonged to Poland, the towns and cities were Polish, the lands owned mainly by Poles, but villages were either mixed or ethnically Ukrainian. After the invasion of Polish territory in 1939 the Soviets infiltrated the villages and instigated the peasants to go murder the landowners. "Do away with those who sucked your blood for so long, we will bring you communist paradise." The propaganda resulted in widespread pogroms.

Thankfully, my mother and her family, who owned the lands for several hundred years, were liked and appreciated by their peasants. I know stories of how our family created schools for the village kids, and were always ready to help the unfortunates. One of my mother's aunts, Janina, went to an agricultural college to study modern ways of farming so that she could educate villagers. Which she did, by opening a free school in the manor house of her estate, which was not far from my mother's. Even the fact that our manor was rebuilt eighteen years after the First World War, which destroyed nearly everything, as the battle grounds were there for a long time, but that the peasants' cottages and the farm buildings had been replaced much earlier, as soon as my grandmother and my mother could come up with the funds needed, speaks about their priorities.

Anyway, a delegation from the village came to the manor, told my mother what was happening, and offered their help. They would bring some simple clothing for all of us, grandma, mother and me, pack all the things mom would want to take into a horse cart, cover it all with a layer of potatoes and take us to town on a market day. We would look like a simple Ukrainian family going to town to sell their produce.

My mother was grateful for their offer. My grandmother had a villa in the neighboring town Łuck (pronounced "Wootzk"), we relocated safely, and at the end of October my sister Isia was born. Happy ending? Oh, no. The Soviets were intent on destroying all possibility of opposition. So the intelligentsia, the families of Polish officers, had to be either killed outright or sent to Siberia for hard work. The Russians came for my mother. Luckily her maiden name was the same as her married name, after all she and my father were cousins. She produced witnesses that she had never been married, just a slut with two kids, as my sister Isia had been already born. No relation to the officer Pohoski. It worked. Of course she knew it wouldn't take long for the KGB to get to the truth, so taking advantage of an agreement between Germany and USSR about repatriation of people who wanted to be under German occupation, my mother applied for a permit to go to Warsaw. It wasn't easy, but she managed to get permission to board a train to central Poland together with her mother and two daughters. She was told the trip might be long — maybe two or three days (a distance of roughly 350 miles), as the civilian trains were often put on side rails to allow the army trains to pass. It was winter by then. With all the nervous tension mother had lost her milk. The baby was on a bottle, and as there was no baby formula to be bought, the bottle had to be filled with boiled cow milk. So, with as much as possible of milk, cloth diapers, food for me and the grownups, with whatever clothes they could manage to carry, the two women with the two children left Łuck. (That name does not mean in Polish, what it means in English. It would be too ironic, wouldn't it?)

Well, the trip in crowded cattle cars, no toilets or water, took several days. My sister, three months old, finished the cold by then milk, used up all the clean diapers and sucked on dry bread for food. She was near death by the time we arrived in Warsaw.

I have been lately asking my friends about their early memories. It seems that a peaceful, happy childhood doesn't help in creating memories. On the other hand, times of upheaval, horror of abuse, being surrounded by war, living through extreme poverty and hunger leave us with indelible memories which hound us to the end of our days. This trip gave me my first memory. When crossing the line between Soviet occupation and the part occupied by Germans, we had to disembark and go through a "cleansing." I remember a big room filled with naked women and crying children. My first ever sighting of naked people. There was also a German woman with a bucket who poured liquid soap on our heads with a ladle. Others pushed us all into another room where scaldingly hot water sprayed out from the ceiling onto our bodies. I remember clinging tightly to my mother's thigh. Her arms were holding Isia and trying to shield her from all that soap and the heat of the water. I was later told by grandma that I had been a brave little girl, that I didn't cry. I suppose I was too shocked to even cry, but this memory makes me shudder to this day. My very first memory.

## SOMETIME LATER

In German occupied Warsaw we moved in with my mother's sister Helena and her husband Tolek. She was a dentist, he was her assistant working on dentures and partials. The apartment was big, one of the rooms served as a surgery, another as a place for my uncle's workshop. My parents' apartment didn't exist anymore. One of the first bombings destroyed it.

When we arrived, my father was there, at aunt Helena's, waiting for us. I did not understand what was happening, of course. I had no idea about Poland losing her freedom, about why Father who I knew had fought with the enemy, was there present in our daily life. Although somehow, subconsciously I must have grasped the situation. I became a quiet, introverted child, observing everything and everybody with a hunger for understanding. The tension in grownups told me not to ask, but rather find the answers on my own. Now I understand what a burden that was for a three, later four and five year old. Then — then it was just normal.

In 1995 I wrote "The Wall," a story that describes what happened in the apartment one day, when, for some reason, only my grandmother and I were at home.

## THE WALL

*I thought it so funny when my father and my uncle started to tear up the floorboards and build a wall. Every day a few boards, so that there wouldn't be too much noise. Preferably when the neighbors weren't at home.*

*It was a fun game. They allowed me to hold the nails and to count — one, two, three. On three they would, both of them, bang on the nails. So that two nails would be hammered in with just one sound. Once again, not to arouse curiosity.*

*When the work was finished, we had a space like a secret closet at the end of the room. It went the whole length of the room, but was no more than three feet wide. Then they papered the wall, to look like the rest of the room, hung a tapestry over its little door, and spread carpets over the bared floor. They even allowed me to play in that secret closet, but I soon became bored. The space was too dark and cramped even for a four year old.*

*The only thing I could not do was talk about it. But by that time I already knew well that I was not to talk about anything to anybody. I was told many times that I would be able to speak freely once the war was over. It was hard to imagine sometimes all those magnificent things that were to happen when the war was over.*

*Soon after, two people were brought to our apartment, a husband and wife. They were led into our hideaway, the door was closed, tapestry smoothed out carefully, a bed pushed against the wall. I was mystified, but knew better than to ask. It was quite queer to play, or listen to stories read to me by my mother, while all the time feeling the presence of people alive there, beyond that partition. What were they doing? How did they manage to keep so quiet? Only late at night, when my younger sister was asleep, and I too was in bed, would my parents let their friends get out of their hiding place.*

*First they would always go to the bathroom. Then they would eat, talk, and then go for a walk. Funny kind of walk. To the kitchen and back, and then again, and again, until my father would ask them* to stop. Once again — the neighbors… But one evening, I remember, the man got so angry, he started to shout that he had enough, that everything was better, that he didn't care anymore, that even death… He was shouting and my parents were trying to silence him, and my grandmother knelt on the floor, her hands joined like in a prayer, pleading with him, through tears, not to destroy us all. For some reason she was constantly reminding him of the children. "Have mercy on the little children, have mercy on the little children…" I got so frightened I hid under my covers shaking, too terrified to even cry. The man finally calmed down. I remember my father speaking about some documents, and about the nose. "With this nose you will be in constant danger…" I became quite fascinated. I forgot about my fear. Were Germans really killing people because of ugly noses? I promised myself to check my nose in the mirror the very next day. Was it too big or too small or what… And then I heard a new word "Armenian." The man was asking: "What about Armenian? Don't I look Armenian to you?"

It was the next day that the Germans came. I was sitting on my potty at the time, right in the middle of that room, when a soldier came in and, slowly and methodically, started looking everywhere. It was just too much for me. I burst out crying uncontrollably. I got blue in my face. I began losing my breath. I don't remember much of what happened afterwards, but Grandma, who was alone with me at the time, told me later: "…and you know what, he must have been a good man, this German. Maybe he had his own kids at home, who knows, but he just turned round and left the room, just like that…and I heard him telling the others 'there's nothing here, let's go.' And they went. Can you imagine? They went. And as soon as they were out, you stopped crying, and as if nothing had happened you finished your poo."

A day or two later my father brought the Armenian documents and took his friends away. I saw them after the war. Their name was Apfelblum.

My father had for himself false papers in the name of Zbigniew Modzelewski, and my sister knew him as our uncle. I did know that he was my father, but was not allowed to mention it except for the time in the evening when Isia was asleep and he took me on his lap to read to me a bedtime story. Then I whispered right to his ear "Tatusiu" (Daddy). Oh how I, and I suppose he too, waited for this little whisper time. "Tatusiu" was the bond; "Tatusiu" was love and pure happiness.

FEBRUARY 2005

I borrowed a new book from the library, *From Dawn to Decadence* by Jacques Barzun. It is subtitled *500 Years of Western Cultural Life*. Barzun says in the author's note: "…this book is for people who like to read about art and thought, manners, morals, and religion, and the social setting in which these activities have been and are taking place. I have assumed that such readers prefer discourse to be selective and critical rather than neutral and encyclopedic. And guessing further at their preference, I have tried to write as I might speak." It is such a joy to read. Only with writers like him do I feel entirely comfortable, as if I was sitting with my father or uncle Mieszek. There is no comfort comparable to the comfort of childhood. Now I can easily recreate the physical comforts, it isn't easy to do so with the intellectual comforts of those years. When I was a child I was surrounded by a family raised in a culture of "only servants speak about people, we speak about issues." Snobbish? Elitist? I suppose so. In my teens and twenties I disliked that saying. I disliked so much about my old great aunts. The damn upper class. Intellectual snobs. And then as I was maturing, although I didn't actually think of myself as better than "servants," I definitely started to value intellectual conversations. Those long talks about "issues." The well educated people surrounding me were exchanging opinions that, by being diverse, were opening my mind, teaching me to think critically. I learned that a conversation between people of different opinions can be enlightening instead of confrontational.

In another place Barzun says that when asked by friends and colleagues how long the book's preparation had taken, he would say "a lifetime." Of course, and that's why a conversation with an older person is usually more interesting than with a young one. They, or should I say we, know so much more, have had time to rethink, revise our ideas.

A few years ago my husband Donnelly and I had a long conversation with my husband's nephew Andy and his wife Robin. Two lovely, intelligent young people. They were going through a very religious period of their lives and called themselves Born Again Christians. At a certain point in the exchange of opinions first they tried to convert us, and then told us they will not be able to visit us again, as they did not want to spend time with such unbelievers as Donnelly and me. They didn't use exactly these words but that was the meaning. I smiled at them, I was not offended, but I told them that they should remember our age. I described how I went through different stages of my belief in the existence of God, told them about my different attitudes towards the Church and how, over the years, I did a lot of thinking and battling with myself. And maybe, when they are in their sixties, if we would be still alive, which I doubted, we could come back to this conversation. Well, they did not stop visiting us, they also changed quite a lot in their attitude to religion, especially organized religion and it didn't take them forty years to do that. They are very good, honest people, great parents of four children, and we are happy to have them in our lives. Yes, it usually takes years to form opinions that we can stand by in our later life.

I am afraid I am too passive now. I read a lot, I think a lot, but I need the stimulation of good minds to come to satisfying conclusions in my thinking. I have spent too many years raising children and earning money to really develop an active mind.

Had I been a university professor as I had planned, it would be different. Do I regret? Never. Jarek, Jan, Iwona and Łucja would either not exist or be part of my life. And now I have to add the next generation too. The choice was right. But when I read a book like Barzun's I know I miss a lot. Is it just the difference between Europe and America, or is it the result of powerful social changes of the last century, the empowering of masses of uneducated people and ensuing dumbing down of the cultures, and what goes with it, the oversimplification of language? As I see it, the books that sell well are those that answer the needs of those who did not grow up with literature, who did not have philosophy in school, who are raised on TV programs. Luckily, if I choose carefully I still find lots of new intelligent writers who write for discerning readers. I just have to look for them more carefully and not on bestseller lists.

## STILL FEBRUARY 2005

I don't think I dreamt when I was a teenager. At least I did not remember my dreams if I had them. I was always envious of people who said they could go on with just three or four hours of sleep. I needed eight or even nine hours to be properly alert in my functioning. Such a waste of life, I thought. One third of my life totally wasted. This is not the case now. I still sleep for eight or nine hours every night, but those hours are my alternate life. I have such magnificent, such interesting dreams. And I remember them so well that it seems quite often that I have lived through what I dreamt.

There are mostly two kinds of those dreams. One is artistic imagery — several years ago I dreamt I saw a statue of a scarab in a tunnel. Big, five or six feet high, around nine feet long, made of marble and encrusted with rubies for eyes, and with gold and many precious stones for its wings. I still can see it in my memory, as if I saw it and marveled at it in reality.

The other kind is even more involving — those are my "film

dreams" as I call them. Quite often I am not in those dreams at all. They are like films, with color and music, with a logical plot, witty dialogues, good wrap-up endings (if something doesn't wake me in the middle of them). Sometimes they are stories in the first person, but that person isn't me. It usually is another woman, rarely a man. Here is an example:

*It all happens in Ireland, maybe seventy or eighty years ago. I see two very young, unsophisticated, village people in love. They walk holding hands, kissing, dreaming of getting married, starting a family, building a cottage. They have no money, so they decide he will go to England to find work and save for their, so much wanted, life together. He goes, she waits. Silence, he doesn't write, she finds excuses — he has never been one to learn much at school. Writing must be difficult for him. He saves, doesn't want to spend on postage.*

*Years pass, one, two, three, four. She waits. All of a sudden there is rumor in the village. He is back. A self-assured man, drinking in the pub with his buddies of old. Parading on the village green in his city clothes. He doesn't visit her. She spends time standing by the window, waiting, her heart beating strongly, hands clenched. She finds excuses — he is embarrassed, he wants her to get used to the idea of their reunion, he is shy deep down under that bravado.*

*In the pub, the publican asks him: "Well, so now are you here to find a wife for yourself?" "Well," the young man answers, "now I am a divorced man I could, but no, I don't think so."*

*Then one day she learns he has left again for England. She is devastated, she blames herself, "I should have gone to him, he was too shy to come, to explain. And now the poor, brokenhearted dear is off again. It's all my fault."*

*She is still a pretty, red-haired, freckled, shy village girl, but broken for life.*

I deeply feel that I know her, that I lived in that village among its people. It's uncanny, how many of my life experiences, memories come from dreams. My brain working overtime? Where do those dreams come from? Is it that my brain has a need for creativity and in my real, daily life I do not give it enough time or opportunity to express itself?

## STILL FEBRUARY 2005

I am getting more and more upset by how my past, and by "my" I mean not only personally mine, but the past of the world in which I lived and which I perceived as real, doesn't resemble the past of other people, or the so-called "history." Right before my eyes history seems to change, to become "what we want to think has happened." I've got to call Wojtek (Voytek), my ex-husband who has such good memory, and ask for a lecture on how and why USSR fell. I remember the growing dissatisfaction of the so called "Satellite States," the weakness of centrally governed economy, and last but definitely not least the Polish workers organizing themselves in "Solidarity," which in turn gave encouragement to other people and states. I remember well the role of the Catholic Church in the creation of that movement. It was difficult, in the years of so-called socialism, if not impossible, to meet in bigger groups than, say, a birthday party. In other "democratic" countries under the fist of the USSR, churches were open only for mass. In Poland we had achieved a relative freedom of religion, which meant churches could be open at any time of day, and could host lessons of religion for children. This meant that people were able to use its facilities to meet, and use its communication lines for their own purposes. In a short time "Solidarity," which availed itself of this, became quite powerful. By the time Reagan became president, the USSR was already as good as fallen. Gorbachev with his "perestroika" and the eastern European countries did it all on their own. Yet in America it is constantly called the big success of Reagan. History as seen by American media and politicians is not the history I lived in. Let's not blame only the Americans, even Margaret Thatcher speaking at Reagan's funeral said that he brought about the downfall of the Soviet Union. The camera showed Mikhail Gorbachev, he was definitely nonplussed. I read a couple days later that he was to speak too. He didn't. I wonder why. And here I am studying history, fascinated by history and historians. Yet if all of it is created the way I see — what is the point? Is there no objective truth? Do we all have different truths, which to a certain degree are truths nonetheless?

There is another point in explaining why the whole, so-called communist, system fell. It is very ironic, but I am pretty sure the collapse was made unavoidable because of education. Schools were free in all the countries behind the iron curtain. Not only K-12, but all daycare, preschool, university, post graduate, and doctoral. Also those who needed it got a scholarship for living expenses. And the level of education was very high. OK, at least in specific academic areas. History courses concentrated on the struggles of the poor with the "bloodsucking" rich, Eastern European literature was taught extensively, but Western European and American were carefully picked through — London, Steinbeck, Orwell, Sinclair were covered extensively, whereas the multitude of others who might have been considered pro-capitalistic were omitted. Yet math, physics, chemistry, astronomy, biology were taught at the highest level possible. And math is logic, and if one thinks logically one is not apt to be manipulable. And if you are not easily manipulated, you are not buying into propaganda. You are critically looking at everything your rulers want you to do, to think, to believe. So it explains on one hand why the Soviet Union was the first in aerospace, but also why Solidarity was created and spread so quickly and so widely. General De Gaulle said once about ruling in France: "It is not easy to govern a nation with a hundred (I don't remember the exact number he used) kinds of cheese." I would paraphrase it to: it is not easy to govern a nation that knows how to think. Is this why the American educational system is so mediocre? Would critical thinking mean that people would be immune to commercial advertising? Would stop keeping up with the Joneses? Would want to have month-long vacations? Well, if it is true that USA is governed by big money, then of course allowing people to think critically should be avoided.

## March 2005

A beautiful spring day. A few filmy clouds in the sky, otherwise clear, warm enough to have breakfast outside. Our fruit trees are in bloom, all pink or white. Forsythia gives a splash of bright yellow. Tulips will open any day now. Finally. This winter weather lasted way too long. In the morning, as we were sitting on the patio, enjoying our orange juice and coffee, we started talking about a woman in her fifties who wants to marry her lover, yet is afraid whether they can make it work. She is Michael Wirth's friend and has asked Michael for advice. Michael wrote with her usual wit a lovely story, using cleaning out of a closet as a metaphor for all the compromises one has to be able to go through. Then she sent it to me, I gave it to Donnelly to read, and today at breakfast we talked about how we had to be open to change, and about our own path to the emotional comfort we achieved. I was, at fifty two, starting a life in a foreign country, which up to the time of our decision to move together, I considered exotic in its customs, way of eating, manners, etc. And when one is in an exotic place, one does not try to fit in, one observes, sometimes with a lot of curiosity, sometimes with laughter, and sometimes with condescension. Let's face it, we often think that our own ways are the right ways. The only right ways. It is pretty hard to accept something so very different from what we are used to.

Donnelly on the other hand had to fit into his life a woman whose attitudes to life, privacy, honesty, and even simply to the kind of order in the kitchen cabinets, were very different from what he was used to. So we talked, reminisced, laughed, and then I said that we could make money in writing a self help book on how to succeed in a "later in life relationship." To which Donnelly said — "If people in their 'later life' want to read such a book, they have already missed the boat. Like in those expensive boutiques — if you have to ask about the price you can't afford it."

There is a lot of truth in this. We have built our coping skills throughout our whole lives. When we are young, very, very young, we build ourselves, our personalities, character, our whole future life on feelings and experiences of that time. That is why, in early youth, one sometimes falls in love at first sight. There is this strong physical attraction, the inner, animal recognition of your own kind — valuable for reproduction of course — but at that time never recognized as such. The teasing in the eye, the warmth of a smile, the touch of a hand — and you feel your whole world is complete and in harmony. There is in us an unbelievably strong need to be loved, cherished, valued, seen as a very special person. After all, what we feel about ourselves is usually that we are unique, different from everybody around us, special. When the person, who is physically attractive to us, responds in kind, heaven starts to be understood. The fact that he or she sees us the way we see ourselves or even better allows us to open up, show our inner selves. In our happiness we are prepared to do the same for him or her — to listen, understand and see that she, or he, is the unique, very special, and absolutely magnificent person they feel they are. And if we are lucky, we build on this. We are open to change, to growth. We can acquire a taste for something we never cared about before. We see as silly, or empty, something that we valued previously.

Happy marriages are built this way. People create a home, a style of life, a set of ideals and scales of values together. Together they grow. First they grow more mature, bigger, then they harmoniously grow old.

But, of course, this kind of a happy ending is rare, very rare. Most of the time, as I see it, those couples who fell in love too early grow in a different way, so that in a few years what, at the beginning, seemed to be made in heaven, begins to feel like a prison. This is what happened to my and Donnelly's previous marriages. We tried hard to make our first marriages work, and when they failed to give us what we desperately needed, we analyzed where and what went wrong and looked inside ourselves, instead of just blaming the other. Both Donnelly and I can truthfully say that we managed to avoid repeating our old mistakes. We are happy, very happy, but most important we are at peace, relaxed, and full of tenderness for each other.

Our conversation about our path to each other led us to discuss the confidence that we have in ourselves. Donnelly asked me whether I had been confident all my life. I laughed, remembering all the pains of extreme shyness in my childhood and how my father cured me.

It was 1947, I was ten, we were in Milan, he had to go to some big banquet and wanted me to go with him, the more so that it was held at our hotel. As he opened the door to the enormous room filled with an elegant crowd I panicked, rushed back and cried that no, I cannot, I will not… My father looked at me pityingly, and said: "You poor little idiot, do you really think that anybody will notice you? For them you are just an unimportant little girl." The truth of that hit me like a ton of bricks. I smoothed my dress and calmly went in. That was the last time I ever had trouble getting into a roomful of strangers. Whenever I felt the shyness return I heard in my mind my father's voice "ty mała idiotko" (Polish for "you little idiot"). This was so different from today's approach to parenting, yet in my case very effective.

Although another day in Milan my newly acquired self-assurance became an embarrassment for my father, or so I think of it now. Once again he was invited to something, this time a grownups only affair, so he put me to bed and promised he'd be back for sure before midnight. Well, it so happened that I woke around one. He was not in his bed. I became furious. My father not keeping his word? How dare he? So I got out of bed, and in my nightgown, hair in two pigtails, fury in my eyes, I went to look for him. Downstairs the restaurant was already dark, chairs upended on tables, nobody anywhere, but some light and noise was coming from another room, so I went there. My father was sitting at a bar with some people, obviously having fun. I came up to him, and, my arms akimbo, told him: "Tatusiu, jesteś świnia" — Polish for "Daddy, you are a pig." There was a roar of laughter from all present, but my father looked at his watch, and said: "You are right, I am coming." He drained his glass, explained the situation to his companions, and came upstairs with me.

As a matter of fact I never heard from him that he loved me and yet I grew up with a firm belief that he did, and that he considered me brilliant. I suppose it was so because he talked to me about a lot of things, treated me as a valuable companion, seriously listened to my opinions, and often, taking on a role of devil's advocate, sparred with me on important issues. Only if I became belligerent in our discussions would he stop, pick up a book, and tell me that a discussion is an intellectual exercise, not emotional, and when I would calm down we could resume. My god, how it helped me in life!

So often people allow a discussion to become a quarrel. So often a conversation becomes proselytizing. There is that enormous need in people to assure themselves that they are not alone in their point of view, that they are right. Yet, in so many cases there is no right or wrong. There are only different views, attitudes, loyalties… Supposedly we shouldn't dispute facts, but how many of us know all the facts about anything? Two years ago I realized that the older I get the more I know, but the more I know the less I understand, simply because I know now how much I don't know. Everything is so much more complicated than I previously thought. I was sure of my knowledge and understanding when I was eighteen! Of course everybody who differed from me in their opinions was just plain wrong. I am glad to say it has changed. Does it make me happier? I don't think so.

## April 2005

I sometimes miss European culture very much. Today I think about its detachment, the ability to understand that life of the body and life of the mind are not necessarily in communion. The deep knowledge that friendship and sexual needs do not have to come together. That marriage is so much more than sex.

I think that the inability to see it is at the base of hatred that the very idea of same sex marriage wakes in so many people.

It was all brought up by something I read about the sex scandals of Bill Clinton. It reminded me of the shock when I realized that quite a lot of people around me did not, could not, understand why Hillary Clinton did not leave her husband after his peccadilloes became public knowledge. For me it was proof that there is so much more that bonds them. This is what I admire in them. I do not cope well with lies, with cheating. I, personally, would much rather have a husband, who if he needed more, or different sex, would tell me so. Then I would be able to decide for myself whether I could live with that or not. What Bill Clinton did was, in my opinion, terrible. But the "terrible" was not the sex, it was the lies that led to humiliation for everybody involved. It was the cowardice of a man who had worked hard to be admired and respected. It was his weakness in the face of lust. Her staying with him was proof of her strength and of the strength of their emotional and intellectual bond. "Tout comprendre c'est tout pardonner." An old French saying: "To understand everything is to pardon everything." I am not sure it is always so, but often, quite often it is. In relationships with those one loves, it usually is. In understanding why Germans started the War it most definitely isn't.

## A FEW DAYS LATER

I enjoy living here. I love the physical space that surrounds me in southern Oregon. The sparse population in the mountains, where one can go into nature and see no people for hours. In Europe, I often become claustrophobic. The density of population in Oregon is around 40 persons per square mile, Germany has more than 350 persons per square mile, in Poland it's around 200. And in Oregon roughly 46 percent live in the greater Portland area. Which, of course, leaves most of the land uninhabited, free for us to roam without seeing another person. To feel totally immersed in nature, be it mountains, forests or desert.

I love the American intensity of involvement, the greediness for life and fun, the "everything is possible" attitude. And yet there is so much superficiality, so much "let's pretend." Let's pretend we are always happy, everything is fine, fabulous, fantastic. It is jarring to hear from people who have no knowledge of the world outside the U.S. that America is the greatest nation in the world. I remember reading somewhere "The most dangerous world view is the view of those who never viewed the world."

So many contradictions. And yet I love this country, and have found so many fine, intelligent, well-educated people. I really feel at home here. Much more than in Poland. Poland has changed so much in the years since I left for America that it doesn't feel like my country anymore.

Two years after I came to the U.S. I wrote a poem describing my feelings of impermanency. I called it "The Visitor":

## THE VISITOR

*I am just a visitor here,*
*All my stuff in cases few,*
*Nothing binds me here to stay,*
*Not a hope of growing roots.*
*I am part of no structures*
*That would fall if I left.*
*Just a visitor, a visitor...*

*Have no home, not a place*
*To call mine, or hide in,*
*Not a wall to hang pictures,*
*Not a fridge to stuff full.*
*I can leave any minute,*
*I can go anywhere, only why*
*Would I want to, or what for...*
*Just a visitor, a visitor...*

*All my friends here are new,*
*Lived so many years without me,*
*Won't be broken if I go.*
*Some will miss me, some will mention,*
*Wonder where or what I do,*
*But my place will vanish quickly,*
*Time will wipe away the print.*
*Just a visitor, a visitor...*

*There's a love here I yearned for*
*Through long years of dreams untold,*
*Love that fills my life with meaning*
*And excites and gives me joy,*
*Yet I find no anchor either,*

*Never an always in all our vows,*
*Always a never at bottom of plans...*
*Just a visitor in passing? A visitor?*

My God, how things have changed since that November 1989! I am still with that love which seemed so impermanent. There is no "never" now. And "always"? Well, we are realists, we know we are mortal.

It was roughly at the same time that I wrote a parable of emigration, of emotional problems with immigration to a very different culture. After all, I came to the States just for a few years, to earn some money, to learn to live on my own, to see how it feels to be independent. I never considered staying for always. I wanted to leave a marriage, not all my children, family, friends. I called the little story "The Train."

### THE TRAIN

*The train was crowded, stuffy, its atmosphere thick with human tiredness, frustration, hopelessness. True, from time to time somebody would play a harmonica, somebody else would start to sing, the mood would ease. If only for a short time. I stood there so very tired. I lost all desire to go anywhere. I didn't even remember well where was it that I was going, or what for. From time to time somebody stepped on my swollen toes, or stuck an elbow in my side. Finally at one of the little train stations I managed to get out. Just for a moment. Just to stretch my back, move my legs, breathe some fresh air.*

*The station was pretty, the sun hot on my shoulders. A little breeze ruffled my hair. Behind the depot building there seemed to be a party going on. I heard unknown to me music, I saw people in fancy costumes dancing, singing joyfully. A man was telling a story to a bunch of revelers, some others watched a magician showing his tricks. I stopped to look and listen, keeping an eye on the train. All my things, my fellow travelers were in that train. I had to go back to all that, I stopped here just for a moment. Well, maybe one more round of dancing, maybe see one more magic trick. Wait for me! I am coming back!*

*But the dance music intoxicates, the rhythm puts me in a daze, speeds up my breath, my blood, creates new bonds with new partners, with the new crowd. And the magicians are showing diabolically interesting sleights-of-hand. So although it is frightening to stay without all that was mine, I look at the train less and less. If it goes, well, let it go. I don't care anymore about belongings.*

*Yet, what will I do when the euphoria of newness passes. How to live without those who were part of the old, the known, the predictable. Can magic join people like sweat did? And tiredness? And common travel to the same destiny?*

I have some answers now. I know that magic, happiness, sharing good times joins people, but in a very different way. The connections that I have with my Polish friends are deeper. It is easier to cut myself off from the relationships here. The exception — Donnelly. And this just proves my theory — we went through several losses, deaths of those who we loved. We also went through some financial difficulties, periods of hard work and tightening of belts. And that strengthened our union.

## April 27, 2005

Today is the eighteenth anniversary of my father's death. I well remember the day of my last visit. I still lived in Poland. I was close to fifty-one, my father was seventy-eight and nearing the end, the terrible end of a long battle (why do we always "battle" or "fight" with cancer, but "have" a heart attack or are sick with flu?) with throat cancer. He was sitting in his room, reading, with the TV on — but only vision, no sound. It was very unusual. My father didn't suffer fools easily, thus he didn't like TV. He used to watch only news, some theater, a concert, very rarely a film. Yet, here he was sitting in his chair with his book and the TV that was changing the atmosphere of the room. That place, which over the years, and especially after his retirement, had become so much an extension of his personality. It was a square, high-ceilinged room, with a very large window and a French door which led to a balcony. There was a wide windowsill with lots of potted plants on it. Beautiful, old, oil paintings decorated those parts of the walls that were not covered by bookshelves. In the corner by the window hung an old, hand-made Arabic glass oil lamp, with verses of the Koran painted on it. One of the plants from the windowsill, a grape ivy, crawled over the wall to a wrought iron hook, on which the lamp was hanging, and created a green mane of leaves and tendrils all around the lamp. Just underneath it stood a ladies desk, one of those delicate structures, inlaid with mother of pearl, with lots of tiny drawers, and carved, ivory columns supporting a narrow mantle for curios — although most of the time the beauty of the desk was invisible under piles of my father's papers and books. A few comfortable chairs, a table and a divan covered with an old Persian *kilim*, on which he liked to take his naps, completed the décor.

    I loved this room, its peacefulness and casual beauty, the smell of my father's cigarettes, of good coffee and flowers that were always kept on the table in the center of the room. So, that first time when I saw the muted TV, I asked him surprised "Doesn't it bother you, all those flickering lights and shapes? Doesn't it invade your reading?" And he smiled bitterly, and said: "I am just doing what I did, more or less, all my past. I am looking at life." There was a long silence, while he intently watched the screen. Then taking his eyes off it and looking at me with great sadness, he added, "Looking at life without understanding it."

    Then he switched off the TV, we went to the kitchen and I helped him prepare some kind of lunch, a sandwich and a glass of beer for me, and for him a milkshake, the only food his poor throat could cope with.

I brought him a large-print book from the British Council library, the only place in Warsaw that had large print. By then his eyes were so weak that he could read only with his glasses and a magnifying glass even when the print was really big.

Over lunch, we talked about books that he enjoyed and that I might find for him, about people, what fertilizer to use best on potted violets, about my children, about what I could bring him for his shakes... And then we were quiet, just sitting there, enjoying each other. All of a sudden I realized how many things about his life I didn't know, how many things I wanted to know, how fast the time was running out.

I knew a lot about his childhood in Egypt, his school years in Paris, about his military academy, and about the fact that he fought in the battles for Poland in 1939. I knew that they lost their last battle with the Germans, I knew that he was taken prisoner. I knew about his being one of the leaders of the Underground, the AK (Armia Krajowa — The Country's Army), but I had no idea how he managed to get out of being a prisoner of war. I had asked him about it several times. He never wanted to talk about it. Once I thought I was near. He was drunk and very talkative that evening, but when I asked, he grew quiet, got up and quickly went to the bathroom. He came out already dressed in his pajamas and went straight to bed. Now, sitting here in this peaceful room, with both of us knowing it would soon end, I knew I had to ask again. It was hard for him to speak, he could communicate only in some kind of a hoarse whisper. Yet, he nodded, "Yes, I think you should know."

And then slowly, interrupting himself every so often, for a sip of water, or just a little rest, he told me the story. They lost the battle, Germans took prisoners, herded them together waiting for orders of what to do with them. They singled out my father as the highest ranking officer there, and two German soldiers, after tying his arms, told him to follow them. My father was fluent in German, so he understood that they had a long trek of several miles to reach the commanding officer who was to "talk" to him. All three of them were extremely tired after a whole day on the battlefield. It was September, but the day was very hot and humid. After some time, his escort decided to stop under a tree for a little rest. They tied my father to the trunk of the tree and then promptly fell asleep in the shade. As tired as he was, he saw his chance. By rubbing the rope against the bark he managed to break it and free himself. Yet he knew that he wouldn't be able to get far enough before they woke. Quietly, stealthily, he moved towards his captors, grabbed one of their pistols and shot both of them.

My father started crying while telling me the story. Nearly fifty years had passed, yet he still could not pardon himself. "It was murder, you see," he said. "It was not battle, it was murder. That is why I had to go into fighting in the Underground. I had to be of use to my countrymen, I had to justify what I did." I understood. My heart went all out to him.

That was the day I did something I never did before. It was not in our family style. I told him that I loved him. I told him that I firmly believed that all that was good in me I got from him. He was visibly moved. "And a fine woman you are," he said. That night he committed suicide. He swallowed a whole bottle of his heart medication, digitalis, that he was supposed to take half a pill twice a day. It was after his death that I decided to leave my thirty year old marriage and try to live on my own.

## MAY 2005

A dream: *Italy, an old people's home, a woman and a man are sitting on a terrace looking at olive trees surrounding the place. He says: "You know, my mother disliked my bride. She refused to bless the wedding dress." She looks sadly at him and says: "Aah, that's why the marriage failed." A moment of silence, then he responds: "Yeah, after 50 years."* I woke laughing.

## May 24, 2005

Today is my name day. We are leaving soon for San Francisco to celebrate at a nice Indian restaurant, then to a hotel, and tomorrow we fly to Frankfurt. My daughter Łucja is picking us up and taking us to her home in Karlsruhe, which is very near the western border of Germany. We'll spend six days there, and then she, her husband Fritz, and the two of us will fly to Spain. There is an apartment rented for a week in Barcelona. Neither Donnelly nor I have ever been to Spain. Łucja and Fritz were there last year, fell in love with Barcelona and want to show it to us. They are good company, and the idea of seeing Barcelona together gives me great pleasure.

## A few days later

This morning Donnelly, Łucja and I walked to the local open-air market in Karlsruhe. The cornucopia of fruits, vegetables, meats, cheeses, baked goods, and lots more, reminded me of how paltry and limited the food choices are in America. Even in a place like Ashland, the fine twice a week farmers' market pales by comparison. The U.S. has enormous grocery stores with row upon row of different cereals, but how about meats? Where is veal, especially veal liver or tongue, or brains, where are the rabbits, venison, capons, fresh not frozen ducks and geese? The fruit ripened in the sun tastes so much better than the beautiful to look at, but often tasteless and aroma-less fruits of our shops. Americans, with all their sophistication, for some reason have never discovered, en masse, the pleasure of food in the same way as the Europeans did.

When I first came to Los Angeles in 1987 I was quite incredulous at how hard it was to find, good, freshly baked bread. Only in a district mostly populated by Russian Jews did I find small bakeries. Now so much has changed, even in our small town there are three or four of them, producing daily fresh breads. In 1989 Donnelly had taken me to a fine, supposedly the best in LA, French restaurant. I was surprised when after dinner I asked for an espresso and was told that they had only drip coffee. And now great espresso coffee is available everywhere, even in little towns. The newly popular trend of eating local produce made good fruit and vegetables more accessible than in the eighties. Yet, we are still way behind Europe in this.

## STILL MAY 2005
Yesterday afternoon we packed a picnic and took a tram to a spacious park to witness Fritz flying in a hot air balloon with eighteen other people aboard. His flight was a gift from his friends, for a birthday he had celebrated a few weeks earlier.

We met at least a dozen of his friends, who came with their families to cheer him. We watched fascinated as the balloon was laid out on the grass, then fan-driven air was blown into it, and finally gas fire made it lift up the gondola of waving and cheering passengers. We could see it fly away for quite a while, then it vanished and the rest of us dug into our food and drink. We talked and sang until nearly dark when Fritz returned, running across the grass and waving his certificate of completion. He was too excited to go back home right away, so we all sat and listened to his tales about the world seen from above until late into the night.

## JUNE 3, 2005, BARCELONA
Łucja, Fritzie, Donnelly and I are sitting on the roof terrace of our little apartment enjoying the evening air after a hot day of sightseeing. Barcelona is a true gem. Our place is off a narrow, old street one small block off Las Ramblas, a famous boulevard. Our apartment is on the fifth floor, no lift but luckily Fritz is strong enough to carry most of our luggage.

The flight from a small airport in Baden-Baden to Girona was uneventful, which means fine. We took a bus for a one hour drive to the city. The country through which we were driving was in stark contrast to the Germany that we had just left. The lush greenery, the freshly tilled fields, well-kept gardens and clean, orderly German villages were exchanged for dry, mountainous views with old, often unkempt, stone houses that seemed not to have changed for centuries. As we drove into the city everything changed again. The old was interspersed with modern, poor with expensive. We found our apartment, unpacked, and went out to reconnoiter. One of the attractions we saw on Las Ramblas was a fiery Spanish woman dancing the Flamenco to the music of a guitar and a drum played by her two companions. What a fitting beginning to seeing Spain. The first two days we just walked around the city admiring, getting the feel, going to the port, taking pictures. We also visited the market. It is housed in an enormous hall and once again we were envious. I would so much like to have the twenty-eight kinds of fish and sea foods (*frutti di mare*) to choose from. And many of the fish are sold whole. When roasting or poaching a fish, those bones inside it add to the flavor. Plus one can stuff fish so much easier if they are whole. I like to fill the fish with herbs and finely chopped vegetables mixed with a little olive oil, salt and pepper. The taste is incomparable to the filleted ones.

 We bought quite a lot of eggs, smoked fish, ham, cheese, bread, olives, tomatoes, and wine for our breakfasts and late night suppers. Both Łucja and Fritz have similar tastes to ours, and just like Donnelly and I, they love to eat. So in the evenings, after an early dinner in some restaurant (oh, how good the food!), after a walk in the cooling air smelling of sea, we sat, like tonight, with the bread, wine, olives and cheese, at this heaven sent terrace, with our feet high.

 On the third day we started on the museums. Admired Joan Miro paintings, ceramics, sculptures, and textiles. Then we went to La Sacrada Familia. The church is not yet finished, although the construction was started in 1882. Designed by Antoni

Gaudi, whom I consider to be a genius of inventiveness, it is still being built according to his plans with quite a lot of input by contemporary architects. Who knows how faithful they are to the original. Anyway, the building is like nothing else I've ever seen. It seems Gaudi tried to replicate nature, especially trees, in brick and cement. It is very impressive and inspiring.

Tomorrow we will go to the Park Guell to see a famous bench designed also by Gaudi. It snakes around a center plaza and is covered with a mosaic of broken pieces of ceramics.

## NEXT DAY

Today we spent several hours at the Picasso Museum, housed in four restored, medieval palaces and showing extensively his early paintings. I had no idea that he went through so many different styles, or that he was such a magnificent painter of portraits before his genius pushed him to invent, to break rules, to become in later years so controversial. I have always liked his paintings, especially the blue period and then cubism, but learned now that I knew so little about his art. It was embarrassing to realize it; it was a very happy feeling to learn so much. I even fell in love with his crystal period of which I had no knowledge before.

In the evening, after a lovely supper on our terrace, we all dressed in our opera finery and walked the short distance to Gran Teatre del Liceu for the performance of *L'Elisir d'Amore* with Angela Georghiu.

After a big fire in 1994 the theater was reconstructed and reopened in 1999. It is a magnificent building with seven horseshoe levels and old style decorations faithfully repeating the interior of the original from 1861, which means with a lot of gold. The acoustics are exceptional. We sat at the next to highest level and could hear Angela's pianissimi perfectly. The other soloists were just OK, but the choir, which in this opera has a lot to do, was magnificent in its power and sensitivity. We like the voice of Angela very much, yet have never seen or heard her live, so we felt very lucky to be able to get the tickets. They were the last four together available.

I love opera, although it wasn't so throughout my life. I first saw a performance when I was ten, travelling with my father. It was in La Scala, in Milan. We saw *Pagliacci* composed by Ruggero Leoncavallo and premiered in the same Milan in 1892. I was absolutely enchanted with the way it was shown and sung. I wanted more, my father couldn't stay longer, as he was on an official trip for the Polish government.

It was only five or six years later that I saw another opera. This one was in Warsaw. It was *La Traviata*, by Verdi. The main heroine, Violetta, is supposed to be exceptionally beautiful, gets sick and dies of consumption at the end of the opera. Here her part was sung by a hefty woman of a good 200 pounds. No possibility of imagining tuberculosis or consumption here. Her lover, on the other side, was tiny although with a beer belly and, in addition he was balding. Well, I was so disgusted by the miscasting that it took me nearly twenty years to see another opera. That one was in Moscow. Elena Obraztseva sang *Carmen*. The Bolshoi renewed my love for this kind of entertainment. During the six years I lived in Russia I was a frequent visitor to the theater. Then came New York in 1981, where I was working and saving like mad, but spending without guilt on Metropolitan Opera tickets. In the eleven months I was there, I saw eight or nine performances. In the nineties I went quite often to the opera in Los Angeles, where Donnelly sang in the opera chorus. I am still a devotee of the opera, on one condition — it has to be high level.

## NEXT DAY, BARCELONA, PARK GUEL

Yes, the bench is a beauty. The park very interesting. The plaza I wrote about previously is in reality on the roof of a big space used sometimes for a market, which is surrounded by artificial caves designed also by Gaudi. As coincidences go, when we walked by one of them we heard singing and discovered a high school choir from Atlanta, Georgia singing at the entrance to one of the caves. Donnelly, of course, stopped to talk to the kids and the teacher. It was a great pleasure for him. Deep inside he still is that choir director and teacher of old.

Later we took a bus and saw some more Gaudi buildings. I love looking at the fruits of human imagination. It all adds up to the richness of the world. It gives me an imprimatur for my own flights of fancy.

## June 10, 2005

We are in Warsaw now, staying with my younger son Jan and his girlfriend Monika. Jarek and Jagoda, his new love, have come to greet us. Oh, how I love those kids of mine. Everybody turned out fine. Touch wood, spit over my left shoulder. (For those who read it and do not understand — it's an old superstition in Poland, to prevent the bad witches from spoiling what you had just praised.)

There were flowers for me, there were stories, hugs and kisses. Then there was a fine dinner.

Jan and Monika had traveled for business to Tbilisi in Georgia just a few days before and had brought fine wines, pickled tomatoes, and a pound of caviar from there, so the dinner was a real feast. Jan and Monika invited us to go (all expenses paid) with them to St. Petersburg in Russia. We'll have to have Russian visas for that. Let's hope it can be done in the few days before they have to leave. Jan is the CEO of Universal Music for Poland and Ukraine and has to travel for all kinds of music fairs, big shows and conferences.

I have been in St. Petersburg twice in the seventies when my first husband Wojtek, I, and the kids lived for nearly six years in Moscow. But Donnelly has never been to Russia and is, of course, very interested in seeing it. He has heard so many stories from me, it will feel like filling up some blanks in what he already knows. And, of course, I will love to show him around. When in America, I always have lots of questions and he is the one who knows how, when, where things were or are done.

Here, in Europe, and especially in Poland and Russia, I can play the role of a guide. Here he has to ask. Here he depends on my translations and explanations.

## June 14, 2005

The days are filled with seeing family. We visited Wojtek who is quite weak after chemotherapy for his leukemia. He is two weeks older than Donnelly, yet looks like there is a difference of twenty years between them. It is so sad to see him in this state. I feel guilty for having left him. Although, deep down, I know that had I stayed I would be by now a very old and bitter woman. Not somebody who can help. Still, that heavy feeling is there. As happy as I am in my new life I do feel guilty about breaking my vow "for better and worse." I try to reason with myself, remind myself that I did stay for nearly thirty years, tried to tell him what I needed, what I so desperately needed.

I left when the children were already on their own, and when all hope that I would be able to lead my life the way I craved was gone. At that time he was a healthy, attractive man. I thought he would be able to create a new life for himself. He was, he is, such an intelligent, well educated and good, honest man. Yet he had always been sure that he was right. He had a monopoly to be right. In order to have peace and joy in the family one had to think like him, behave according to his views, like the things he liked etc., etc....

The first twenty-five years of our married life were filled with love, happiness, and furious quarrels. Well, furious is maybe not the right word. He never raised his voice, he was able to quarrel in whispers. It was I who yelled. There were times when he would bring me to such a state of fury that I could hardly manage to be sensible. And yet I knew he loved me.

In fact his actions saved my life several times. Whenever I was sick, and sorry to say I did have quite serious problems with my health, he was the best caretaker.

My first big health problem happened roughly a year after we married. I had no idea I was pregnant, all the normal signs of pregnancy were absent, yet there was a fertilized egg which lodged itself in the fallopian tube and grew there until the tube broke. The first we knew that something was wrong was at a dinner we had at a nice restaurant in Podkowa Leśna where Wojtek and I lived. In the middle of the meal I became very nauseated, tried to get to a rest room, found it occupied, so I rushed outside and vomited under some bushes growing in front. I remember there were some women walking by who commented: "Look at her, so young and already so drunk." Wojtek took me home but I was feeling worse and worse and with terrible pain in my belly. He wanted to call for an ambulance, I didn't allow him to, as I was sure it was just food poisoning. Wojtek called a doctor whom we knew well, a gynecologist, to ask what to do. The doctor, his name was Fitkał, told him where to push on my belly what to observe and report to him, and in a few minutes decided the situation was grave and he would wait for us at his hospital.

Did I mention I am stubborn?

We didn't have a car, I refused the emergency ambulance, I wanted to go by train to Warsaw (fifty minutes). There was no discussion. Hardly able to walk, gritting my teeth I allowed Wojtek to take me to the station. In the train I fainted and, at the nearest station, he carried me out and laid me on some grass. When I came to, I still didn't want an ambulance, but this time Wojtek hailed a passing taxi, put me in and with the horn on loud and the pedal to the metal, we reached the hospital. Dr. Fitkał was waiting. After a short examination I was taken to the operating room, cut open and saved. There was enormous bleeding from the ruptured fallopian tube. I was recuperating for a very long time. From a weight of 130 pounds I went down to ninety. Also the doctor told me that as soon as I gained a little of my strength I would have another, this time small, surgery as he discovered a cancerous growth on my cervix. I was told that having only one ovary and one tube, with a scarred cervix, I would have a hard time having children. Yet, what do you know — every time I forgot my diaphragm, or we were in too big a hurry, I became pregnant.

In Moscow, in 1972 I had an unusually strong headache, went to a doctor who told us he was sure I was having a stroke.

He called a colleague to confirm it, that one though was absolutely sure I had a bleeding in my brain. Faced with such diverse opinions Wojtek called the preschool to take care of our kids for forty-eight hours (yes there was such a possibility in the preschool!), a friend to pick up Jarek from school and care for him, took me to the airport and a few hours later we were in a hospital in Warsaw. There I was diagnosed with meningitis, stayed for some time in hospital and was later taken in by my sister, Isia, while Wojtek flew back to Moscow and the kids.

Then in January of 1987, when my menses became irregular and I was sure the menopause was starting, it was Wojtek who insisted on taking me to the best doctor we knew and the result was another cancer diagnosis and a total hysterectomy.

I know I am alive because he took much better care of me than I did. The only problem was that he did what he thought I needed or wanted all the time, not only in emergencies. And if I wanted something different? He knew better. It was in the last five years of our life together that I grew tired of fighting. Tired of having to push against the tide. Tired of not being able to do what I wanted to do. Wanting so much to think on my own.

When I finally left, I promised myself — never another man in my life. It felt so good to be my own master, or should I say mistress. It was two years later that I met Donnelly. I fell in love like a teenager — head over heels. Luckily for me he fell in love with me. Now, after sixteen years together, I think I can say "...and they lived happily ever after." I had never dreamed life could be so easy, so peaceful, so good. Now that I have total freedom I often bend to Donnelly's wishes. But it is always my decision to do so, or not. A big difference.

Another sad meeting has been with Isia and Staś. She is my younger sister, yet she shows signs of senility. He is ten years older than she and luckily is just fine, both mentally and physically. It seems that after sixty or so the number of years spent on this earth doesn't tell us how old the person is. There are some ninety-year-old people who are young, and others who at sixty are already far downhill.

The best proof of it was our visit at my aunt Helena's. The same aunt in whose apartment my parents, my sister and I lived in 1940. She is ninety and still full of energy. She made a dinner for us — appetizer, soup, main dish and dessert, all from scratch, all fresh and very tasty. She also told us, when we commented on her not wearing eye glasses, that she still works as a dentist, "but only twice a week, and only half time." Well she was my role model since I was a small child. My mother, although I loved her, was somebody whom I didn't want to emulate. Aunt Helena, her younger by eight years sister, was as different from her as two women can be. I just hope that I got some of my aunt's genes. Although we never know, do we?

## JUNE 15, 2005, ST. PETERSBURG
Our flight to St. Petersburg was fine. The airport bigger and more modern than I remembered, but nothing to write home about. Then a long drive in a taxi. Kilometers of monotonous, nearly identical apartment buildings, built with only one goal — housing as many people as possible. No money or thought were spent on the idea of comfort or beauty. No wish to make them diverse, interesting. Typical for not only Russia,

but all the previously "socialist" countries. Then the city itself came into view. And here a surprise: the old buildings that I remember as totally run down, are now in either a very good state, or surrounded by scaffoldings, obviously being renovated. Those already done are very beautiful. After all, this was, in pre-revolution times, a rich city filled with fine architecture and art. We stopped at the rental agency where we had made our reservation for an apartment, and an employee got into the taxi with us to take us to our place. At first we were not sure we could accept it, the building on the outside and the staircase were badly run down. The front door of the building was painted Russian style — meaning, many layers without a scraping off of the ones from before. Then she opened the door to the apartment and we had a big shock. The apartment had not only been renovated, it had been made into a gem of modern, high-level fashion. Fine wood floors, bathroom tiled with Spanish tiles, under floor heating, heated towel racks, kitchen with everything one might need, and fine furniture. Even the bed linen was ironed to perfection. Flowers on the table in the living room!

It is such a different Russia from the one I knew. The nearly six years, from November 1969 to August 1975, when Wojtek, I, and the children had lived in Moscow were the times of Leonid Breznev. It was the time of great shortages of food, clothes, appliances or gadgets. Flowers, fruits, or vegetables were a rarity. The attitude of sales people was generally unpleasant. As they had to be at work in regular work hours, yet the shortages of merchandise were such that they had to constantly answer customers' questions with a "nyet" — no, we don't have it, no I don't know when it is going to be available, etc., this attitude was understandable. All the luxuries were suspicious. Why do you need a color coordinated skirt and sweater, be happy that you can buy a skirt. Why would you think it preferable to have a smooth coat of paint on your wall, be happy you have a wall...

Of course I exaggerate, but that's how I remember the years I lived there. Capitalism — as much as I criticize its greed, its lack of compassion towards the poor, its coddling of the rich, I have to admit, has many good sides. One of them visible here in this apartment — caring about what you do for profit and how you do it. Today it is to our benefit.

Jan knows an Armenian restaurant that he likes, so they are taking us there for the evening. No protests here. I have always liked this kind of food: grilled or roasted lambs, meat-ball type kebabs filled with aromatic herbs, spicy sauces and all that washed down with fine red wines. To say nothing about aged cognacs for the after dinner drink.

## NEXT DAY, ST. PETERSBURG

We had a lovely evening yesterday. In the restaurant we met some German musician friends of Jan and Monika. The company was interesting, the food delicious, the wine was poured liberally, so when we left around midnight we were in very good moods. We took a slow walk to our apartment. Midnight, but the upper stories of buildings were still lit by setting sun. At last Donnelly saw the white nights. The streets were full of strolling people.

Today Jan and Monika are going to be busy with their music fair so we will go alone to town. I want to show Donnelly the Russian Museum. If I remember correctly, it shows a lot of Russian history — old village houses, furniture, tools, clothing, toys, and games etc. I remember especially the Russian art — how until Peter the Great the paintings were mainly icons in Byzantine style, then after Peter opened the country to the west (around 1700) everything changed, the art started to imitate the western European style, especially the Flemish. It was Peter who brought the western European artists, architects, shipbuilders to, very isolated until then, Russia. I had been surprised, never expecting that something could change in such a short time so drastically. I wonder how Donnelly is going to react to it. It is all so different from what he knows in America. Although he has been to Japan and China, to say nothing about many countries in Europe, the Russian culture will hold many surprises for him. After all, when we see people as different from us as the Asians or Africans are, we are prepared to see their culture, manners, traditions as exotic. The Russians look like us, eat like us, dress, especially now, in similar fashion, so it is hard to get an understanding of how very different their world view is. I remember how surprised I was in the early seventies, when Wojtek and I lived in Moscow, to find that many people still adored Stalin. When asked why, they responded "He made the whole world respect us. Even Churchill and Roosevelt respected him." Now, when we in the West criticize Putin for limiting freedom of his citizens, the majority of Russians are approving of his rule. Of course if you remember that they never in the past had democracy, it is easier to see why the difference in world view is so big, but still the difference is there and often makes it impossible to find a common ground. But when I think about all the differences between Russia and the United States, I have to agree that there are also some similarities. One of them is this idea that "the bigger, the better," and the feeling that "we are the best," which in both countries is firmly rooted in the undereducated masses.

## JUNE 17, ST. PETERSBURG

The Museum was everything I expected. It was good to be reminded of many things I had forgotten, and Donnelly was fascinated. There is, in one part of the museum, the history of the siege of Leningrad (it lasted 872 days) during the Second World War. The photographs of emaciated people, destroyed buildings, even a book of music, of German lieder, shot through with fragments of a bomb that destroyed the music academy. Historical proof of horrors, like the extermination camps or this siege, are imperative to remind us of what atrocities humans are capable of committing.

I wonder, have Bush and Cheney ever seen, ever learned, what wars do to people and how totally ineffective they usually are in attaining goals for which they are started? Have they ever had history lessons in school?

While there, I couldn't help but think of children in Afghanistan and Iraq. We often speak about those who were killed or maimed. We do not mention children who, as I know from my own experience, are emotionally maimed for life.

As Donnelly was avidly taking in all the expositions of life in old Russia, I sat on a bench to rest my feet and was filled with memories. I can remember now the war without dissolving in tears. But that was made possible by a certain night in Mt. Shasta six or seven years ago. It was the night before the fourth of July. I was awakened by sounds that made me shake, made me literally paralyzed with fear. I could not move. Only when I realized what those sounds were, only after I was finally able to get out of bed, only after I sat for several hours and wrote four stories, I stopped shaking. I also, for the first time in my life, became able to speak about war, although I still often cry when I do speak. For some reason it is much easier to remember the war if I write a short story about it. When it isn't so much baring myself, painful pulling things out of my heart for everybody to see. Is it easier pretending I am dragging them out of somebody else's heart? And this comes from me who hates the "Let's pretend culture." Go, figure. But the ease comes also from immersing myself in creating proper sentences, in making decisions about the right tenses to use, about how the whole structure of the story works, in trying to avoid clichés. It does lessen the emotional impact for me. Here is a story from that night in Mt. Shasta.

## THE SUMMER NIGHT

*I never know when it will hit me. I sleep peacefully. The man I love breathing evenly by my side. The house quiet. The only sounds those of the brook, wind, slight rain drumming on the leaves.*

*I have come a long way. I have built a life for myself. A life to dream of. Enveloped in a cocoon of contentment, I never even think about those long gone years.*

*And then it happens.*

*The sound of flares being dropped from an airplane. Their light invading the darkness of the night, exposing my street, my house, baring it all for the eyes of the killers. Then comes the next sound. Loud, menacing, piercing my ears, filling me with fear, fear beyond any possible description.*

*How do I even begin to describe the stiffness of my body, heartbeat so fast and strong that it seems my heart wants to escape, just rip the cage and flee.*

*How do I even begin. Every word is finite in its meaning. Every sentence has structure, and that fear has no beginning, no end, no shape. There cannot be any structure to something so complete, so overwhelming, so homogenous.*

*The sound.*

*The whistle of the bomb.*

*Seconds like ages, when I wait — will it hit us or our neighbors. And the all-powerful desire — let it be them! Please God, please God, let it be them!*

*I wake. Reality comes to me in a fraction of a second. It is no bomb. It's just some drunks, in our usually peaceful neighborhood, shooting fireworks at three in the morning. Now they are yelling with joy. Happy with the lights, the ruckus they create in the stillness of pre-morning hours. Drunk with alcohol and the power to change the chemistry of the night.*

*Yet, this knowledge is only in my brain. My heart still races and tries to flee. My body rigid. Nausea flooding my throat.*

*After sixty years my body still remembers that night when it wasn't our neighbors.*

This is the kind of future all those kids in Afghanistan and Iraq are going to have. Some will want to fight, because it is the only thing they know, the only thing that is "normal life" for them. Some like me are going to have nightmares all their life. That terrible night in Mt. Shasta I realized that except for one occasion, I had never spoken about war to anybody, not to Wojtek, not even to my children, until Donnelly heard a little snippet of it on one of our first dates. The one occasion was in Moscow in the seventies. I became very friendly with Marcia Baker, a woman from the U.S., who was there with her husband and children on an exchange program with the Soviet Academy of Science. Both physicists, professors at University of Washington, intelligent, sophisticated, modern people, they lived in a neighboring apartment building. We met through our children who befriended each other on a playground, and the four of us quickly became friends. They both spoke Russian, which was a boon for Wojtek, who was never comfortable with English.

That memorable day, Marcia came with a cup in her hand to borrow some sugar for something she was cooking or baking. I was just making tea for myself, invited her to join me, and she agreed after telling me it would have to be short, as she is quite busy. We sat down and she, unaware of what she was opening, asked me something about the war. Well, an hour or maybe two later, with both our faces streaming with tears we finished talking. Or rather I finished talking. It was unstoppable like a flood. Yet it didn't change my unwillingness about telling others what I went through in those years. Even just mentioning something was hard and brought tears. Here in St. Petersburg I could not join Donnelly in looking at the ruins, at hunger, at pain so vividly portrayed in the memorial exhibition. I know it,

I have it in me, there is no way of escaping from it.

It all started in 1942 when we moved to Lwów. I was used for some deliveries of papers or ammunition. I had been given a doll and a little perambulator in which I was to take my doll for walks. Fun? Well, no. I knew what was under the covers of the little carriage. I knew I could not trip. And all around me was war. Here are two more stories about my war experiences that I wrote that memorable night in Mt. Shasta in 1995.

### TOYS OF WAR

*It was a beautiful winter day, yet there were not many people in the street. Among the few pedestrians, a tall, thin woman walked slowly with a little girl, maybe five or six years old. Somewhere from a nearby park came happy sounds of children sliding down a hill. Snow crunched pleasantly under the feet of passersby, glittering in the sunshine, as if made of a million pieces of shattered mirrors, but the little girl was not looking. She was pushing a baby-doll carriage. A pretty doll with a little painted face complacently stared from a pillow. A colorful, quaint quilt covered her body. Such a happy, peaceful scene. The girl, the doll, sunshine and snow… One hardly noticed the pockmarked walls of buildings. Even the still steaming ruins of a house, bombed just the other night were not so blatantly visible in this sunshine. The happy yelling of the kids in the park belied the ever present fear and hopelessness.*

*Except for the little girl. Something in her face, maybe the immobility of it, maybe concentration, made her look much older than her age. Stiffly, carefully putting her feet, one in front of the other, one in front of the other, she walked down the street. Carefully, carefully, so that she wouldn't trip. Carefully, carefully, so that the carriage wouldn't overturn. And yet something did catch her eye. In different times, what she saw would make her think of a doll's house, but here it was just terrifying.*

*A big apartment building had lost its front wall. Everything in-*

side was now open to the human eye. *Little rooms with beds and tables still standing. Some pictures still hanging on the walls. Doors, some closed, some gaping open to unknown depths beyond. And a bathroom with a white metal tub, a toilet, and...what was that... what on earth could it be...a silhouette of a man on the wall behind, just to the left of that toilet...a dark, brownish* silhouette... "Mother! Look, what is this? How was it done?" *And the mother's fear. How could she explain, what was she to tell her daughter? With nausea rising in her throat, she tried to make her go on. Don't look, she wanted to yell. Don't look, it will haunt you to the end of your days!* "It was a man," *she finally said.* "A bomb killed him. It squashed him against that wall. Let's go. We have to go. We have to deliver the things on time."

*The girl's face closed even more.* "Yes, Mother." *She moved on. Mechanically, carefully she pushed the carriage. She knew about the guns, the ammunition, the papers under the doll's mattress. Those had to be delivered. And what better, safer way than in a doll's carriage. Nobody, but nobody would suspect a child walking with her toys. Oh, how she hated dolls. Never, never would she play with dolls. As a matter of fact, even as a grown up woman she would have a hard time buying dolls for her daughters.*

### THE CELLAR

*– So, what about those tiles?*
*– You know, I think I've changed my mind.*
*– But you wanted to see them. You've been talking about an antique tile fireplace for so long, and then when that guy took us to the basement to show them...*
*– I don't want a tile fireplace anymore. Now, look here at that picture. Wouldn't you agree that it looks better between the windows?*
*– Well, I don't know, perhaps...but the colors were more vivid in that other place. Mother, what was it yesterday? What happened in that basement?*

– Oh, nothing much. I just felt faint.
– You aren't sick, are you? You look OK now. Something happened there. You looked awful, white as a sheet. I got really scared. I've never, ever seen you like this. What was it?
– Leave me alone. Can't you see I don't want to talk about it? It was just the smell.
– Oh, come on Mum, you are way too strong to faint because of a smell.
– You just don't understand anything. That smell — it was the smell of death, it was the smell of war.
– You are right I don't understand. But whose fault it is? You have never told me anything about the war. I do want to know what you went through. Why don't you ever talk about it? Why don't you ever watch war films? Isn't it time I knew something about your childhood?
– I know, I know, you are right, but it's so damn hard…
– But look here, if I am ever to understand you, I've got to know things. Maybe you could start with that cellar. You are not afraid of the basement here, at home. What's the difference?
– I told you, the smell.
– What about it?
– Our basement here is just a few years old, it has relatively big windows, it just smells of home… Oh, well, I'll try to explain, just don't rush me, OK? The building we went to yesterday, it reminded me of the one I lived in during the war.
– Yeah, it was quite nice. Must have been pretty elegant in its day. But what a difference between the apartment where we talked to the guy and that basement where the tiles were.
– Well, only servants used the basement and nobody in those times paid any attention to the comfort of servants. Those basements were used for storage and for laundry. Our basement consisted of a big room with a sink, a few stone or metal tubs, a wood or coal burning stove… you know, all the paraphernalia of pre-washing machine laundry, and of a tiny room with a toilet. Most of the time it was quite smelly.

– *So?*

– I must have been, what, five or six when the bombardments started. Russians bombing our town because that's where the Germans were. Your Aunt Irene was just a toddler. You know, she slept so soundly, she never woke, during the worst noise, she slept all through it.

– *Oh, Mother, here you go again, describing Auntie's toddlerhood. The basement, please.*

– Ok, Ok, I told you don't rush me. I promise I'll tell you. I suppose it'll do me good if I speak about it, but it is so hard. Have patience. It was that laundry room that was used as a bomb shelter. On the outside the windows were covered with sacks filled with sand. Big piles of them. Inside there were wooden benches under the walls. Whenever the alarm sirens went off, everybody went to that cellar. As my mother had this sleeping baby in her arms, and me, people let her have the most comfortable seat — the wooden cover of the toilet. The door to this cubicle was long gone, maybe burned for warmth, who knows, but still it was sheltered from drafts, and I suppose a little safer.

And then came the night when a bomb hit us… you know I still can hear the long whistle of the bombs… and how it usually ended with a boom, sometimes even with a shaking, when the hit was near… but this time it was different…

– *Oh, Mummy, don't cry, oh Mummy, I am sorry, I love you Mum, here, have a tissue…*

– See? I can't even speak about it without shaking and crying. But this time I will go on, just bear with me, so, that night, the whistle became a roar, a boom surpassing all other booms and a quake incomparable to the other quakes. The sand bags must have been blown away from the window, because a powerful blast rushed in. People were flung against the walls, and one lady, who had been standing in the middle at the time, was hurled onto the floor and spun round…just like a toy top… round and round and round…and my mother grabbed me and tried to cover my eyes…but I wouldn't let her, because it was fascinating to watch… something queer was happening to that spinning lady... she was losing her face... and her arms... she was becoming bloody pulp... right there... in front of us... And then she slowed, and slowed, and stopped, and after all that movement, she was just lying still. I wanted to run to her and tell her it's all right, she could get up now, but I didn't, because what was lying there didn't resemble her at all. And then somebody yelled that our building was on fire. People rushed up a straight staircase toward a sturdy wooden door leading into the backyard. My mother didn't budge. She must have been afraid of us getting trampled. I don't know, but we just stayed there in our little haven and looked at all the others rushing to the exit, opening the door... we heard the roar of the fire, and then we heard the staccato of machine guns. The Russians were flying over us again and gunning down all those who were escaping the burning structures. It was just like it is in films, people are standing, then...ta...ta...ta...people are lying on the ground. Only it wasn't films, and anyway I didn't know about films. The only thing I knew was war. War and death. War and death and the stench of that cellar.

In the fall of 2003, when the bombings were still a daily occurrence in Iraq and our then president, George W. Bush, who was responsible for all the dying, the pain, the maiming that was happening there, was telling us that we need "small precise nukilar (sic)...," and daily on the public TV — PBS they were showing in total silence pictures and names of our fallen young soldiers, I wrote a poem. It was so bitterly ironic that we were able to enjoy ourselves, to not think about what was happening there. Yes, in political discussions among friends, we criticized Bush, and even went so far as to insist that he, Cheney, and Rumsfeld should be tried as war criminals. And then we would proceed to the table, to eat, drink and be merry. So here is the poem:

## WHY DO I LOVE LIFE

*Why do I love life — you ask,*
*It's the shape of clouds in the sky,*
*It's the sound of wind in the trees,*
*It's the wine in my glass at dusk,*
*And the warmth of your eyes when you*
*Look at me from across the room.*

*Why do I love life — I don't know.*
*How can I, when bombs are falling*
*Daily in Iraq, and here "in silence*
*Are nine more fallen…" — nine lives,*
*Nine loves, nine stories in the making,*
*And "we have to develop small, precise, Nukilar…"*
*How can I, with all the hunger, hatred and fear…*

*Why I love life — I wonder,*
*Maybe 'cause it's so easy to forget.*
*I remember the ecstasy of birthing*
*But not its pain, sweat, blood.*
*Chopin sounds exquisite when*
*The bombs are in my knowledge, not in my ear.*
*No memory of hungry, rickety children*
*Spoils my dinner tonight.*
*So here's to life. L'chaim to forgetfulness.*

## STILL ST. PETERSBURG

The evening after visiting the Russian Museum we walked for quite some time to the Neva River, looked at the Winter Palace which houses the famous Ermitage, took a bus home to rest and eat a bite, and once again a bus to the Church of the Savior on Spilled Blood (*Tserkov Spasa na Krovi*). The church is so named as it was built on the exact place where Tsar Alexander II was assassinated by an anarchist in March of 1881. It is a spectacular example of medieval Russian church architecture with multi-colored onion domes. It is now a museum of mosaics, and those mosaics are so magnificent that it became one of the major places for tourists to visit. In its history it went from being a church before the revolution to being either closed or used as a warehouse in the years of the Soviet Union. During the siege it served as a mortuary. Restoration began in 1970, ended in 1997, but the church was never again consecrated. That evening it was to be a concert hall.

After getting our tickets (and I had a pleasant surprise when the woman selling them thought that I was a Russian, my language was so good), we entered the overwhelmingly beautiful interior. The choral concert was the best I have ever heard. It was sung by the Mariinski choir, which had the privilege of holding the first ever concert performed in the Church on Spilled Blood. They performed an a cappella work by Alexander Kastalsky commemorating the dead heroes and victims of all wars and terror, "Those who have died at the time of man's choosing, not God's," in the words of the composer. It is sometimes called the Russian Requiem. The choir of 100–120 men and women, with women standing behind the men, made perfect use of the crystalline acoustics, with expressive singing, ranging from a nearly inaudible murmur to climactic fortissimi. In those moments it seemed to be filled with outraged anger, a guttural cry that sounded like it was coming from the surrounding mosaics. We left the church speechless with emotion. Walked home and on our way bought a bottle of cognac and some chocolates with which we ended the night.

Today, we finally went to the Ermitage. It was opened by Catherine the Great in 1764, and is housed in the Winter Palace which was built at the beginning of eighteenth century, and magnificently restored in the 1960s. One of the good sides of socialism was that no money was ever spared on culture. When the government decided that museums or theaters were important for the people, they would spend generously. Now the old palace is literally breathtaking. The architecture and interior design have been reconstructed on such a scale and so lavishly that it is hard to find anything similar in other old palaces. At first, what one sees is the amount of gold and marble. Only later one perceives the details and proportions. As we would have needed at least a week for sampling all the exhibits, we decided on concentrating on French impressionists. But first I wanted to start by taking Donnelly straight to Picasso's "The Drinker of Absinthe" from 1901, my beloved picture. I literally ran through rooms until we reached THE ROOM. This is a picture that moves me every time I see it. There is something in the expression on this woman's face that speaks of the depth of her feelings. She is unhappy, she is depressed, she knows she should stop drinking, yet she is too weak to do it. How did Picasso manage to put it all in her face, in her eyes, just by employing some brush strokes on a flat canvas. He was a genius. Then more slowly we went through all the impressionists. It took a long time to do so. There are so many of their paintings there. Just the first room contained ten Cezannes. Well, Ermitage has the biggest painting collection in the world. If one never saw another museum, one still would have a very good understanding of all the history of art.

## STILL ST. PETERSBURG

And now the big day of going together with Jan and Monika to the Summer Palace. Jan has rented a car with a driver and after a breakfast at our, by now, beloved Boulangerie Francaise, off we went. The palace is situated twenty-five kilometers southeast of St. Petersburg in a place called Tsarskoe Selo (Tsar's Village). When we arrived, we found that we had to stand in line to get tickets to see the interior. The wait was long. We reserved our place in line and went to the gardens, and my, oh my, was there plenty to see. An oblong, artificial lake branching out into several canals with arching stone bridges. The garden itself with gazebos, statues, and well-kept trees, shrubs and flowers gave us a lot of pleasure. Filled with appreciation for its beauty we returned to our line. Finally at 4:45 we managed to get in. That was the last group allowed in, the rest, and there were still many of them, had to come another day.

The interior was worth the wait. There was a palace here starting from 1717, but it was demolished by Empress Elisabeth who ordered Bartolomeo Rastrelli to build a new one in the Rococo style. There was no limit to the amount of money spent, obviously, as the decorations on the stucco façade and sculptures on the roof were covered with a hundred kilograms of gold. And that is on the outside. The inside is just as opulent. There is also a very famous amber room, which has its own history. Created in the 18th century, it was the biggest amber chamber ever. The walls, ceiling, frames of windows and doors, everything was built of amber. During World War II it disappeared. Most probably the Germans dismantled it and took it back to Germany, but it has never been found. It is thought that the ship carrying the amber had sunk in the Baltic Sea on its way to Germany. So as part of the restoration process the Soviets decided to reconstruct it exactly as it was. It has been open to the public since 2003. Thank God for that.

Tired like hell, we ended the day at a Georgian restaurant. We enjoyed the food so much that I bought a Georgian cookbook. We'll see how I will be able to replicate those magnificent dishes. It won't be easy, as quite a few of the ingredients taste differently in the U.S. I might also have problems with some herbs. Anyway it'll be good to try.

## June 20, 2005, St. Petersburg

The last day — another visit to the Ermitage, then a little

shopping. I bought loose leaf tea, Donnelly got a *rubashka* (Russian style man's shirt) for himself. Tomorrow back to Warsaw.

## JUNE 24, 2005, WARSAW AND PLUSKI

It is Jan's name day today. The day was spent mainly on packing and then travelling to the village I love, Pluski. We celebrated his day with a lovely fish dinner at an outdoor restaurant, and then sat on the terrace overlooking the lake. The evening was calm and warm. The water smooth, with a ripple only where a swan family of four swam. Standing later on the little pier in front I felt so happy, so relaxed, so without a care. My normal Pluski feeling which had begun so many years before.

I still remember how I disliked vacations with my parents. Their idea of a good time, with one exception about which I'll write later, was to go to some nice mountain town, stay at a hotel and spend days walking in a park, sitting at an outdoor café with their coffee and cognac, and then in the evenings my father would lie in bed reading, while mother would play bridge with some new acquaintances. Boredom of the highest degree for both my sister and me.

The second summer after we returned to Poland from Egypt, when I was seventeen, friends of my parents, Stanisław Lachowicz (in our family always called Bambula) and his wife Alianka asked me if I would like to go with them somewhere to a lake to fish. Well, that seemed like a big change, a new challenge, a gift from heaven. Yes! I did want to go with them. They had heard of a village away from everything and wanted to investigate. Fine, I was all for new adventures. The village, called Pluski, was seven kilometers from any means of transportation, so we took a bicycle, some bags with our clothes and fishing utensils, boarded a train, and off we went. After we reached the station of our destination, we hung the bags on the bicycle and started walking. Soon we entered a forest.

Big trees, lots of underbrush, birds singing and otherwise quiet, peace, beauty. The day was hot, the bicycle heavy to push, so we took turns. After what seemed like twenty kilometers we saw water glistening behind trees. Then, the whole of the lake came into our view. No people whatsoever. Great! Half an hour later we saw the village. Small, relatively poor looking, but very picturesque. There was a shop. We entered and asked a heavy set, middle age woman who was there whether she knew of a place to rent a room or two.

"No," was a short and rather unfriendly response. Could we buy some food? "There is nothing."

At that point a little kid came into the shop. Bambula pulled a handful of candy from his backpack and gave it to the boy. The joy on that little face brightened the whole room. Even the ogre behind the counter lost her angry look. Here Alianka, with the nicest of smiles, asked the woman could she have a glass of water, as she was very tired and thirsty. All of a sudden the atmosphere changed. The "ogre" became human, brought some water for all of us and said that maybe, just maybe the Brauns would have a room for us. She gave us directions and added that if we did stay, we could come in the evening and she would find something for us to eat. Well, the Brauns were a mother and her four children of roughly my age and younger. They had plenty of rooms and no money, so they gladly rented two nice rooms to us.

That was the beginning of my love for Pluski. The whole summer Bambula and I fished, or all three of us gathered berries and mushrooms in the forest. I, who all my life had a very hard time getting up in the morning, here arose smiling at four or five, to hunt for worms with a flashlight, and then sit for hours on an old wooden rowing boat. And sit in total quiet, so as not to scare fish. Bambula taught me how to fish without a rod. I just had a spool of fishing line with a fishhook on the end. I would thread the worm on the hook, and then depending on how deep I expected the fish to be (or rather what Bambula told me to expect), I released an appropriate length of fishing line. Then the sitting started. The line was in my hand, the finger served as the alarm sensor. I could very well feel delicate tugging as the fish checked the worm. Then came the moment when the poor creature would grab the worm in her mouth, and sharply and quickly I had to lift my hand to hook it on, and then pull it in as fast as possible. It was so sensual, so much me against the prey. Literally, my whole body was involved in the hunt. I fell in love with water, with fishing, and with the slowness of the passage of time.

Later in the day, I often would take the boat, a book, some food and drink, and row against the wind, then stop rowing and just lie down on the bottom of the boat to read and let the gentle waves carry me back home. To this day I can hear in my memory the rhythmic slapping of the waves on the side of the boat. Feel the sun on my skin, the joy of totally uninterrupted reading or thinking. My time, mine alone. Not always was it this good though, as sometimes the wind would change directions and a sweaty and angry Joanna had to row against the waves again.

Even with those mishaps, I fell for this kind of summer, to the point of going to Pluski the next year alone, and spending long days on a boat, or in the forest all by myself. In the evenings I either stayed with the Brauns, who by that time became close friends, or went to the village hall which had the sole film projector and where one could see some terribly old and badly scratched films. That village hall was the source of a long, still lasting friendship.

On my evenings there I became aware of a boy, roughly my age, who kept looking at me. I started to see him in other places and his eyes were always looking at me. So one day I talked to him. He was not somebody I could become romantically interested in. Too much of a country boy for a girl like me, yet there was some sadness, some intensity in his gaze that affected me. So I said something, I have no idea now what I said, but he responded and we got into conversation. Later on, whenever we saw each other we would exchange a few words, and at the film showings he would sit by my side. In summers to follow we would greet each other like friends. His name was Rudolf. He still lives in Pluski, he still is alone and lonely, he still is a friend and he always shows his friendliness whenever I come to the village. For years he was there to babysit when Wojtek and I wanted to go somewhere without the children. At first to pick mushrooms and wild strawberries, and later on when we sailed on the lake. Finally when we decided to build a vacation home, he was there to help with the building of it.

In time we were able to reciprocate. One year Wojtek and I got a telephone message from one of his neighbors that Rudolf had surgery in which a big part of his stomach was taken out and he was in a very poor state. Winter was coming, we knew that the only heating in his little house was a wood stove for which he needed to cut the wood. What's more the house had no running water so he'd have to pull it up from a well. Wojtek and I decided that we could not allow it. So Wojtek drove to Pluski, brought Rudolf to us and he stayed in our house near Warsaw the whole winter. He recuperated fine, and I had all the torn children's pants, all the missing buttons sewn. He was a great helper this way.

That was also when he told me why he never married. When the Red Army liberated Pluski from the Germans, they were raping and plundering with a furious vengeance. After all, that part of Poland before the war was the so called East Prussia, belonging to Germany. He and six of his siblings were present when the Russian soldiers gang-raped their mother. It was so violent that she died there under one of the beasts. The children were later taken to an orphanage, raised pretty well although in very deep poverty, but never got over the trauma. None of them could create a comfortable life for themselves.

In time, my parents also started to come to Pluski for their vacations. Although my Father's idea of enjoying the forest was definitely different than mine. Especially his mushroom picking remains vividly in my memory. In the morning, around ten or eleven he would start preparing a picnic lunch basket. There were sandwiches, salads, and an absolute necessity — half a pint of vodka. If we reminded him, he'd include some water or tea for the rest of us. Then, taking a blanket and, in addition to the above mentioned basket, some smaller baskets for the mushrooms that we were supposed to pick, we would all go to the forest. There, we all, including him, looked for mushrooms for maybe fifteen minutes, after which he went back to where the blanket and food were left, spread all the feast on the blanket and called us to lunch. Lunch eaten, vodka drunk, by him of course, he would lie down for a nap, while the rest of the company went off on a serious mushroom hunt.

Sometimes my school friends, and later on, college friends would come, and finally my husband Wojtek and the children. Pluski had become our beloved summer home. The only place on earth where I was always happy with a deep peace in my heart.

For a long time we spent our vacations in rented rooms. Then when Jarek was born, I became painfully aware, for the first time, of the flies, dirty outhouses, doubtful well water. I especially remember one day when I had to go to the lake to rinse Jarek's diapers and there was nobody to take care of the baby. As there was no running water in the house I was renting a room in, and all the water had to be pulled up from a well, I used to do the wash there, but the rinsing I did in the lake. Sometimes my landlady watched the baby for me, sometimes Rudolf dropped by and I left him with the baby, sometimes I took Jarek with me. This day I noticed that a grassy enclosure, where usually geese or goats were kept, was empty. Knowing that the little boy, just barely crawling at that time, would be safe, I left him there. Can you imagine my horror, when on coming back I found my precious baby, whom I tried to keep so clean, sitting in the grass and joyfully eating little dark pellets — animal feces. Well, there were no bad consequences to this feast and to this day he has a pretty strong digestive system.

Anyway, both Wojtek and I agreed we should build a summer house for ourselves. The only problem was lack of money, but when young we do not let that deter us, do we?

As often happens in life, fate intervened. Another family in Pluski, the Storks, contacted us. Mrs. Stork had just been diagnosed with cancer and was told she needed surgery, but the provincial hospital was so overworked, they could schedule her in six months at the earliest. Mr. and Mrs. Stork were simple, uneducated people, but even they knew what a six month wait could mean for a cancer patient. They wrote to us asking for help. The next day Wojtek got in the car, drove to Pluski, brought her to our house on the outskirts of Warsaw, and two days later she had her operation. She then stayed with us for a month while we were taking her to the hospital for radiation and checkups.

She survived, she got well, and one day she told us, that if we still wanted to build, they could give us the land, half an acre on the lake shore, right across the road from their house. They used that piece of land only as a pasture for their lambs. We were in seventh heaven. We started right away.

By that time Jarek was nearly three and we had another son, Jan. The money was still hard to come by, but we managed to buy the needed wood, and a friend of ours, an architect, drew the plans for free. Well, free if we didn't count endless suppers with lots of vodka, while we discussed the architecture of the dream house. Next summer, with the help of a village carpenter, we (and I mean we, Wojtek and I, who had never before used a hammer for anything more serious than hanging pictures on a wall) erected the frame. A year later, by now parents of three, as our daughter Łucja joined the boys, we, with the help of family and friends, covered the roof and walls. People were coming with baskets of food, tents and air mattresses. They would cut the boards, dip them in a preservative fluid, nail them on to the frame. In the evenings we used to make a big campfire of all the small remnants of the wood we had cut during the day. We roasted sausages, cut thick slabs of fresh village bread, drank lots of beer and vodka, and sang and laughed of course. The lake served as bathroom for washing off the sweat and dust, the weather cooperated, everybody was happy, and by the end of summer we were done.

The house had a roof of corrugated asbestos (yes, nobody told us then how dangerous it was), outer walls, doors and windows. It totally lacked inner walls, floor or ceiling. It had no electricity, and no plumbing.

We managed to build an outhouse which was officially opened by cutting the ribbon, in reality it was toilet paper festively wrapped around the structure. Amid lots of very pompous speeches stressing the fact that socialism will bring a marvelous future, the proof of which is this architectural marvel of an outhouse, we celebrated our new possession. Even a small bottle of vodka was broken on its walls, while a friend, serving as a godmother named it Slavoyka. Then Wojtek inaugurated its use by peeing inside, with the door open, so everybody could see that it worked well. It was our only toilet for the next thirty years or so.

Yes, that number is right. For the next thirty years we were spending our summers in this unfinished shell of a house, and we were very happy.

The year following the building of the house, we adopted two children from an orphanage, Darek and Iwona. That was also when we moved to Moscow, where Wojtek became foreign correspondent for his newspaper *Zycie Warszawy* (*Life of Warsaw*), and I, to a certain degree, a stay at home, full time mother of five. I say "to a certain degree," because I soon started freelancing for several Polish newspapers and magazines. With all that work and all the children, and the need to build a much bigger house than the one we lived in near Warsaw, we never had time or money to finish the Pluski house.

We all loved it. There was no housework — all the floors were just loose planks of wood laid on sand, so sweeping the floors meant going with a broom and waving it from side to side. I have always liked spiders and taught my kids to respect their lives. So of course, the windows could not be washed, because that would have destroyed the spider webs. All our bathing was in the lake, so no bathrooms to keep clean, no scum on the tiles to fight with. The cooking was done on a two burner propane stove. On very cold days we simply didn't wash, and, of course, the children loved it. On the whole it was all beneficial, both for them and for me. They had nearly total freedom without being nagged about the mess that kids naturally create, and I had my days of peace, of reading and thinking uninterrupted.

People now talk a lot about the need of meditation. They sit in a certain way, close their eyes, repeat some mantra, all to get rid of tension. Well, Pluski was my way of keeping sane. The hours on the rowing boat, walks in the forest, or simply lying on the grass (unmowed of course) in the sunshine and allowing peace and calm to overtake my whole body, readied me for months at home, for months of taking care of the family, house, and working for money.

Now it is hard for me to understand how I was able to cope with it all in those months of work, school and generally "normal, everyday life." Just imagine — five kids, big house always kept clean, cooking (of course from scratch, as there were no frozen meals in Poland in those days), laundry (until the kids were six to ten, it was done in an old washing machine, which had to be filled with water and later emptied by hand, and as it was very slow, the clothes, towels, bed linen had to be rinsed in a bathtub, wrung, and hung out to dry), and afternoons spent on teaching English, French, translating, and writing. I did have a busy life, yet usually I also found energy enough for a social life with friends.

Yes, I needed Pluski the way it was.

Quite often some friends would come to visit on weekends. Then we would have long into the night conversations by a bonfire. I remember a funny moment of an anti-compliment. One evening some friends from Warsaw brought an unknown to me journalist with them. We spent some hours by the fire, we had fun singing and talking politics, then they slept in their tent in our garden before heading back to the city in the morning. A month or two later Wojtek and I attended a big party in Warsaw. Imagine my surprise when this new guy came up to me and started to introduce himself. But we know each other, I said. I reminded him of Pluski and the evening he had spent with us there. "Oh" - he said - "I had no idea you were so beautiful." Just shows you what some makeup and clothes can do to a woman.

Later when we were back in Poland and my kids were teenagers, they would bring their friends to Pluski, and I would have not five but seven or eight kids spending the summer with me. I only told the parents of girls that I do not take responsibility for their virginity, so they better take care of educating their offspring. I suppose it was easier in Poland than it would be here, as we had fewer sexual hang-ups there.

All that was then. Now the Pluski house is totally different.

When I left for America, leaving all our worldly possessions to my husband, he sold the house to our younger son Jan. Jan and his family enjoyed it the way it was for a few years and the house was still in its unfinished state when Donnelly and I came for the first time to spend part of the summer with my kids there. I have a lovely memory of our first morning. It was cold. It was windy. Nobody wanted to go to wash in the lake except Donnelly. We were all sitting at the table having a nice, filling breakfast and looking through the French doors at their new stepfather scrubbing away all the civilized dirt off his body, then taking a plunge and a swim, coming out into that icy wind and fiercely drying himself with a towel. As he ran up the hill to the house, my otherwise serious, adult kids started applauding loudly, clapping, and then yelling, "Yes, Mama, you have chosen well. He passed the Pluski test."

It was in 1992. The next time Donnelly and I came to Pluski was three years later. An enormous surprise awaited us. I knew something was in the air when Jan didn't want us to drive to the village on our own; he insisted that we wait for him. Finally the day came. Jan, Magda, his then wife, and their two children, the two of us, and Łucja and her then-husband Paweł and son Olaf, all arrived together. The house was there, but what a difference! From outside it was what in real estate lingo is called "half timber," white plaster with exposed dark wood beams. A new roof cover. Great new windows. But the shape of the house the same as before. More surprises inside. All the inner walls and floors put in. Not only beautifully done in wood and tile, but there was under-floor heating. The kitchen finished in gorgeous Spanish tile, the bathroom likewise, a loft above the kitchen and bath, skylights and a big terrace overlooking the lake. It was a shock. The more so that it was done exactly the way I had always dreamt of. I turned to Magda and asked how she knew about my past plans, to which she smiled and said, "I was spending summers here with you since I was sixteen. I listened."

I had always loved her, but at that moment she became my daughter. She still is.

There is another memory from that day. Łucja, who also had no idea what Jan and Magda were doing, at first looked in amazement and awe, then her eyes filled with tears. Donnelly asked her why. She said, "My Pluski is no more." Yes, the place that was such a love of their young years had vanished.

Donnelly went into one of the bedrooms and roughly half an hour later appeared with his guitar and sang a song he had just written about it. The song is called "Nothing Lasts Forever." It is now the title track on his CD.

Yes, our Pluski is no more. Now, so many years later the owners are Jan and Monika. Monika is a very fine young woman, beautiful and generous, with a fine taste. She has made the house even more beautiful than it was before. And yet, for me — a sadness, a missing, a "my Pluski is no more." There seems to be no place on earth that is as it was in my youth. Well, nothing lasts for ever.

## Ashland, September 2005

I remember how often in my previous years, the time of work, children, travels, friends, I dreamt of some peace. Of some boring time when nothing would happen. Yet whenever such a possibility of quiet comes, I immediately fill it with business. Same thing happened now.

We came back home in July and right away got immersed in our normal life. Donnelly had to get back to his work in academic counseling with students and writing a newsletter. I became, once again, a dutiful housewife. Housework, garden, friends — and so much joy and so much work. I don't like cleaning the house or doing the laundry, yet I love my rooms to be clean and filled with flowers. I do like gardening, yet my back aches after an hour or two of weeding. I like cooking and feeding my friends, especially if the conversation at dinner is interesting, which it usually is, yet, of course, after a day spent in the kitchen and an evening of being with people I am tired. All the "likes" outweigh the tiredness, so we entertain a lot.

There were a few of those busy things in August that I would like to record. On Saturday we were invited to have dinner with Sean Curry and Mary Pfister to meet their friends from Berkeley, Joan Finton and her husband. Joan, we were told, was a painter, and there was a showing of her work at one of Ashland's galleries. Fine, but we wanted to see what kind of painter she was, so as not to make a faux pas in conversation. We went to the gallery, not expecting much, I don't know why, maybe because we knew a few local painters of cute little kittens and such. Great surprise! Joan Finton's work was very good. Especially one picture of a dwarf piano player caught our eye. We came back to view it several times. OK, but we have all the paintings we want, we don't have money to spend on art, we have no space on our walls, so went our reasoning why, for sure, we wouldn't be even thinking of buying the painting. We left the gallery, got into the car, started driving home. Oh, was I sorry we couldn't buy that picture! But then, I thought, I did have some money that Jarek gave me as a gift. If Donnelly would consider adding some…and maybe if we moved the portrait of an old guy from where it was over the sofa to above the fireplace there would be a lovely space freed for this pianist… My brain was in turmoil. We stopped in front of a red light. Silence. All of a sudden Donnelly, who had been quiet all the time, cried out "we'll buy it!" made a u-turn and the picture is ours. Joan and her husband proved to be fascinating people and we had a fine evening.

Another event worth mentioning is water rafting. We have beautiful rivers here in Oregon and there is rafting on several of them. I had never done it before. One day, both Donnelly and I decided to go do it. The more so that my fourteen-year-old grandson Olaf was spending his vacation with us and was willing to go too. So one day we paid our participation fees, and were taken to the river in a little bus. The raft that awaited us there was for eight people. Seven of us were amateurs, one a professional guide. Everything started nicely with our guide telling us about the necessity to have our helmets on all the time, instructing us to remember that if by some mischance one of us would find himself/herself in the water to try to float with our toes pointing the way the current of the water went. We all relaxed then with some jokes, splashing and teasing by the guide who asked who was brave enough to jump into the river. Not saying anything I just bent backwards and fell overboard. I love water, am a pretty good swimmer, and I like jokes, so we all had a good laugh, and then the trip downriver started. The first few of the rapids were fairly small, the water twirled rather than boiled, the sound was pleasantly scary, but not hair-raising, so everybody relaxed. It was fun. Then came a serious one. From afar we could see the river narrowing, big rocks sticking out of the water, no passage visible, the noise of swirling, rushing, tumbling water telling us of danger, plumes of white froth shooting up into the air. The guide shouted instructions, everybody held their oars a little tighter so as to be ready — and then came a big jolt and I was out of the raft and into the rapids. My first thought was "Good to have that helmet" as I hit one of the rocks hard with my head. Second thought was "Hell, of course grandma couldn't cope, how embarrassing," only then remembering the direction of my body, pointing my feet with the current. I resurfaced soon after and was I surprised that in addition to me, my grandson, another young man and the guide were also in the water. Simply everybody sitting on the right side of the raft had been thrown. We did manage to get back onto our craft, and of course the excitement made the whole adventure even more fun. I promised myself to go again soon. Donnelly wasn't so sure. The next day I wasn't so sure either.

 And I still sometimes think how nice it would be to have a quiet, uneventful period. Such an inconsistency of our perceptions about ourselves. Except for Pluski summers, I usually coped with a few days of "nothing happening" and then found myself creating "happenings." Like this rafting. I just hope I won't lose the taste for diverse adventures. Anyway winter will come and with it theater, concerts and long evenings with friends, or books, or TV. How tame it sounds now.

## Ashland, November 2005

We talked today about sincerity, about how many people always play a role they created for themselves. Pretending to be who they would like to be, not who they really are. Some of those pretentions are harmless, like makeup, dyed hair, hiding inner insecurities. Some do bring harm — either to the pretender, because he or she is not able to acknowledge his/her need and thus seek help, or to others who are misled as to the true intentions of the poser.

I was of an opinion that some play acting, wearing a mask, as I called it, is very beneficial. I gave example of myself, as that is who I know best. I even found a paper I wrote years ago. I wanted then to show Donnelly who I truly was, yet up to now never showed him what I wrote. Today I read it to him. Here it is:

*You tell me that I am strong, brave — and yet it is only a mask. Yes, a mask my dear. You know, some people put on masks to hide their ugly, their stupid side. They put them on to be accepted, admired. I put my mask on to cheat myself, you know.*

*A mask. Of course I wear a mask. Without it I am so vulnerable, and often in such pain. I hurt for every person who is unhappy, ill, crippled, unloved, lonely, desperate. For every unloved child. For every beaten animal. For every crushed ant. And I need love so much. I want to be the small, helpless, little me, without the fear of being trampled by those who want to take advantage of my weakness. Sometimes the pain is unbearable. And the mask? It is not for other people. I suppose they might have liked me more if they saw the real me with all my weaknesses, failures and doubts. They don't often like the cocksure, opinionated woman they most of the time see. No. The mask is really for me. I suppose I am a good actress in this respect. I can get into my role so completely. I am strong! I can do whatever I choose. And I usually choose to do such a lot. Only with this mask I am able to stop feeling sorry and start doing something to help. To add my own little brick to the edifice. To help where help is needed and not whine that it is such an infinitesimally small percentage of what needs to be done. And in my mask I am happy, I can enjoy life — with its sunshine and flowers and rustling of leaves. I can enjoy other people, because my strength gives me tolerance and enables me to see the good sides of my brethren. And I can enjoy me. My acute love of good sounds, views, smells and touches. Oh, the touch of sunshine on my skin! And the touch of a loved hand! And the smile of a loving child! But all this is possible only in my mask. So are masks bad? Maybe only when they pinch and restrict breathing? When they are worn because of fear of being unaccepted?*

Today, I know how far I came from the time I wrote it. Today I can truly say I do not wear masks anymore. Oh, OK — maybe sometimes. The big difference between my previous life and now is Donnelly. He made it possible for me to accept my weaknesses. Possible to realize that I have two sides, strong and weak. The strong woman is not a mask. How is that dichotomy possible? Why those two sides do not cancel each other? How did I develop their coexistence?

I think from early on I was obsessed with the idea of strength. It was my father's doing. He talked to me about freedom and slavery. In his opinion a person who is strong is always free, a weak one is always a slave. Always bends under pressure of other people, of times, of conditions, or even under his or her own weaknesses. It made enormous sense to me. I did want to be strong. I did everything possible to become strong.

He also talked often of the ability to tell oneself only the truth. To never lie to oneself. That latter is the more difficult. I have tried all my life. And yet I still catch myself in creating myths.

I know I am a strong person. I think about how it started. Was it just genetic, or did it develop slowly? How about all the stories I heard from my mother describing me as a particularly stubborn child? Is stubbornness the name we give to strength when we do not want to recognize it as such? Isn't stubbornness in children a manifestation of a need to be in control? Of course it isn't always so. Sometimes it becomes passive-aggressiveness, resentment, not strength. Strength has to be developed and realized. One has to know one is strong in order to make certain decisions, to be in control of, at least, one's own life.

And what is the role of fear? Can one be fearful and strong at the same time? Well, the fear problem has been taken care of, in my life, by the war. To live the first years of one's life in constant danger takes away any fear one could have later on. I feel though, there must be much more, there must have been events that made me strong in this steady, calm way that I am now. Events that have given me the confidence to insist, to persist, to win. Big things, small things, they all have such influence on us. When I try to remember what made me go this way I come up with several examples, several such moments, about which I can say now — that's it, that's when I changed from a helpless child into the woman I am now. One of them is cold showers.

There was a time when I stopped washing myself. It was as if I had a need to be dirty. Maybe it was a need to rebel against my parents. Against all those: "A young girl should...a young lady shouldn't...." Anyway, whatever the reason, I started to go to bed without washing. I was eleven or twelve at the time, we lived in Cairo, where my father was a diplomat at the Polish Embassy, and my parents had a lot of night life going on. After the infernally hot summer days, especially August when the Nile flooded and the air was resembling a steam bath, September brought nights that were pleasantly cool, with a slight breeze coming in from the desert and the town would erupt with garden parties. Everybody tried to cram in as much fun as possible and my parents were going out nearly every evening.

I still remember sitting silently on my mother's bed while she was getting ready to go out. I loved to watch her putting on some shimmering silk dress to which she would pin a brooch or a spray of flowers. Then I would help her zip it up in the back, and being so close to her I could smell her perfume. She always used "Soir de Paris." Now it seems to me disgustingly sweet, cloying, but then it was simply heavenly. The smell of my mother, the smell of grown-up life, of partying, of a big world which someday, in the impatiently awaited future, was going to be mine. I was usually allowed to pick her shoes for her, find a handbag to match, put a few drops of perfume on a clean hankie. I loved telling her that she looked beautiful. And then, when she and my father left, I felt so good, practically elated with all the elegance I had just witnessed, I would go to bed without washing, with the dust of the whole day clinging to my sweaty skin and feet black from running around barefoot. Why? I have no idea. Asserting my separateness? My individuality? Maybe. I don't know.

Well, one night, after coming home late from some party, my father came in to check on my sister and me, or maybe he just wanted to kiss us goodnight, anyway he saw that my feet resembled more our mother earth than the feet of a young lady. Next day we had a long talk about cleanliness, hygiene, manners and so on, after which I promptly went to bed without a visit to the bathroom.

Once again they were late from some theater or party, once again my father saw my dirty feet, but this time he took me out of bed, carried me to the bathroom, put me in the tub and turned on the cold water. I screamed bloody murder. I cried. I hated him and wished him dead. I sobbed, sure that nobody loved me, that I was in the hands of a monster, that life wasn't worth living, that I would kill him. Yet, I had to wash myself before he allowed me to return to bed.

Next evening, still hating him, I swore he was not going to break me and went to bed dirty. The story repeated itself. It repeated itself several times before I understood my own helplessness. Only then I devised a crafty plan: I was going to take cold showers everyday, even several times a day, for as long as I needed to develop a liking of them. Then I would go back to my dirty habits, and if he gave me cold showers — hey, no problem. I would be laughing, joking. That would show him who was stronger, wouldn't it?

That is how it started. Everyday, gritting my teeth, shivering and unhappy, but as time went on, more and more proud of myself, I was taking the damn cold showers. Slowly the shivering ended. Then the unhappiness went away. When I finally achieved my goal and started to actually like the cold water and the surge of warmth and energy that comes after a good rub with the towel, I didn't remember or care about showing anything to anybody, about proving things. What's more I started to enjoy going to bed fresh and clean. There was something my father never knew: I did feel strong, maybe even stronger than he. I realized my own power and it did come in handy several times in my life.

Another time of transition from girl into a strong woman was one summer when I was fifteen. My father, his friend Janusz Witomski, and I went to a lake deep in the forest of northern Poland. We were supposed to camp on a lovely, uninhabited island on the lake, known to Janusz from his previous summers, and the forester, who was taking care of the woods there, was to give us a rowing boat for the duration of our stay. It all went very well, except for the fact that the forester wanted to be taken to the other side of the lake before he relinquished the boat. My father saw no problem. He said his daughter would take the guy to where he needed to go and bring the boat back. The men would wait and rest before having to set up the camp. The only problem I could see was that I not only didn't know how to row, I also had never seen a rowing boat in my life. Did I mention this to them? Oh, no. That would not do. Of course I could do it. Luckily the forester was very nice and sat down to the oars himself. I watched him attentively. It seemed to be quite simple. One just dipped the oar blades in the water and pulled, then lifted them up, moved them to the back and repeated the whole thing again. The boat ran smoothly and quite fast. In less than half an hour we were at the other side. The water was smooth, the sky blue, the world beautiful, life was great.

Then I was alone on the boat.

The forester was kind enough to turn the boat around before he left, I lifted the oars, dipped them in water, pulled, the boat moved. For some reason it didn't go far, maybe an inch… I lifted, pulled stronger, the boat moved a little more, but why oh why did it turn, as if it wanted to follow the guy? It took me an eternity to find a way of going in a relatively straight line. Another eternity passed before the speed was a little more than a snail's. Finally, finally, tired like hell, I approached the little pier where my men were waiting for me. (They later told me it took me three hours.) As the boat neared it, I stood up to pull myself closer so I could get out. I accidentally did exactly that — I pulled myself, not the boat, so I plopped into the water between the offensive, dumb, stupid, beastly thing and the pier. So what did my father do? Calmly he told me to go swim to that floating device and bring it within his reach. I did what he wanted me to do. Once again I hated him with all my might. Once again I didn't say anything. After we loaded our things into the boat, my father sat at the oars, smiled nicely and said: "Thank you, I really needed that rest, you were so brave to go on your own. Thank you." And I loved him, I was so damn proud of myself. I knew I could do whatever was needed. I was strong.

This feeling is deep in me. I am strong. I think I proved it to myself countless times. And yet I still have butterflies in my stomach before any big decision, before any big undertaking. That's why I always give myself time to think things over, to try and see as many pros and cons as possible. But, up to now, the decisions I made seem to have been the right ones. I would like to say I never regret them, but it would not be true. I can think of one that did go wrong, and had I been wiser, less emotional, I probably wouldn't have made it. The decision to adopt Darek.

## A FEW DAYS LATER

There are so many things in our brains, in our past, that we like to sweep under the carpet. Not to see them, not to recognize that they are part of us. When I wrote the sentence about adoption of Darek, it stunned me. I have never consciously accepted it as a mistake. I know why we adopted him. It was for the purest of reasons. It was supposed to be good not only for him, but also for the whole family. And yet, young and inexperienced as I was, I was mistaken in my belief that love and a sense of security would be beneficial for him to the point of overtaking his genes, his first years of life, his whole past. After all he was at that time nearly seven years old. Seven very formative years.

In December 1968, I read in a newspaper a heart wrenching article about children in orphanages. How they never learn the stability of a good family life, responsibilities and benefits of a loving relationship, attachment to one person. I showed the article to Wojtek, he reacted in a similar way — we have to do something. We had three kids, a nice, if small, house in a lovely little town near Warsaw. We loved each other, we had love to spare. He called the orphanage and offered that we could invite a kid for Christmas. A kid would have to be a boy between four and six, the ages of our two sons, so that the kids could play together. Łucja was only two, we did not think she would mind.

On Christmas Eve, Wojtek went to the orphanage to pick up the boy. As he was waiting for the paperwork to be done he noticed a little girl crying softly and holding fast to the boy that was supposed to go. Wojtek asked why she was crying. The teacher explained that she was his sister and was, of course, upset that he was leaving. So, my husband, who had a very big heart, told the teacher that he was willing to take both. That's how Darek and Iwonka entered our life. We knew nothing about them, they knew nothing about us, yet the time they spent in our home was a great success. We fell in love with them. They fell in love with us. After just a few hours they started calling me Mama, and Wojtek became Tata (Polish for daddy). Darek was a bright energetic little boy, but he had a heart problem. Some time in his early childhood, while still living with his mother, he had a bout of rheumatic fever. Untreated with antibiotics it damaged his heart. He couldn't run. His face, especially around mouth and nose would develop a bluish tinge and he would pant hard when playing some active game. Iwona on the other side was a pretty, dimpled little girl but she was very quiet, a sweet child not taking any initiative in play, just smiling and following others. She was nearly four, yet did not speak. She understood when we talked to her, but never responded verbally. Just nods and smiles. There was another strange thing. When kids that age cry, they usually do it very loud. Especially when they know somebody is in the vicinity. It is only the old people who cry in total silence, with tears streaming down their faces. Yet Iwona cried like this. Quietly. Preferably hiding in a corner. I had never thought it possible, and it was heartbreaking to see. On the whole though, they seemed very happy being with us. Especially Darek, who was so curious about every little part of daily life. How cooking was done, how the heat in the house came from a furnace that had to be stoked with coal and coke. It was the first time he saw a whole loaf of bread, which had always been served sliced in the orphanage. He had never seen how his clothes were washed. So many new discoveries! Trips to the grocery store were adventures. The fact that we were constantly there, not coming and going in shifts like the teachers in their orphanage, made them feel secure and happy.

Problems started when after the New Year we told them that the Christmas visit was over, and they had to go back. Darek was incensed: "Why Jarek, Jan and Łucja stay and we have to go?" How do you explain such situations to small children? Well, we told the truth. Both of us grownups worked, we had too small a house for the seven of us, we would be visiting them often, they would be visiting us often…

And so it was for the next nine months. Then an unexpected complication came. Wojtek was to become the Moscow correspondent for his newspaper. We were to go with him, live in Moscow for the next five or six years. What about Darek and Iwona? How can we just vanish after all the attachment they developed? We started thinking adoption. Not an easy decision. After all we already had three children. We worked hard. How could we contemplate taking such a new burden on ourselves? But could we abandon the other two? Could we live with ourselves if we did? And what about legality? After all they had a mother, whose parental rights were limited, but not totally taken away.

Then came another change. The orphanage called to tell us that their birth mother had improved her ways to the point that a judge allowed her visitation rights and she would be taking the kids to her place for Christmas. Well, a load off our shoulders. The kids are getting back their mother, we are not needed anymore. We knew she was alive, but as she had been an alcoholic, prostitute and thief, the kids had been taken away from her. Now apparently she had changed, we hoped it would work, we hoped the little ones would be OK. We hoped she was capable of change. Hoped, hoped.

Both Wojtek and I went to Moscow to set up the office, to find a place to live, to research the conditions. Our kids stayed at home in the care of family and a neighbor, Irena, who had been our beloved helper. We came back a few days before Christmas, to pack and then move the whole family to a new place a thousand kilometers away.

Once again Christmas Eve. In Poland this is the biggest day — a traditional supper, giving out the gifts from under the tree, singing carols. The supper is supposed to have thirteen dishes, for Christ and the twelve apostles, although no meat or butter are allowed. The preparations are long, the festive spirit alive. The kids would gladly skip the feast and go straight to the mysterious packages under the tree. The grownups tired but happy, look forward to a peaceful night and a relaxing holiday of two more days (in Poland both Christmas and Easter are two-day holidays). That year the weather cooperated. It snowed for two days before, after which came freezing temperature. The whole world was white, the nights starry, the air crisp, the trees carried enormous white hats, which they from time to time released in unexpected snowy showers when the wind shook the branches. We were looking forward to a walk to the midnight mass through this wintery paradise.

All of a sudden late in the evening as we were getting ready to go to church, a telephone call. The lady working at the orphanage was crying, could we come and pick up the kids? Their mother took them, yes, everything seemed to be fine, but at ten at night a police patrol found a little girl walking in the street barefoot, in a thin dress, crying. The temperature was around minus twelve degrees Celsius (10F). The policemen took the child, she was not able to tell them where she lived, but they found markings on her clothes that pointed to the orphanage. They brought her there and learned that her brother was most probably still with that mother of theirs. The police, together with the teacher, went to the mother's address and found the woman totally drunk, asleep on the floor, a man in similar state by her side. Both of them badly scratched, bloodied, obviously after a fight. Darek frightened to death was hiding under a bed.

Now both kids were in a state of shock. Could we please save the situation and come. Of course we did.

It was frightening to see their enormous eyes, devoid of fear or comprehension. They were both ashy pale, and very, very quiet. Didn't seem to react to our hugs. Didn't want to eat. After we put them to bed, they just lay there staring at the ceiling.

The next day Iwona had a high fever. She developed a dangerous pneumonia. We postponed our moving to Moscow for as long as we could. She was very sick for a long time and was still recuperating when we absolutely had to leave in the middle of February. She was too weak to go with us, but she did understand our promise that as soon as we were settled we would come to fetch her. Darek went with us. The kids were our kids, that was that. Of course an enormous amount of red tape ensued. Their mother was totally stripped of parental rights. We started adoption proceedings. Finally, in 1970 the kids' names were changed to ours and we were a legal family of seven.

That's when real problems started. But about that I shall write later.

## Ashland, December 2005

It is so hard to go back to those years. I still don't know whether I could have gotten different results had I been wiser. I still blame myself for a lot. Yet can you blame a lame person for limping?

Well, so we started our life in Moscow. The authorities gave us two apartments joined into one so that we had enough space for the seven of us. In those days all the foreigners had to live in special apartment buildings with a policeman at the front door, officially for our safety, but as we understood it, so that we wouldn't contaminate the good Soviet citizens with our ridiculous ideas of how life should be lived. The policeman checked everybody entering the building, especially those who looked suspicious to him.

To give an example — one day a group of first graders, colleagues of Jarek wanted to come to play with him. They were stopped and turned away. Our safety? Separation of Soviet kids from "bad" influence? What influence? That they might see how others live? A multiple-room apartment occupied by one family? Who knows what was on the minds of those responsible for the separation of Russians and foreigners. That day one of the little boys managed to sneak in. While the policeman was occupied with shooing others away, he came up, told me what was happening and I rushed downstairs and started yelling at the man. That is when I learned that yelling in the USSR helped. The police, the clerks, sales people obviously think that if you yell, you must have a right to do so. Everybody else would be afraid and cowed. Anyway I was allowed to call back Jarek's friends. They all had a great afternoon and I learned a valuable lesson, that I used several times afterwards.

We do not remember the name of the courageous boy. Yet we know that one of those little ones became a famous writer, Yegor Radov. He became quite known for his rebelliousness, so it seems quite probable that it was he who sneaked that day into our apartment building, but of course this is just a conjecture. Sorry to say Yegor Radov died at the age of forty-six. He visited Jarek in Poland when they were both in their thirties, their friendship still strong, yet Jarek told me then, quite saddened, that Yegor drank heavily. Oh alcohol, the drug of choice in Russia. How many lives were shortened by it. Yet, could those people survive the systems, first the tsarism, then communism, without the oblivion they found in drinking?

In the Moscow apartment, we had the space furnished with all kinds of household necessities made in Poland and sent by our newspaper according to my specifications. The furniture was quite comfortable, and as I brought from our own home some antiques and beautiful paintings, we felt at home quite soon. The younger kids were accepted to a lovely, regular, public

Russian preschool and Jarek went to a Russian elementary school. Everything seemed to go smoothly.

Just the previous September Jarek had started Polish school, first grade. He had learned the Roman alphabet and rudiments of reading and arithmetic before we left for Moscow in February. Now he had to learn the Cyrillic alphabet and was exposed to a new language. His teacher asked me whether it would be OK if she kept him in class for an hour after other kids left so that she could teach him more in a one-on-one situation. Of course it was all right with me, and I told her I would like to pay her for the time. She was offended. It was just her duty to see that all the kids in her class graduate to the next level. She succeeded. By the end of the school year he spoke Russian and was good in reading and math.

Kids learn so easily. Which reminds me of my grandson Oskar. When he was five he, his mother Magda, and older sister Łucja, (yes, the same name as her aunt, my daughter — we started speaking of them as little Łucja and big Łucja), came to Mt. Shasta, where Donnelly and I lived at that time. The idea was that all three of them would stay with us for a year and learn good English. Magda enrolled in ESL classes at the local community college, Łucja went to the elementary school to age-appropriate sixth grade, and Oskar, who was five and knew no English, was enrolled in a private school, in kindergarten. After around two or three weeks, Donnelly sat him on the sofa and speaking very slowly, asked him — "Do you understand me?" To which Oskar replied, — "Piece o' cake."

It took much longer for his mother to be able to be fluent.

It was similar for us in Moscow. The kids, all of them started speaking fluently very soon. I felt comfortable after a year, or later, although I had had some Russian in high school.

The Moscow years were in some ways difficult, in other ways very pleasant and memorable. The difficulties were mainly because of shortages even bigger than we had in Poland. Lots of things were simply unavailable, for others we had to stand in long lines. Once, shortly after we came, I saw a very long line in front of a department store. I stopped and asked people what was it that they are waiting for. We don't know yet, was the answer, but there are trucks being unloaded in the back. How sad, to be in a situation where whatever was going to be sold in the shop you needed. Some foods were in the shops nearly always — milk, bread, potatoes, sugar, flour, kasha (buckwheat), butter and cheese. Some meat products were often available, although for all those we had to wait in lines. Fruit and vegetables were basically nonexistent. For these I had to go to a farmers market. A place where one could buy tomatoes, carrots, grapes straight from the suitcases they were brought in from Georgia. Everyday flights from Tbilisi were filled with entrepreneurial Georgians bringing fresh produce to the capital of the great USSR. You can imagine how expensive that was. But we, the foreigners were paid well enough to be able to give our children the vitamins. What about the locals? Well, I did see some Russians buying the fruit, but not many.

One day I was buying quite a lot, my bag became very heavy. The seller — a young handsome Georgian — offered to carry it to the car. I gladly accepted. On seeing my Fiat he whistled, and asked "*Pokatay myenya*" (give me a ride). When I refused, he added "*Kuplyu tyebye marozhenoe*" (I'll buy you an ice cream). I still refused to give him that ride. Yet to this day I remember how handsome he was.

Our building had around a hundred apartments, all occupied by foreigners. Everybody had a car. Winters were very cold, our cars were not easy to start in such temperatures. The Germans are known for fine organizational skills, and here they proved to be exactly that. They came up with the idea and made a box in which we were supposed to put our car keys on nails numbered with the license numbers. Then everybody was assigned a time that they were to go out and switch on the engines during the night between 10:00 p.m. and 6:00 a.m. Wasn't too difficult — you started at one end of the parking place and by the time you came to the last car the first ones were already warm, so you went again through the whole parking switching them off. It was considered to be enough for the cars to get warmed up every three hours — three times in the night. As there were some hundred apartments, that meant every person had a duty roughly once a month or less. The cars were no longer a headache. Everybody was happy.

We also have some funny family memories. Once when my children were playing outside and I was at home, there was a doorbell. I opened the door and saw a bunch of kids supporting my son Jan, at that time six or seven. Jan held his belly with both hands, was obviously in great pain. I became very worried and when I heard something about a car I became sure that he had been hit. I was about to call the ambulance when the kids started to explain that, yes, it was a car, but a parked car. They were chasing each other and Jan, while looking back at his chasers, had run into the car at full speed. The poor boy had a black and blue belly for a long time, but learned a good lesson in the necessity of looking where one is going.

Another funny memory with him was when kids came to tell me that Jan was on top of a tall tree and seemed unable to come down. OK, Mama went to the rescue. As soon as he saw me he said with great resignation in his voice: "Mum, I don't think I will ever be able to come down." I did stand there for quite some time directing him move by move, leg by leg, hand by hand, until finally I was able to hug a very relieved little boy. As you see Jan was (and still is) quite adventurous. With time though he became more reasonable in his decisions. He is a fine driver. He drives fast but very sensibly. Same with skiing. And he did sell his motorcycle. I feel very safe with him in the driver's seat.

Another thing worth mentioning is pre-schools. The one

closest to our house, open to everybody in the neighborhood, was so fantastic that I used to joke that if the Rockefellers opened one for their kids and their friends' kids, they couldn't do a better job. The whole thing was big — for somewhere around two hundred children. They were divided into groups of no more than twenty kids. Each group had a playroom, a dining room, a nap room, and a room to change out of outdoor clothes. Each group also had an outdoor, fenced in little garden play space with the usual swings and sand boxes, but also some flower and vegetable beds for the kids to plant and care for. There was also a medical center with a nurse on constant duty and a doctor visiting when there was a need. There was also a dormitory for children to stay in when there was a serious illness in the family or a single parent had to travel. Even my kids were put in it once, when I had meningitis and Wojtek had to fly me to Warsaw.

Normally the preschool was open from 6:00 a.m. to 7:00 p.m., with parents deciding how many hours their child would stay. Paradise? Well, you have to consider that it was also the perfect way of subjecting the young ones to propaganda. I remember Łucja when she was four asking me to read to her. I was, as usual, extremely busy, so shooed her off with, "They read to you a lot at the preschool, don't they?" "But I want you to read a real book, Mama. They always read about Lenin, baby Lenin, lovely little Lenin." Or when I was helping her to put on her boots in the cloak room, a colleague of hers asked me where we were from. I said we were from Poland. And he nodding seriously said: "Oh, I know, we are helping you." And that at a time when Polish shops had no meat as our whole pork production was transported to USSR, same with coal and many other products.

My years in Moscow are also memorable for gaining two friends who became very important to me — Moira Cunninghame-Stramentov, a correspondent for *Financial Times*, and, already mentioned, Marcia Baker. Both those women are still in my life. I love them, respect them, and admire them very much.

## December 13, 2005

We went yesterday to Havurah Shir Hadash to an evening with a Klezmer band. What fun! I react to this kind of music with a joy permeating my whole body. I think it is because it combines the sounds of Middle East and Poland, so it takes me back to my young days, the days of dancing, of laughter, of young love. Anyway, whatever the reason, my body reverberates with those rhythms still.

The coming week is going to be quite full, what with starting private Pilates exercise class, SORS (Southern Oregon Repertory Singers, the choir Donnelly sings in) concerts, and a party for the choir on Sunday after the last performance. And then, quite soon the Christmas season. It does help in overcoming the blues of the short, darkish days of December.

## Next day

I woke in the middle of the night with an urge to get up and write what was on my mind. Here it is:

> *I am clad in a blue dress. Blue.*
> *That's the color of my eyes.*
> *That's also the mood I am often in.*
> *Does this mean I am depressed?*
> *I don't think so,*
> *Even in these moments of sadness*
> *I can hear the joyful sounds of a bird singing,*
> *I can see the beauty of a tree tousled by wind,*
> *I can feel the tenderness of my lover.*
> *Yet I perceive with clarity the big*
> *Unimportance of my existence.*

> *Not only mine. As individuals*
> *We are all unimportant. Well maybe not all.*
> *There are these rare, extremely rare persons,*
> *Personalities who are capable of leaving*
> *An imprint on human development.*
> *But without us, without the unimportant*
> *Individuals, would there be humanity?*
> *After all we are the pieces of this mass*
> *We call humans. But this I know on days*
> *That are not blue.*

## DECEMBER 31, 2005

Another year is ending. I am sixty-nine. Never in my wildest dreams did I think I would feel this young, energetic, in love and loved — at this age. Sixty-nine. Until not long ago I thought that sixty nine was the age of decrepitude, of giving up on so many things in life. Ha! We had a fine Christmas, with the eve supper I love and that Donnelly came to appreciate, with a traditional Polish Christmas Day brunch of many kinds of cold meats, vegetable salad, gold beets, pickled mushrooms, salted cucumbers, beer, and then fruit cake and coffee. Debbie and Brian Tingle and Chris Dahl were with us. All of them are singers so there were carols sung and Chris sang a Norwegian carol and some spirituals. I never could sing, but always loved to be among those who do, and that quartet was very lovely to listen to. Donnelly even sang some Polish carols that he learned while we lived there. What a fine day it was.

Yesterday was our fifteenth wedding anniversary. I am so happy. What will the next year bring?

## JANUARY 12, 2006

I had an interesting day at the library. I was there doing my volunteer job putting order on book shelves when the director of the Library, Amy Blossom, stopped by and told me that some people were expressing interest in a serious book club. There are apparently many book clubs in Ashland, but they tend to be shallow in their readings, and soon become wine and gossipy conversation clubs. Amy was complaining that although she would like to start something serious, she had no time to do it. I just blurted out: "Well, what about me? This is something I would enjoy very much." She seemed to be very receptive, we agreed I should think about how, what, and when. Then we made a date for February seventh, as I'll be in Portland for the next week or more. I am quite excited about it. I have read so many good books and would love to be able to discuss them and the issues they deal with, with some intelligent people. I already have some ideas how I will run the discussion group. First of all, I definitely will enjoy being the dictator as to what books we should base our discussions on. Then there is another idea — what about not talking about books, but about issues based on books that deal with those themes? Yes, these possibilities excite me. I'll talk to my friend Margot about it, she might want to join with me in the organizing, and it would take some pressure off my shoulders. I already have the first themes. The first will be *The World is Flat*, a new, fascinating book by Thomas Friedman. Very timely as problems with globalization keep people very unsure of what to expect. I might also try to do a discussion about totalitarian systems, basing it on *Reading Lolita in Tehran* by Azar Nafisi, and then on how people can be manipulated into wars, which I would like to base on *Stones From the River* by Ursula Hegi. This is also something perfectly described in Joseph Conrad's book *Under Western Eyes*. Somewhere in it he writes: "The belief in a supernatural source of evil is not necessary; men alone are quite capable of every wickedness."

It is nice to think that he was a Pole (Józef Konrad Korzeniowski). He emigrated from Poland as a seventeen-year-old, studied in France, became a sailor, worked for a long time as a ship captain, and only later in life settled in England

and started to write. Another interesting thing about him — he wrote only in English, but when speaking insisted on using French.

Do I compare myself to him? No, I do know how little talent I have, if any at all, but do I hope that some readers will enjoy my musings. Of course, I do.

For the time being I wonder what will come from the discussion group I'll be starting at the library. We'll see how it develops, how people will react, how many will come, how lively the discussion will be. I am looking forward to doing something intellectual again.

## END OF JANUARY, 2006

January is a good month for Donnelly to take some time off work in his business of counseling high school students in their choices of college, in the rather complicated process of applying to the chosen school, in finding financial help, editing their essays, etc. By the end of the year all the students' applications for colleges have been sent, new work can wait for a week or so, thus we are free to go somewhere. This time it was a resort named Whispering Pines near Portland, at the foot of Mount Hood. While we rested at the resort I had one of those fantastic dreams of mine. I woke in the middle of the night and had to get up and write it down lest I would forget. It was complete, I didn't need to add or subtract anything. Why, oh why do the stories and poems so often come to me in dreams? Well, whatever the reason they are welcome. So here is that dreamed story, for whatever it's worth:

### MIDLIFE CRISIS

*"I enjoyed my thirtieth birthday very much. I was at that point in life when I needed reassurance that I wasn't immature anymore. My first book had just been published. It hadn't been a best seller,*

critics weren't raving about it, but those who wrote, wrote positively, encouragingly, the book was selling and my friends were using superlatives when they talked about it. Even my mother acknowledged it with a satisfied: 'Well, so you are not totally wasting your time.' So, I actually enjoyed being thirty. That was ten years ago. I do not like the idea of forty. Not at all. My books are going well, thank you, but all of a sudden professional success is not that important anymore. So, fine, I have the money, I live in the Marina district in a lovely apartment, I buy my clothes at the trendiest boutiques, and so what? There's no one to share my joys with, no shoulder to cry on when I feel like crying, which for some queer reason I often do, lately. Oh, don't misunderstand me, I do go to parties, I do have 'dinner out' invitations. There are plenty of people who like to be seen with a relatively famous writer. There are plenty of those who claim to be my friends, but whose eyes glaze over if and when I start saying something that may require real listening. Or, heaven forbid, getting involved with. I know, I know, it is all my fault. I am odd. I don't like to go to bed with guys. Nor with gals, either, for that matter. But what can I do? I haven't met that person yet who would wake the urge in me. Can you imagine? A virgin, at the age of forty? In the twenty-first century? Not even raped? Not even sexually abused?"

Alice got up from her computer and went to the kitchen to pour herself a glass of merlot. She didn't particularly enjoy spilling her guts on paper, but knew from experience that it often led to some good writing. She could be annoyed with herself, annoyed with the very idea of writing, yet it became such a habit by now that sometimes it felt as if it was the only way she could deal with reality. She eyed carefully the shelves filled with bottles. Which was it to be — Forest Glen or Kunde? Forest Glen, it was a damn good wine. Back to the kitchen, put some almonds in a wooden bowl, open the bottle... Struggling with a corkscrew she remembered Cindy. Cindy's eyes never glazed over. Cindy listened. Oh, God, How, how long ago was that? She hadn't seen Cindy in what, twenty years? Even *more. She didn't even remember why she never wrote to her. After all, wasn't she her best friend? Was the new college so enchanting? Did New York turn her head so much that she wanted to cut all ties to the simple provincial life she had known up to that time? Or was it that Cindy was so unsophisticated, so real, so down to earth that subconsciously she feared Cindy's remarks, her response to what was happening inside her, Alice? Well whatever the reason she never wrote, never called. Now all of a sudden she regretted. Now it seemed like Cindy was the very person she should be talking to. Was it too late? What if she were to go there and just knock on the door, and say, "Hi, I miss you. I want to talk to you." Idiotic. But not out of the question. She hadn't been anywhere farther than Carmel in a long time. A big gulp of wine and her hand was reaching for the phone. Air tickets, car rental, the excitement of a rash decision, the fun of doing something unexpected, wild, it was worth it even if she didn't find Cindy. Or worse, if Cindy didn't want to talk to her. She knew something would come out of it.*

\* \* \* \* \* \* \* \* \* \*

*The room in the motel was just like any other motel room she ever woke up in. The smell was obnoxious, the prints on the walls sugary sweet, the pillows lumpy. She sped through a shower, dressing process, wanted to get out as fast as possible. In the café she was nastily surprised by the watery coffee and amount of grease and sugar in everything. The typical American small town breakfast. Eggs and bacon and fried potatoes… Alice started feeling as if she were in a strange foreign place. She got so used to San Francisco, to her bohemian latte and brioche, lately. This here was really exotic.*

*The fat blonde behind the counter was serving her nicely enough, but Alice could feel her curiosity. With amusement she decided to play right to it. "You know," she began," I lived here in my young days." The woman was all ears. Looking at her, trying to decide whether she could recognize her. "I wonder if you know a Chinese family who used to live here, the Lee family. I am looking for the daughter, for*

*Cindy Lee. Would you know, are they still here in town?" The blonde was all smiles now. Yes, she said, she knew Cindy, but hadn't seen her in a good fifteen years. She heard Cindy got married, had kids, lived in Boston, or maybe New York. Her parents had died, both of them, but her older brother was still here maybe he would be able to tell... "Only," she was continuing in a theatrical whisper now, "he became, how to call it... a weirdo...you know, he hardly ever goes outside, never married, doesn't have friends...."*

*Alice thanked the lady politely, and all of a sudden had this strong urge to go see Kai. She barely knew him. He was four years older than Cindy, and when they were teenagers that was a big gap. Now that gap would be nonexistent. A weirdo, the woman called him. That might be interesting. She decided to walk.*

*The town had changed so little it was real fun to relive all the walks she had taken in the old days. All too soon she saw the white clapboard house surrounded by a profusion of peonies in full bloom. She remembered those peonies. They were the pride of old Mr. Lee. He used to tell her that peonies were very much Chinese flowers. As proof he showed her some Chinese paintings of them. It didn't really interest her then. Now she smiled with a touch of tenderness. They were the palest of pale pink, and weirdo or not, Kai must have been taking good care of them. They were simply gorgeous.*

*She had barely knocked when the door opened and there he was, his arms wide open, a happy smile on his face. Not a shade of surprise. Just greeting Alice with joy. "Come in, come in, I did wait long enough." Alice felt slightly embarrassed, but Kai took her in his arms, into a big long hug. Then, putting his arm around her shoulders he led her into the living room, sat her in an armchair and dropped on his knees by her side. Seeing her embarrassment, he started to laugh, and caress her calves. "It's okay," he said, "it's okay, I know you need a little time to realize why you came. I do know how to wait, although we have wasted too much time, as it is." Alice's first reaction was, of course, surprise mingled with fear. Was he sane? Was she safe here in a house with a lunatic? But then, very unexpectedly, there* was an enormous surge of tenderness, a feeling of being in the right place, and she relaxed and allowed herself to be caressed. *He spoke to her as if they were the closest friends. He told her of the years he had waited for her to come, as he knew she would do. He spoke with utmost certainty of their togetherness. He seemed to know all about her life.* It wasn't surprising in itself, a lot was written about her after every book. Yet he seemed to know about her loneliness, the deepest fears. In a short time she stopped being frightened. When he started to undress her, it felt like the most natural thing in the world and she watched with fascination as he took off his clothes. His body was strongly built, he was slim and tall for a Chinese. His sex loomed there above her and she wanted him very much. Kai was tender and slow in lovemaking. Alice was a virgin, yet there was no pain, only pure joy. They were lying on a big white sheepskin in front of the fire, and its softness added to the feeling of comfort and security. Such an atavistic feeling.

For a while all her problems vanished in the peace that surrounded them. But then Kai took her hand and led her into the bedroom. A big room filled with sunshine, the bed covered in snow-white linen, flowers in abundance and in the corner she saw an exquisite cradle. It was carved out of light wood, covered all over with intricate vines and flowers.

– What a beauty, she exclaimed.

– I made it, he said with a smile. It took me ten years to carve it. It's for him of course.

– For whom?"

– Well, for our son.

– ?

–The one we have just made. Don't you feel you are pregnant? But don't worry, I will be a good father. I will take good care of him. And you, if you will want it....

Usually after I write down what came in my dream I am able to go back to sleep. This time I was under such impression of the story that I stayed up for a long time. I felt like I knew those two, Alice and Kai. I felt for them, I wished them happiness, yet wasn't sure whether he was sane. Had this story come to me in the daytime, I don't think I would have written it. I would have felt it was too weird, too contrived. Is that my problem? The self-censorship? Is that why the stories, the poems come in my sleep? Is my inner censor switched off only then?

## FEBRUARY 7, 2006

I had a great meeting today with Amy Blossom and Margot. So the discussion group is being started, its name (which Margot came up with) is going to be THE ELASTIC MIND. I think it is perfect. We'll start on the second of March to give people time to read the first book *The World is Flat*, and also because Jan, Monika and Oskar are coming on the seventeenth to spend two weeks with us, so we cannot begin earlier. Monika wants to have some good immersion in the language, and I found a tutor for her to teach her the grammar and proper usage of words. It is going to be such a happy time for me to have the three of them with us. The seventeenth is Jan's birthday, I am going to prepare his preferred dinner — roast leg of lamb with roast potatoes, ratatouille and golden beets and goat cheese salad. Then a chocolate cake that I had always baked for him while at home. He is going to be forty-one. As usual, I think of his birthday as my day too. Forty-one years ago I went through a very traumatic time — it was the middle of the eighth month of my pregnancy and I stopped feeling any movement of my baby. He had been quite a boisterous little one up to that day and all of a sudden became quiet. I called the doctor, he ordered me to come right away to the hospital. On my way there I started to have birthing pains. By the time the doctor saw me, the birth was in progress, and within two hours the little boy was born. He was premature but weighed five pounds, everything seemed to be fine. He cried, moved, yet a few minutes later his heart stopped. The doctors tried to reanimate him, nothing was achieved, and after seven minutes, as they later told me, they decided to do an experiment. That year our hospital was in cooperation with some American research institute which sent them, an untested as yet in humans, preparation which was to revive a heart. It was to be used in a hopeless case. The doctors decided to use it on my little boy. He got an injection straight to the heart. It worked. He has been and is a joy to be with, an intelligent, energetic, charming, successful man. His birthdays are celebrated by me with great gratitude for the unknown to me American team of researchers.

## MARCH 2, 2006

What a day, Monika, Jan and Oskar left in the morning and at one in the afternoon we had our first meeting of The Elastic Mind. There were fourteen people, all of them interesting, well read, and willing to tell us their views on the whole problem of globalization. I am glad to report that I had no difficulty starting the meeting with an introduction and then with keeping everything flowing nicely. The good old brain hasn't lost its elasticity.

After the meeting I was too excited to go home, so Margot, Donnelly and I went out to lunch and to talk it all over.

Next meeting is going to be based on *Reading Lolita in Tehran*. It combines my interest in Middle East and in totalitarianism. Both were such a big part of my life. Both are to a certain degree unknown here. Even those who are well educated know it theoretically, but usually cannot understand it in the depth that comes with experience. They were, and are exposed to so much of propaganda — either of the political, cultural or religious kind.

Even Donnelly, when in 1991 we went for the first time together to Poland, was very surprised with the amount of culture he saw. He told me his idea of that country was of babushkas and horse carts. First I showed him our bookstores and he was astounded. He counted, in just the first one, some ten foreign languages from which the books were translated. To say nothing about Polish writers.

Then we saw opera, went to a concert or two, visited some homes of my family and friends. Homes filled with exquisite furniture, fine art on the walls, and tons of books. And when joining my friends for dinner he was exposed to such thin porcelain, silver cutlery, embroidered table cloths, and gourmet food, to say nothing about the level of conversation, that he marveled about it all for a long time afterwards.

That's when he fell in love with Poland and Poles. He even joked, well I hope it was a joke, that if I leave him (a euphemism for when I die as I have no wish to leave the man I love so much) he would find another Polish wife for himself. I sometimes think he likes Poland more than I do. Which is quite understandable; he has no bad memories from there. For me it is difficult not to think of the war, of Stalinism, of very hard daily life, without the comforts of full stores, washing machines, refrigerators, ease of buying clothes instead of having to make them, and even this only possible if one managed to procure cloth. We didn't have those things, or later on, when they appeared, one had to stand in long lines to be able to buy them. For our first fridge Wojtek had to stand in line the whole night. Of course it wasn't literal standing. People brought chairs, blankets, food, and thermoses with something hot to drink, they read, talked, complained, and started friendships. When the store opened in the morning there were so few refrigerators that he was the last one who actually got a fridge, all those who joined the queue later than him had to go home without one. Yet, some of them had spent the whole night in front of that store. And all this makes it so hard to explain how the kind of life we had behind the iron curtain changed our whole perception of what was important and what was not. How can I ever communicate to my friends why the clothes I wear, the make of the car I drive, the street on which I live are ultimately of no importance to me. Things come and go, the secret of happiness is not to get too attached to them.

You know, there is something in humans that, in my opinion, allows them to survive anything — and that is the ability to joke in the face of danger, hunger, or just difficulties of life. Even in those very dangerous times in Lwów, when my father's role in the underground fighting created a lot of tension, when we were living through all those bombardments, we still had plenty of laughter.

There is a funny tradition in Poland, that on Easter Monday (which by the way is a holiday in European countries) everybody is allowed to pour water on anyone else. It is called Śmigus Dyngus. The greatest day for kids. Can you imagine being able, without punishment, to splash water on your parents? On your friends? On strangers in the street? Well, that is something! But if you think that only kids do it, you are grossly mistaken. This is a day when a big portion of grownups allow themselves to revert to childlike behavior. One such occasion happened in the middle of most terrifying war times in Lwów. My parents decided to visit some friends in the evening of such a Monday, leaving Isia and me in the care of one of our parents' friends and co-conspirators, the aforementioned Bambula. He came up with an idea of removing the middle section of my parents' three piece mattress, putting a big bowl of water in its place, then stretching the sheet very taut so the bed looked normal. There was no way either my sister or I could go to sleep, of course. We couldn't stop giggling as we waited for our parents to come home and go to bed. Finally they did come. Mother, quite upset that we still weren't sleeping, started to deal with us, while father got in his pajamas and… the yelling could be heard for miles. There mustn't be much as shocking as getting your butt in cold water when you expect to be touching a nicely made bed. Father chased Bambula all over the apartment, first yelling that he wanted to kill him, then joining with the rest of us in laughter. Much later, when the life in socialist Poland became so very difficult, when even getting food was an ordeal, we had plenty of fun with our friends. One couple, Ewa (Eva) and Andrzej Ciałkowski were our companions par excellence. They both worked as attorneys, were quite busy, but often came in the evening for a bite and some wine or vodka. We loved talking. They, just like us, were big readers, loved poetry, had similar political views, so we enjoyed each other's company very much. I remember one evening when I read in the newspaper that *Fiddler on the Roof* was to be shown on TV. Wojtek and I did not have a TV. Andrzej and Ewa did, even a color one at that. We called to ask whether we could come watch it with them. They, of course, said yes. Yes, but they were already in bed prepared to watch it there. We didn't think long — I put on my nightgown, and as I was to go visiting I added lots of jewelry and a feathered hat; Wojtek dressed up his pajamas with a gaudy tie, fedora and a cigar and we went to our friends, joined them in bed and had a great time seeing the famous film.

Another time our talking and drinking went on for quite a long time. At around 1:00 a.m. we decided we absolutely had to go visit another couple of our friends, Ewa and Wojtek Janikowski. We were in such good spirits. It was selfish of us not to include them in our fun. We immediately took action. As I usually didn't drink, I became the designated driver. Already in the car on the way to our friends, being the one sober, I thought of the fact that our friends were most probably already sound asleep.

"We need a reason to come to them in the middle of the night," I said.

That put a damper on our spirits. Luckily not for long, as Wojtek had just noticed at the side of the street a stack of wood, which looked like old telephone poles cut nicely and obviously

prepared for somebody to pick it up in the morning.
"Here!" he yelled, "Look, we are bringing them wood for their fireplace!"

And so we did. I stopped the car, all four of us got out, everybody picked a log, got in and we happily continued on our way.

Imagine Wojtek Janikowski's face, when awoken from a deep sleep by a doorbell, he saw on opening the door, four of his beloved friends thoughtfully bringing him some wood for his fireplace. Well, both he and his wife rose to the occasion and we spent the rest of the night by the aforementioned fireplace drinking hot cocoa, talking and singing.

Yes, we knew how to enjoy life. But when we hear about life in a totalitarian state, we hear only about oppressions, jails, fear. I know from experience that lack of political freedoms affects in a terrible way those who are prepared to risk their lives to end the oppression. Everybody else lives a relatively normal life. After all look at us here in America — how many feel the need to publicly criticize the government? Of trying to change our political system? We can't even make the effort of voting in our elections in sufficient numbers to call our system a real democracy. People in totalitarian regimes are even safer in their daily lives than what we have here now, as with a lot of police one does not worry about burglars, about being accosted on a late night walk etc. People's life or death depends on their decisions, on what is most important to them. It is something quite shocking to my American friends when I oppose calling the invasion of Iraq the "freeing of Iraq." In Iraq now, one has no ability to control one's fate. It doesn't matter what you decide, you or your children might be killed on your way to work, to school, while you shop for food at a market. Even during the worst of the Stalinist era, had you asked us if we wanted to be liberated at the cost of war, of bombs, of stirring up all the fanatics with their exploding devices, the answer would be a resounding "NO."

Right from my early childhood I have learned, and throughout my whole life tried to prove it to be true, that most valuable lesson — what kind of life I have depends to a high degree on me. It's always about the choices that one makes. The choices of values, of people, of expectations. Even in situations totally out of our control, like war or natural disasters, a lot depends on our choices, our decisions.

I suppose I have shown that I know how to choose. Was I always happy? Of course not. Quite often the unhappiness came as a result of choosing values that were more important than my own happiness — like not divorcing until my kids were on their own. Was the choice of my husband wrong? No, look at the fine children we produced. At the time of my falling in love with Wojtek I had no way of knowing that eventually we would be changing in such different ways, directions, that at a certain point we would become incompatible. Had I known, would it have stopped me from marrying him? I am pretty sure it would not have had any influence on my decision. After all I was very much in love, we did have many years of very good life together, and we do have the children that are our joy.

And now look — all those memories came just because I was thinking about *Reading Lolita in Tehran*.

## APRIL, 2006

I have already mentioned my being with my father in Milan in 1947. How did it happen? Well, he was there on government business. It all started with the Soviets taking Lwów from the Germans. One of the first things they did, just like in 1939, was to arrest all those who might have wanted to oppose them. Of course those who had fought with the Germans were in the first line, I suppose rightly so, if one looks at it from the Russian point of view. After all, as the people in the Polish Underground had opposed German occupation, they would have opposed a Soviet one too, and thus, of course, were considered dangerous to Stalin's plan of incorporating Poland into the USSR or creating a buffer zone separating them from the "dangerous" West. But this was something known to the Soviets. Our side in their naivete, in their belief of honor, in their belief in trustworthiness of Churchill and Roosevelt, thought that now they would join forces with the Red Army in fighting against Wehrmacht. So when the Soviets' call went out for the underground fighters to come out of hiding, the leaders of AK (Armia Krajowa — the Country's Army) went to the Russians to talk about how they could plan to work together against the Germans.

My father, together with others, was promptly taken to prison. He was transferred to Kiev. They dug a hole in the prison yard, three-feet by three-feet by three-feet. My father was put in it and told that he would stay there until he delivered all the names of his "co-conspirators," and the addresses of places where the documents of their "subversive" deeds were kept, where were the guns and the ammunition. He was interviewed, he was tortured, lost all his teeth and one kidney. To keep sane, he remembered later, he braided some straw on which he was sitting. Braided and unbraided for hours. The interrogations usually took place in the middle of the night. The Russians were relentless in asking, threatening, torturing or pretending they were his friends.

To give up the documents would have meant to put the others in danger, which my father knew very well by that time. To give up the places where arms were kept would remove any possibility of resistance to what he now knew to be another enemy occupation. Yet, at a certain point my father realized he wasn't going to live long enough, so he agreed to their demands. But he insisted that in his state of health he had forgotten where the locations of the documents and arms were. He might remember if his captors took him back to Lwów and walked him in the streets. Which they did. He counted on his colleagues to be able to free him if they saw him paraded under guns of the Russian soldiers. What happened next is uncertain. My father told the story of how he managed to flee from the villa where he was kept. His companions told a different story, which as a matter of fact is much more impressive, so I'll tell their version.

The AK people on seeing him, came up with a fine plan. Having discovered that he was kept on the top floor of a villa occupied by officers of the Red Army, they sent a striptease dancer, an accordion player, and one of the underground fighters, pretending to be their impresario, with a proposition to give a show to the soldiers. As expected, the officer in charge wanted to see what they could offer. As expected, hearing the music and seeing a partially naked woman brought everybody to the downstairs room, leaving the rest of the house free for the Poles to spirit my father out. They hid him, they took care of his health, they fed him, and when he was finally able to go on his own, they helped him to get out of Lwów. Knowing the Russians were looking for him, he walked the whole distance to Warsaw, around 240 miles, hiding in forests and small villages whenever there was a need. By the time he reached the city, not only his shoes were worn to tatters, but one could say he was worn to tatters too.

The house where we had lived with my aunt and her husband in Warsaw had been destroyed, but my uncle managed to put up a notice in the ruins telling where we could be found. My father did find us, the family finally got reunited, everybody took care of him. Yet there still loomed the danger of the Soviets finding him. Something had to be done urgently.

At that time there was already a new, installed by the Soviets, government. He knew one person from before the war, Edward Osóbka-Morawski, a good Polish patriot who was now the Prime Minister. Father decided to trust him. They arranged a meeting and my father told him about having to hide from the Russians and why. Luckily for him, to the Russians he was known by a name on his false, wartime papers — Modzelewski. Now Mr. Osóbka-Morawski officially changed his name back to his real one, Pohoski. Shortly afterwards he sent him as a government emissary to France, Switzerland, Italy, and Egypt, with an understanding that as soon as the diplomatic relations normalized and a Polish Embassy in Cairo would be opened, he would be the first commercial attaché there. And so it happened. In December of 1946 my father and I left Poland on a train to Paris. Why me? My sister was very sick at that time, Mother had to stay with her. Father wanted to take at least one of us to some kind of normalcy. I was ten, healthy, open to everything new. I know that he never regretted the decision. I, for sure, benefitted immensely.

Sometime much later, when I remembered the day of our departure, I tried to write about it. Now I found a piece of paper with these words: "Standing there at the window of the train, clutching her father's hand in both of hers, she was filled with awe. So she was leaving. Going away with the one she loved most of all. Her father. She was leaving behind so much — her mother, sister, grandma, auntie, uncle. But also the country which in her short life gave her so much pain. The fear, the pervading, physically felt, mentally perceived fear. Her own, but even more important, the fear felt by others. Death, which was so common, so often seen, yet never becoming unimportant, had filled her young heart with constant tension."

To this day, I remember my happiness when, in that train, we were passing Berlin. Totally ruined Berlin. I suppose the area by the railroad was especially destroyed, maybe had we stopped there and visited other places I would have seen some buildings still standing, but by the train tracks it was all piles of rubble. After having seen Warsaw, of which 84 percent had been destroyed, realizing that a similar thing happened to Berlin made the little girl very, very happy. I remember standing by the window of that train, jumping up and down and yelling "Yes! Yes! Yes!..." The word "schadenfreude" describes it best. It is really untranslatable, in essence meaning the joy one feels at somebody else's unhappiness.

And then we were in Paris. Seemingly untouched streets. An elegant hotel. Beautiful, clean bed. And the next morning a breakfast of brioches and Ovaltine. With sugar! With jam made of real fruit! I became ecstatic. Dinner in a restaurant, served by a waiter in a dark suit with a white napkin over his forearm! There was no end to the magnificent things happening to me. In the evening Father took me to a movie theater. I had never seen a movie in my whole life. We entered while the movie was already in progress. Laurel and Hardy, or Flip and Flap as they were called in Europe, were driving in a convertible, and bungling as they were, they entered a sawmill, drove under an enormous vertical saw which cut the car in half, so that one of them veered to the left, while the other went to the right. My first impression was shock, but within seconds I was laughing so hard I could not stop. That first movie scene stayed with me. Even now it makes me smile. I have to check it out. Will it be as funny to me now?

The next big event was a visit to the Louvre. Well, to speak of a visit is a euphemism. Remember, my father was in Paris as a working man, he had to do something about his daughter, to find a safe place for her to stay while he attended to business. The next morning after breakfast he took me to the Louvre, gave me a paper bag with a sandwich and some lemonade, told a nice old docent that I would be staying there till afternoon, that the only language I spoke was Polish, but that I was a good girl and that he was sure they wouldn't have any problems, and he left. I was not upset. There were so many beautiful pictures. I had never seen anything as fascinating before. I remember that after a certain time I began to make up stories about the scenes, the people in the pictures, the animals. I found that I could make up different stories about the same picture just by changing the way I looked and interpreted it. I think it was my first big lesson in relativity. I had a great time. Some docents, bored as there weren't many visitors, started to teach me French, showed me where I could eat my sandwich, where was the bathroom. They became my friends. I suppose they must have been quite amused by the situation. Anyway this hungry, tense child filled with hatred for the Germans, was transported into a place rich in culture and food and the feeling of safety, and she took to all this like fish to water.

By the end of the three months we stayed in Paris I spoke quite passable French, felt comfortable in hotels, restaurants, and museums, knew the difference between Classicism and Impressionism, admired Michelangelo and Benvenuto Cellini. I even fell in love with a statue of a boy picking a thorn out of his foot. He sat to the left of the entrance so I saw him every day as soon as I came in. And here is a funny part of it — now as I researched his name, Lo Spinario, on the internet, I found that he is in Palazzo de Conservatori in Rome, another one is at the Uffizi Gallery in Florence. I was upset by it, after all I do remember how I loved him, how I talked to him. On further search though, I found that several copies were made and one of them was given as a gift to King Francis I of France in the sixteenth century. So it was quite possible that my memory is right after all, that I did see him in the Louvre.

I said I felt quite comfortable in my new surroundings. Sometimes I was too comfortable, especially in the feeling that nobody could understand me when I spoke Polish. One day in our hotel while waiting for my father, I sat on a bench in the vestibule next to a very old, ugly, and heavily made up woman, literally covered with jewelry. When Father finally came I told him what I thought about the ugliness of my neighbor. I did not mince words, I remember calling her "an ugly, repulsive cow." When I finished, the woman turned to my father and, in perfect Polish, told him what a disgusting brat he had for a daughter, and wished him well in all the problems he was going to have while raising me and trying to teach me some manners. I did learn my lesson; never again would I take it for granted that people did not understand my language. Have I stopped having sharp criticisms of things and people around me? No way, I still am quite often, overly critical. I just learned to keep my mouth shut.

After several months in Paris we went to Bern, Geneva, Milan, and finally to Rome. There my language abilities grew even faster than in France as the hotel we stayed in, Albergo Paradiso, had a fine back garden in which I played for hours with the children of the staff. Well, I did not spend my whole time there. My father remembering the success of the museums of Paris, took me quite often to the Vatican Museum. The docents there were young clerics, and they enjoyed very much having this curious child under their care. They even took me a few times to the papal gardens where they introduced me to Pope Pius XIIth. Not that it made a big impression on me.

On the whole I loved Rome. My father must have been less busy so that he had time to take me to the Forum Romanum, the Coliseum, the Catacombs, Villa de Trevi, Villa Borghese and many other places about which I later read fascinating things. Finally came the day when we were to fly to Cairo as his new job in a freshly created Polish Embassy was to start. My uncle Mieszek lived in Heliopolis, which is a suburb of Cairo, worked at a French bank, Credit Lyonnais. So my father bought the tickets, sent a telegram telling his brother, with whom we were supposed to stay, the details of our arrival, and we were ready to go. On the day of the flight he had to do some errands and told me to stay in our room and pack our suitcases. When he came back he found me sitting there, doing nothing, not having packed anything. He grew angry, wanted to know why. I told him calmly that I was not going to fly. You can imagine his anger then! An up to that time nice, obedient child telling him she was not going anywhere. Well, he yelled, started packing, and then something very strange happened. I lost consciousness, had something similar to an epileptic attack. A doctor was summoned, gave me some kind of an injection, and hearing the story about what led to the seizure, he told my father not to make me fly. He said that after the injection I would be sleeping for some time, but had I woken in the plane the consequences might be dire. My poor father had to cancel our flight, find a ship that would go to Egypt, take me by train to Marseille, as that was the nearest port with communication with Egypt, and six days later we finally landed in Alexandria. Then another train to Cairo. In all that hassle he never thought of sending another telegram to Mieszek about the change of plans. Anyway, seven days after his brother and his wife awaited us, we showed up at their doorstep. Rang the bell. The door was opened and seeing us, Mieszek nearly had a heart attack. They had just returned from church after attending a mass for our souls. The plane which we were to take fell into the sea; there were no survivors. I had never before, or after had any fear of flying. I had never again had a seizure. Coincidence?

## STILL APRIL, 2006

I found a scrap, literally a small scrap of paper with these words written in my handwriting: "When you give love you hope it will return to you like a boomerang. But just like a boomerang, it may strike you, knock you down, be the tool of your destruction. And what if you give a lot, so much that you empty yourself and are left with ashes? What then?"

I have no idea when I wrote it. What was the occasion? Was I afraid of loving? Or was I thinking how my great love for Wojtek had changed over the years, leaving me feeling alone and not understood? Was I thinking that my situation was hopeless? Was it the same time I wrote the poem "The Fog," when I was so lonely after starting my life in this country?

### THE FOG

*Fog, impenetrable fog*
*Tiny drops on my face*
*And somebody's touch*
*Soft, connecting, I don't see whose*
*I don't know for how long*
*And when it disappears in the milky mass*
*I won't find it, relive it*
*Because of fog*
*Thick, impenetrable fog.*

But that was sometime in 1987 or 1988. The time of my father's death, my cancer, leaving Poland... I knew I wanted to be alone, independent, yet sometimes it was very painful.

### JUNE, 2006

I am rereading a novel by Andrzej Szczypiorski, *The Beautiful Mrs. Seidenman*. A fine book about the war, about Jewishness, about good and about weakness. We usually juxtapose good with evil, I like to think about another pairing. Good and weakness. Isn't it more true? What is the nucleus of evil if not deep fear, so deep that it overcomes decency, compassion, love? And fear that leads us into evil is possible only in weakness, isn't it? The author also deals with past, present, and future in a very interesting way. He says: "Life is that which has been realized, that which can be remembered... the future cannot be my life... because I am not present in the future; I feel neither hunger there nor cold nor warmth. That which will happen somewhere and sometime is still beyond me, concealed behind these walls and bars, beyond the space I occupy and beyond my understanding...." And later he says, "I have experienced nothing but that which I remember." We often tend to think of life as the present, yet as some philosophers tell us, there is no such thing as present — the minute we think about it, it already has become the past. Then there is that problem of memories being constantly changed, either by slightly manipulating them in retelling to make them more palatable, easier to live with, or simply that the retelling, even to ourselves, changes some small seemingly unimportant details and after time we do not remember the first version of the story.

## NEXT DAY

We have spent a lovely day with Debbie and Brian Tingle. They treated us to breakfast and then we played Ligretto, after which Debbie and I played Scrabble while the men watched sports on TV. I am glad to report that I won both of the two Scrabble games we played. I am always very proud of myself when I win in Scrabble with an American, especially with Donnelly or Debbie who are so well educated and so well read.

Debbie talked about the time they had spent in Poland in 1976. Both the Tingles like to remember that time because that is where their romance started. They were there with a choir in which they both sang, travelling all over Poland to sing in different venues and to see the country. Debbie remembered an occasion which baffled her. She needed to go to a public restroom, was surprised at a *babushka* sitting at the entrance taking some money for the usage of the facility and giving out pieces of toilet paper to the people entering. That was a surprise in itself, but imagine her astonishment when, upon exiting, when she praised the old woman for a piece of embroidery on which the woman was working, the embroiderer looked around and then quickly, surreptitiously handed Debbie a long piece of the toilet paper, while putting a finger on her lips. I laughed at this memory and explained it to her. There were two points to this: One was the presence of the worker taking money. In other European countries there were little automatons on the doors to the cubicles into which one had to insert a coin to open the said door. In Poland we had a constitutional right to a job. The state had to provide a job to everybody who wanted one. Thus we had a lot of jobs that could have been either taken by a machine, or cancelled. I am sure that this *babushka* cost much more than what the facility got from the users. She had to have, like everybody else, a month's vacation, health insurance, and eventually pension.

The second explanation was a nearly constant shortage of toilet paper. The shortages were so bad, that had the paper hung inside the cubicles, it would have been stolen by every user. I suppose me included. At home we quite often had to use newspapers. They were bad for reading, but also quite uncomfortable for that other usage. The shortages led to funny changes in human behavior — I once got as a birthday gift twelve rolls of toilet paper. Just imagine somebody, in this case a well known lawyer, coming to a birthday party with a necklace of the aforementioned rolls, which he had dressed up with a little posy of flowers. Oh my God, what an affront it would be here in America, what a faux pas that would be. Well, there, then, I was very happy to receive the rolls, and the gift created a lot of laughter and questions from the other guests as to where did he get them.

There were other instances of the changes in human behavior that would be difficult to understand in today's America, or even for the young people of Poland, the way life is there now. One day as I was busy in the kitchen cooking dinner for my kids, as they were to come from school at that time, I heard singing from the street. Some people were singing the melody of "Ode to Joy." Such an unexpected sound. I looked out the window and, to my enormous surprise, I saw both my daughters, two of my sons, and quite a few of their male friends walking in the middle of the road, holding some packages triumphantly above their heads and singing loudly. Well, the packages they were so proud of were — women's sanitary napkins! Apparently, as they were passing a drugstore on their way from school, they saw a queue. The said napkins were being sold. A rarity! Everybody had a right to buy one package! So my girls asked all available male friends to stand in line with them and to buy them the allotted amount. Well, my grandsons now wouldn't be caught dead with a package of feminine hygiene stuff. *Tempora mutantur et nos mutamur in illis* (times change and we change with them).

## STILL JUNE

We went out to dinner to Chateaulin. Both Donnelly and I like this restaurant very much. The food is delicious and the ambiance elegant yet warm. I always feel there as if I were in a European restaurant, something in the way it is decorated, the way waiters move, speak, wait for the customers to make a sign before the waiter approaches the table, reminds me of all the good places I frequented in Europe. As we were eating I was watching a couple at the table right across from me. Of course I couldn't hear most of what they talked about, not only because they were quiet, but also because Donnelly and I were having a conversation. Still, the other couple was interesting enough to make an impression on me. As soon as we came back home, I sat down and wrote a short piece.

### *A RESTAURANT SCENE*

*He was tall. His brows black and bushy contrasted interestingly with a white beard and salt and pepper hair. Dark eyes, intelligent and animated, rested on his companion, a very lovely woman roughly his age, with eyes just as bright, just as thoughtful, just as playful.*

Her white, nicely starched shirt and a pair of good blue jeans, in no way belied her age, they were quite compatible with her vivacity. No spring chick here, but no teenage recidivist either. They took the table close to us at the restaurant. I noticed first the handsomeness of the man. Then tried to find, to no avail, something to criticize, or make fun of, in the woman. They ordered, drank some wine, ate the appetizers. Their conversation seemed to be animated, easy. They laughed, they became calm, all in a relaxed manner. And then they became serious, very serious. The man extended his hands over the table; the woman took them in hers, one could feel the tenderness that was emanating from what the man was saying. There appeared an uneasiness in the woman's eyes. She asked him something, she laughed, he seemed to relax, and then she asked something to which he replied "yes," but the joy left his eyes. His shoulders visibly slumped. She started to talk. She talked much louder now, she was speaking about her sister, tried to make it all lighter again, told some other story... His face was falling, he was aging in front of our eyes. His hands went back to his lap. That was it. A few minutes after she finished her main dish, a salad, she left. On her way out she stopped for a second and kissed his bald spot. He stayed. A sad, sober man. The waitress tried to cheer him up with a dessert menu. He chose slowly. He was in no hurry to go anywhere.

## JULY, 2006

I tried to translate my Polish poems into English. Impossible. It brings to my mind why I always think that the available translations of Pushkin, Anna Ahmatova, Wislawa Szymborska are so inadequate. I really do not think it possible to translate Slavic poetry into English. There is an enormous difference in speaking about feelings between Germanic and Slavic languages. In Polish or Russian one indicates one's attitude towards words, quite often, by changing the ending of the word. Just to give a small example — "dom" which means house, becomes "domek" if it is small, or "domeczek" if it is small and you like it. It becomes "domisko" if it is big and you do not like it, so one would never use this word for one's own home, unless the house is too rambling, too much to take care of etc. And this is just a small and not very important word in the realm of feelings. When we start to speak about love, fear, abandonment, loneliness, that difference becomes crucial. In English we have to use whole sentences to describe something that can be put in a word or two in Polish, or Russian for that matter. So when I read a Polish poem and compare it to the English version, I see two different poems written about roughly the same thing, with the Slavic version much more lyrical, much more heartfelt. Let's not forget, though, that English has become an international way of communicating in aviation, science, or politics. Those are spheres where accuracy, precision are of the utmost importance. We do not want to know how the traffic controller feels about the path an airplane is taking in approaching landing. All this I know, I love the languages I speak, I love reading novels, poetry in them, but it does bother me that so many things have a different feel in different languages. Is this the reason why people have problems with understanding other cultures, other sensitivities? Is this why Europeans are more internationally minded than Americans? After all, in all of Europe children learn foreign languages early enough to be fluent in them. They also usually learn two, three, sometimes four languages. Only now I realized that at home with my parents we used freely many expressions in several languages. In my first years in America I suppose I must have been perceived as a snob because instinctively I used them. I remember how surprised some of my friends were, when I spoke of a "pied-a-terre" (a small apartment in which to spend some of the time, when for instance one visits a city, while having a home somewhere else), "si non e vero e ben trovato"(even if not true it is well received), "lasciate ogni speranza, voi ch'entrate"("let go of all hope, you who enter," the writing on the gate to hell, as imagined by Dante Alighieri in his famous *Divine Comedy*). Those expressions are usually known to anybody who went through high school in Europe and read the proscribed literature. I don't do it anymore. I have learned my lesson.

There is another question in my mind — how did the different languages develop? I would think that words were invented when there was a need to name some thing, or emotion... Could the differences in the richness of certain languages point to differences in national characters? In Slavic languages we have a word, which in Polish is "tęsknota," in Russian "taska," which has no equivalent in English, German or French. It names the feeling of a great missing of a person, place, food, animal etc., which one particularly loves. So for instance, living here in America I miss (tęsknię) my children and grandchildren, I miss Pluski. And yes, I say "I miss," yet it is very different, because the Polish word packs a lot of emotion, which the word "miss" doesn't. After all you can miss having coffee after dinner, a book that you have lost on a train, etc., etc.

Does it mean that Slavs are, or at least were, more emotional? The Germanic people more accurate? I would love to meet a linguist who researches these themes, who could answer me, explain. I suppose there are universities in which I could find the answers, yet at my age and with the level of my financial resources this is rather out of the question. Oh, well, so many things that are fascinating will remain unanswered, and it has to be OK.

Anyway, going back to where I started, meaning poetry translations, I did an acceptable job with two or three of my Polish poems, so I want to share one of them:

## A SUMMER NIGHT IN THE CANYON

*Monotonous and even*
*The crickets sing.*
*Like a canvas for the hooting*
*of my neighbor — the owl.*
*For the rustle of wind*
*and the cat scratching rug…*
*Peaceful, every night sounds,*
*sucking me into the depth of sleep.*

*And then a jolt, coyotes' yap,*
*They found their prey, and they attack.*
*Their hungry, piercing, laughing bark*
*brings to me the other's silent fear.*

*I bleed its wounds,*
*I hurt its pain.*
*In panicky wait for the final calm*
*My heart is racing for it'll mean death.*
*My sleep long gone*
*For the truth is bared*
*Of all the frills in which we hide.*

## NEXT DAY

I read what I wrote yesterday and thought about how many other "translations" are very problematic. I remember how long I had an unhappy time with maps. I started learning about the world on a globe somebody gave me when I was six. I was fascinated by it, but it got lost in one of the bombed houses. Then a couple years later I received a flat map. It baffled me why the world was so different. My father took a potato, peeled it and showed me how difficult it was to put the peel, the surface of an orb, on a flat surface. It did speak to me, yet for a long time I considered flat maps a lie, which in reality they are. Even more problematic is the transferring of our cultural notions. We grow up without doubting the moral, the traditional, the usual ways of behavior that surround us. In Cairo, one of my parents' friends was a lovely Egyptian woman doctor, Mrs. Habibi. She had studied in Paris at the Sorbonne, then in medical school somewhere in the US. Beautiful, sophisticated, speaking several languages, spending her free time in Europe, yet dressed in a chador. I was so curious why, that one day I did muster some courage and asked her. She was very gracious in answering me — it was much nicer, she said, to be noticed and admired for who and what she was and not for her sex-appeal. "You see," she said, "when I was in the U.S., I constantly felt I needed to convince others that I was not an empty-headed pretty doll. Here in this dress they listen to what I have to say, they respect me for my knowledge, for my wit, my character. How I look doesn't enter the picture." It was a big lesson for me. Even now, or maybe especially now, when we often hear that we have to free the Muslim women, I remember Leila Habibi.

## AUGUST, 2006

A funny thing happened today. I was reading a story in which the author remembered her mother singing to her a French lullaby "Au claire de la lune mon petit Pierrot…," and to my surprise I read it not just as words on a page — my brain put a melody to it, I heard these words as a song sung in my father's voice. I do not remember him ever singing to me. I must have been a baby when that happened. He often, in later years, read French poetry to me, but never, ever sang. Yet it was definitely in his voice that the memory came. What's more, the story I was reading gave just those few words, yet when it came to me as his singing, I heard the whole song. I immediately went upstairs to my laptop to check whether I remembered it all correctly. I found it on YouTube, and yes the memory was right. So, sometime early in my life he must have sung to me, and although I did not know French at that time, my brain stored it faithfully, yet not in my conscious memory bank. I wonder how many other events in my life I have stored there beyond everyday reach. I am amazed and hopeful that they will eventually reappear.

I have said several times in this memoir that I am what my memories are, but what about those unlit crevices of my brain? Are the memories that I consciously know nothing about still forming who I am? Is that why we sometimes surprise ourselves? Why do we not always know why we do something? Why the instant likes and dislikes? Why so many things come out in dreams?

## A FEW DAYS LATER

I have heard, I have read that writers, the dedicated writers write every day. A day not spent on writing is a wasted day. Well, that means that I am not a dedicated writer. Maybe not a writer at all. There are days, sometimes weeks, when I do not feel like writing. Just today, having a choice of going upstairs and putting my thoughts and ideas into the computer or sitting here on our patio with Donnelly, I chose the latter. How can you beat it? The day is hot, but the heat is not oppressive, there is a lovely breeze, which means that the sound of wind in our aspens is blocking the sounds from the freeway. I am, or rather we are, reading the Sunday *New York Times* and whenever we find something that strikes a chord we exchange remarks, or simply read a sentence, a paragraph to each other. This often leads to a conversation. Why would I prefer to sit in my study and write? This here is living life, up there is reliving it. But then why am I writing this thought about not writing? *La donna e mobile qual piuma al vento*... A woman is fickle like a feather in the wind.

## September, 2006

So, Donnelly had his birthday, he is now officially seventy-two. I like that from now until the twenty-second of December he is three years older than me. Silly, isn't it?

Both his kids were here for the occasion. It is always nice to see them, good for Donnelly, yet I have to watch myself very much as Laurie is very sensitive and it is easy to hurt or offend her. She acts as if it was me who destroyed the family, yet Donnelly had been long divorced before he met me. Louise, his first wife and the mother of his children, is very friendly towards me. Whenever we visit Los Angeles we are welcome at her home, their home in the old times, or we take her out to lunch and then visit. She often plays the piano during those visits, he sometimes sings, while I serve as the audience. For a long time I could not, for the life of me, understand Laurie's attitude. Now I have a suspicion that it has to do with the obvious happiness her father shows in his new life. Oh well, we are not going to change this, are we? Anyway, I do appreciate her visits. I like her and her intelligence, her reading habits, which make for interesting conversations. She is a lovely woman. I would love for her to visit more often. Even if I have to curb myself in speaking in my normal opinionated and outspoken way.

## October, 2006

Łucja is taking her final exams for a master's degree in Slavic Languages at the University of Heidelberg. First the written exams, then orals. For a graduation gift Donnelly and I decided to give her a two month vacation with us here in Ashland. She must be worn out, working at a job and keeping house for her man and son all the time while studying. It will be good to be able to pamper her a little. After all what are mothers for? But for the time being I am nervous and thinking about her so much. Not that I have any doubts about her passing those exams, no, I suppose just feeling her own tensions. This is an emotional umbilical cord that never gets cut. In this respect I am glad I live far away from my kids. Had I been in Poland all those nineteen years, I would worry every time they were sick or quarreled with their spouses, lost their job, etc. This way I am not aware of things small, and in reality not very important. They usually call me to brag about some achievement. And that is fine, as I do not want to become a meddling mother, or, even worse, a meddling mother-in-law.

## December, 2006

So, all the exams are behind her, she has done brilliantly, and bought a ticket to Ashland for the tenth of January. I am so happy. Christmas is going to be filled with joyful preparations for her visit.

## Later

I think I already have mentioned a Polish saying, "Man shoots, God carries the bullets." So, the plans were made and all of a sudden we had a call from a dear friend that his wife tried to commit suicide, she is terribly depressed, doesn't want to go for psychiatric help, and when pushed said that the only place she would feel safe was with Donnelly and me. Could he ask us to take her into our home for some time? We do love both of them, so the answer was of course "yes."

For obvious reasons I don't want to use her name, let's just call her AB. She came in a frightful state. A fine, pretty, vivacious, intelligent woman was turned into a haggard, wrinkled, shaking uncontrollably, always feeling cold, unhappy creature. When they showed me her pills, I could not believe the medley prescribed by her doctors. Something like thirty pills a day. She had a headache? Here are pills for migraine. A nerve inflammation in your face? No problem, take those painkillers. Cannot sleep? Well, there we have sleeping meds, etc., etc.

I am so sorry for her, I try to help by slowly taking her off of certain medications, but I am not a doctor so I have to be very careful. I also try to make her eat and drink, as she had become emaciated. And all the time there is that fear that when my back is turned, when I sleep, she might again try to kill herself. All her pills are hidden well, but if one is really intent on doing it there are more ways to commit a suicide. I am beside myself with worry. I am also feeling for her, for what she must be going through. Oh, if I only could be sure I am helping. That what we are doing is the best for her. I love her, and she is in pain, and quite often I feel helpless. I wish I had more medical knowledge. I wish I had more trust in medical doctors, but what AB is going through does not inspire that kind of trust.

Also what am I to do about Łucja? The peaceful house we promised her is gone. Even the only guest room that we have is taken.

## January 2007

Łucja is here. Every morning we have to fold up the bed in Donnelly's study. This means she has to get up relatively early, which I am sure she hates, but Donnelly cannot stop working, seeing his students, answering their emails, etc. We have to fold up the bed and move it to the garage, take all her stuff into our bedroom, and still try to have her be relaxed and happy. It was not supposed to be this way.

Łucja is a very good person so she immediately pitched in with help for AB. I am trying to convince AB that she needs more professional help. I am sure she needs a closed rehab center with proper doctors to take her off most of those pills she is taking. I cannot do it. What we did manage to achieve is the limiting of meds, feeding her a little, having her stop shaking, and getting her to the point of talking to us and listening. She is even able to converse with Łucja, and today I heard them laughing. It was so good to hear that.

## A FEW DAYS LATER

J, AB's husband, found a place for her. An extremely expensive rehab in Malibu. They do have the money to pay for it and she is on the verge of accepting the idea. Let's hope it will be what she needs. The place has both medical treatments for addictions and psychological help for the mental and nervous problems. She needs both approaches very much.

## STILL JANUARY

AB has gone to Malibu. What a relief. My God, how difficult the last twenty days were. Now it's all about Łucja and relaxation, and having fun. We all need it.

## FEBRUARY 28, 2007

Łucja left today. It was so good to have her here. We went to theater, we attended concerts, we had friends come to dinners, went visiting. There was even a very special evening in the Weisinger's Winery, an evening of "drinking songs." The Southern Oregon Repertory Singers, the choir in which Donnelly sings, performed, the winery served dinner and wines. Donnelly sang the "Libiamo" aria from *La Traviata* in duet with a lovely young soprano. Oh my, how well he sings. If not for the fact that I already am in love with him, I would have fallen for him for sure. Good to know that he is mine!

I think I loved most our own, private, family evenings with her. We reminisced about the years spent in Moscow, especially the first one or two, which she can hardly remember. I told her the story of how she earned her first prize for dancing. She was not yet three when we arrived there. Our apartment was not yet ready so we had to stay in a hotel, which was not bad, but the food situation was quite miserable. The restaurant didn't serve any fruits and very limited vegetables, only cabbage and beetroots. I tried to buy fruit in shops and was mortified realizing that there were none to be found. Anyway, one evening when we went to the hotel restaurant for dinner there was some kind of a banquet going on. A long table was set beautifully for around twenty-four people. Baskets of gorgeous fruit made the table look very festive and appetizing. Men and women sat around it. All the men were dressed in military uniforms with lots of medals decorating their chests. At the head of the table sat a heavy, big man with general's insignia. A band was playing music, some of the military men were dancing with ladies looking like their wives. How do I know? The women were heavy, not very young, and dressed richly in showy brocade dresses, which I knew were unavailable at regular Moscow stores.

It so happened that just before we left Poland my children performed in a little New Year's show in their preschool, and Łucja soloed in a Russian/Ukrainian dance "kazachok." Here, when the band started to play the known to her melody she slid off her chair and started dancing in the middle of the dance floor. Grownups moved to the side and began to clap, soon the whole room was clapping, my little girl was beaming with pleasure and dancing very prettily, and towards the end of the melody the general himself got up, picked a big pineapple from a basket nearest to him, stepped on the dance floor, knelt on one knee in front of a bewildered little dancer, offered her the fruit and kissed her hand. What a moment! And yet she knows it only from our stories, she doesn't remember it at all.

She does remember though all the songs and lullabies she heard every night on Russian TV. The TV there had only three or four channels, but was pretty good if one knew how to choose. There was a lot of great theater, concerts, ballet and opera shows, and children's programs in addition to unacceptable propaganda. I allowed the kids to watch every night a half hour "goodnight" program that was especially well made. No violence, just soothing cartoons, or stories about animals, plenty of lovely songs, and it always ended with the same lullaby, "Spiat ustalyye igrushki…," which means "Tired toys are sleeping…" and which ends with telling the kiddies that tomorrow is another day…. Łucja sings those songs very beautifully, and I was surprised that I also remembered them and could join her in singing. Donnelly praised us very much.

Łucja is a fine cook, so when we entertained she made several dishes that were unknown to Donnelly and me. All the more enjoyable, because of that, and easier for me, as I didn't have to cook alone.

She even went to the Elastic Mind meeting with us. Talked very well and, of course, I was mightily proud. This time the theme was "Pros and cons of democracy." It is something very important to a Pole. After all Poland was one of the first democracies in Europe in modern times. Yes, we were a monarchy, but our kings were elected from 1370, when the last king of the Piast dynasty died. At first the electors were only a small council, but gradually that privilege was given to all "szlachta" or nobility (pronounced shlahta in English). Yet, as often with translations, "nobility" does not give a true picture. Nobility, in Poland, was given to a person for good deeds for the country, usually for valor on a battlefield, but it was not limited to fighting. What's more, the sons of the nobles inherited the title. All the sons, not just the eldest. Daughters inherited the title but not the rights — for instance the right to vote. By the middle of sixteenth century there were around half a million nobles, some of them poor peasants. A far cry from aristocracy, from the rule of landlords, princes, earls, and so on. As a matter of fact, in keeping with the idea of equality among the nobles, no titles below "prince" were allowed in Poland. We did have some barons, marquises and others, but they, or just their titles, had to come from some other country.

Ironically enough the democracy that we had was the reason of our downfall. Towards the end of eighteenth century, it became known that the three powerful neighbors of Poland

— Russia, Prussia and Austria — connived to attack Poland and divide it between them. Being forbidden by laws to act unilaterally, the king convened the Sejm (the lower house of the national assembly) to get permission to raise taxes for the army. Well, we know even today, how the parliaments react to the very idea of raising taxes. The Sejm was still discussing the need when the attack came. Poland was taken and partitioned between the three who had kings unencumbered by democratic notions. It regained independence only after the First World War, more than 125 years later.

I am glad to report that, after all, Łucja had a good rest in Ashland. She left very happy and ready for a big change in her life because her husband Fritz got in the meantime a very good job in Zurich, Switzerland. Before her is the move from Karlsruhe to Zurich and looking for a new job there.

## March, 2007

Another discussion of democracy at Elastic Mind. This time "Is Democracy a Utopia?" It was based on two books: *The Electronic Republic* by Lawrence Grossman and *The Silent Takeover* by Noreena Hertz. I started it by reminding people of the definitions of democracy. Yes, plural. There are four main approaches: 1) Making political decisions directly by the whole body of citizens. Or rather those recognized as responsible persons, which in old Greece meant only free men. Possible to achieve in Greek city-states, where there were rarely more than 10,000 inhabitants, and where women and slaves had no right to vote. 2) Representative democracy in which people rule through their representatives chosen by and responsible to them. 3) Constitutional democracy — the powers of majority are restrained by constitutions guaranteeing every citizen some inalienable rights. Even the minorities are protected in their right to free judicial systems, freedom of religion, etc. 4) Social democracy, which tends to minimize social and economic differences between citizens in addition to the ability of choosing one's representative and president.

We always hear a simplified definition: democracy is one person, one vote. Nice, but like a lot of things not true. Just take our American style of elections. We vote supposedly for our president and then our votes are translated into electoral votes that get counted as the only valid votes for the president. Electors are chosen by the two political parties, yet there is nothing in the Constitution limiting the way they are to vote.

Each state decides it on their own, with forty-eight states and District of Columbia giving all their electoral votes to the presidential candidate who won the popular vote in that state. The rule of "winner takes all." That means disregarding say even 49 percent of voters, as case might be. Only two states select the electors proportionately to the results of the popular vote. So, in 2000 Al Gore won the majority of popular votes, yet George W. Bush became president. Or going back to 1992 — a third candidate — Ross Perot won 19 percent of popular votes but none of the electors. Democracy? Then there is that problem with social democracy. It would seem to be the best in theory. At least from our Christian society's point of view. You know, love thy neighbor, etc. Some dare say that Jesus was the biggest socialist of all. The camel and the needle…. But let's not mix religion and politics, nor stray away from reality. Social democracy seems to be impossible in our culture of adoration of financial success, in which those who achieved it think, delude themselves, and try to browbeat others in thinking that they are in such a good position due to their higher intelligence, industriousness, and other superior traits of character. In other words they are better than those who are poor. This "browbeating" if done well is, I suppose, the reason why the majority votes so often against their own interests. Those in the upper financial class have the means to hire good propagandists, to own newspapers and TV stations. Maybe even just pay for TV programs aimed at general population, to make, as we say in Poland, "soup of their brains," or convince the poor undereducated guy that he or she has a chance of becoming a millionaire, a CEO, a president, or at least a TV anchor. Thus, no higher taxes on the rich, although it's only through raising taxes that we could have better roads, safer bridges, school buildings that would not fall and crush children in a hurricane, or public transportation which would enable us to live in a healthier environment and in a more relaxed manner. Have you noticed that the word "socialism" has become a bad word in America? That anything "social" is, at least, suspect?

Why did Europe manage to make their democracy, their capitalism, so much more humane? Whenever I go there, which is roughly every two years, I marvel at how much easier, more relaxed is the lifestyle of people in Switzerland, Germany, Sweden, or even Poland. The comfort in which people in those countries live, the good and easy access to healthcare, the four to six weeks of paid vacation time, long paid maternity leaves, all this makes me wonder. Why cannot we? Why and how could they? Is there something in the national character that makes people more tribally minded? We like to put family among our most important values, yet we do not have those four or six weeks of leisure to spend with our spouses and children in an unhurried way. We always hear that maternity leave would damage small businesses, but why doesn't it damage German business? And what about those children that grow so much healthier, both physically and mentally, with one of their parents taking care of them at home in their first years, instead of in a daycare? How come German or Polish doctors can visit their patients at home if need be, and ours cannot? How many illnesses are caught in a doctor's waiting room, when a person weakened by some other illness sits there for often a long time? We have this dislike of learning from others, it seems we are capable of learning only from our own mistakes, and even this not often.

Look at geography. Social democracies succeeded in central

and northern Europe. We always read in our newspapers about the "nanny states" like Sweden or Finland. Usually it is written with condescension. We are pitying the people who are, supposedly, treated like children, stripped of freedom of choice, of individuality. Yet in truth, if we look at it closely it is they who have more freedom to think and act in an individual way because the "nanny state" frees them from worry about their and their families' health, education, or old age. Those same ideas of social democracies are failing in the south of Europe. Should we pay more attention to innate characteristics of people before we think what political system would work? I know, I know here I enter a very politically incorrect area. Yet if we are to come even close to truth we have to reject preconceptions, especially when they are based on fear or guilt. All those problems and more were discussed at our Elastic Mind meeting. Did we find any panacea for the ills of democracy? Fat chance of that, but the conversation was lively, and, I think, we all learned something and enjoyed the process very much.

## STILL MARCH 20, 2007
Donnelly and I were today the guests of Joe and Michael W. at dinner in Chateaulin. The food was so good I became ecstatic and joked that I want Donnelly to bring me to this restaurant once a week in the future when, due to our age, we won't have sex anymore. It was greeted with a lot of laughter. As well it should have been.

## APRIL, 2007
On the sixth, on Good Friday, at around ten at night, as I was already in my dressing gown, the telephone rang. It was Jan telling me that they are in Spain for the Easter weekend, wishing me happy Easter, asking me what our plans are.... At the same time the doorbell rang. I got worried. At ten? Something must have happened to some neighbors? Holding the receiver to my

ear, I rushed to the door, opened it and...there were Jan and Monika. He was still with his phone to his ear, she had a little basket filled with colored eggs in outstretched hands. My god, what a surprise!!! Spain! Ha, ha! They came all the way from Poland, then had a long drive from San Francisco, just to spend Easter with us. I love it when they come, I love spending time with them, enjoying our easy and lively conversations.

We usually have great food, as we all like to eat, and Jan buys expensive wine, and as he has a great instinct in choosing it, we do have feasts. They know how to enjoy life, are easy to laugh with, and thus are fine company. What good children I have! How lucky I am that they like Donnelly so much and that Donnelly likes them very much too.

It isn't the first time they surprised us so. In 2004, in December, roughly two weeks before our fourteenth wedding anniversary, Jan called to say they wanted to give us a gift of the very best restaurant dinner for the occasion. Could we choose a place and make the reservations and then tell him, so that he can give his credit card number to the restaurant to put the tab on. We were very happy, as our favorite Chateaulin is too expensive for us right now. We made the reservation for the thirtieth and joyfully awaited a fine evening. Well, at seven o'clock on the memorable day we showed ourselves in the restaurant, and the maitre d' led us to our table. I was dismayed on seeing that there must have been a mistake. The table was set for four, and a bottle of a very expensive champagne was cooling in a bucket of ice. I said it must be an error — to which the maitre d' smiled and pointing to the bar said: "no, no, it is that couple at the bar who ordered it all." We looked — and there were Jan and Monika sitting, enjoying a drink and smiling the loveliest, most tender of smiles. My god! I started crying, people in the restaurant applauded, obviously everybody except us was in on the secret. The young ones flew from Warsaw to San Francisco (sixteen hours), rented a car, drove for another five hours, had to change in the car, just to be with us on this important day!

Yes, I do have the most fantastic kids. It also helps that they can afford such extravaganzas and they are young enough to be able to physically cope with such adventures. Just imagine the jet lag — their bodies felt as if it was four o'clock in the morning. Yes, there is a nine hour difference in time between Poland and our West Coast. We had a great evening and the next five days of their visit.

## May, 2007

Once again we are in Poland. On the twenty-second we will fly to Rome. We'll spend a week there alone in an apartment that Jan rented, then he and Monica will join us and after three or four days we shall all drive to Venice, stopping on the way in several places of interest.

For the time being I am visiting family and getting emotional. It is hard not to, as I see them so rarely.

## Rome, May 24, 2007

It is again my name day. What a place to celebrate! Our rented apartment is in an old building, lovely with the elegance of an aged, wrinkled grande dame. Furnished with antiques, with some good oil paintings on the walls which makes it feel so sophisticated. Although we were told to use the bathtub sparingly as it leaks. Didn't I call it a grande dame?

The apartment is situated near the river Tiber, just across it from the Vatican City, and a walking distance to St. Peter's Basilica or, if we go the other way, the center of the old town. For me Rome has a ton of memories from the three times I was here with my father. Donnelly is here for the first time. Among my memorabilia I have a photo that my father took of the ten-year-old me in the Coliseum. That was on our first trip. I have it now here with me so I can stand on the same spot again. I am quite excited by that possibility.

We walk so much that from time to time we have to give some rest to our poor feet. It is pretty hot outside, the weather is gorgeous, but luckily for us there are so many magnificent churches everywhere with interiors that are cool, quiet, and filled with art. They provide us with rest stops that are very welcome.

I am sated with museums. I've seen too many of them, I suppose. But churches, streets, architecture of buildings, parks and mainly the people — their moods, customs, way of life — are of great interest to me. In Rome many churches are so rich in art that they can be considered museums, yet I love seeing them. After all, during long periods of time most paintings, sculptures, or music were commissioned by the Catholic Church. The church had the money. I often wonder whether the idea of filling churches with art came to priests, bishops and popes because they were art lovers, or because they knew that when people are in awe they are easier to be manipulated. I would rather vote for the latter. Whichever the reason though, we are the beneficiaries.

There is another reason for my liking old churches — I always feel in them a very different kind of energy enveloping me. I know that a scientist would pooh-pooh my belief that all the people praying and meditating over centuries have left their imprint in the walls of the buildings. Energy stored in the walls? It does sound crazy, yet this is what I feel when I sit quietly in an old pew in one of those churches.

I remember what a strong impression "Pieta" at the St. Peter's Basilica made on me. Why was it? Did I, ten years old, remember all the dead I saw during the war? Could I, at that age intuit the pain of a mother losing her son? Who knows. The fact is I still remember the enormous feeling of compassion that swept through me at seeing it. It is even today overwhelmingly sad for me.

What is my attitude to church as an institution? My ideas about religion? I often describe myself as an agnostic if anybody asks. Normally that name is given to a person who doesn't believe in God, but also does not claim the nonexistence of God. It's from Greek agnotos — unknown. Saying that we humans cannot have claims to ultimate knowledge. In all spheres of knowledge, not only in religion. And I like that wider definition. Our senses are so limited. Our brains are astonishingly developed, yet also limited.

Humans do not hear sounds that many animals hear, we know how flawed is our perception of colors, of time. Is there anyone who does not feel the slowing down of time either when bored or in a dangerous situation? And time flies so much faster when we are in a hurry to do something, to go somewhere. And how about the radio or TV waves? We have to have manmade receivers to hear or see, without them we cannot get those waves, yet they are all around us, all the time. So how many other phenomena are real, exist in our world, yet we have no notion of them? Slowly, very slowly at first, we develop our knowledge of the world we live in. Of course if we compare the tempo of this development now to the one, say a hundred or a thousand years ago, it seems very fast, but we have to remember the constantly growing base for this knowledge. A good example would be our ideas about the existence of extraterrestrials — we can only imagine things that are close to what we know, we picture them with weird eyes, limbs, antennas, yet still those are eyes, limbs, etc. All the things that we know. And what if they are just small bundles of energy, or even small bundles of something we have no idea what? I suppose that is why all our knowledge develops in small steps.

We can go into unknown territories but only a small piece at a time. How then could we be sure about existence or non-existence of God? How could we be sure about our origins? How can we even define the word god. Over the history of religions men pictured "God" in such different ways. Just think of Zeus the lascivious as compared to God the Father. Or the seemingly impossible idea of one god who at the same time is the father, the son and the holy ghost. So when we think about creation, how can we imagine the creator — person? energy? spirit? accident? combination of those? And when we come to the question of the beginning of it all, we cannot overcome our feeling that everything had to have a precursor, everything had to come from something. Just like what we know from our own life. No wonder priests always tell us not to seek knowledge about those big problems, just believe. But for me, personally, belief is a copout. I want to know. Even if I accept that most of those unknowns are not going to become known in my lifetime. The more we know about space, the more we know how little we know. Same goes for a lot of other scientific research. Not a month passes by without some new revelation about how our brains work or how genes seem to switch themselves on or off and what happens when they do. Yet we still cannot cure a simple cold, and are helpless when confronted with some viruses.

What creates consciousness, memory? How come we move before we consciously perceive the need for movement? How come we, sometimes, get a brilliant idea, an already well-formed idea, before we even know that we had started to form it?

Often I feel as if my brain is totally independent. It just allows me to use it from time to time, but mostly it works for itself, by itself. My whole body is just a tool for the brain to exist, move, be fed. Yet, at the same time the body influences the brain. It can impair it, it can stimulate it, it can finally kill it. And another problem — who am I as a person? Am I just the brain? It seems obvious to me that the real me is the combination of the two. Not always a peaceful combination, not always productive, but always the two together. Although why do I so often feel that my body betrays me by getting old and infirm? Even the way I put it — I feel…it betrays me. Not that it betrays itself. So? A conundrum. Wiser people than I tried to answer the big question "Who am I." I suppose it'll bother me to the end, until there is no more an I.

Yet, back to religion, to church. I do have certain beliefs. One of them is that there is no "personal god." The very idea of an all-powerful, all-knowing and all-good god seems to me to be ludicrous. Remember? I went through the Second World War as a child. If there were such a god, if he knew everything and if he were so good — could he not have intervened? Could he have looked at the slaughter of innocent people, innocent children and do nothing? Either he didn't know, or he was powerless, or he didn't care. The only other possibility is — he doesn't exist. Then another tenet I was taught in my Catholic school in Cairo — a child who was not baptized cannot enter heaven! Why? Where is the goodness? Or the very idea of the primeval sin? Why should we pay for our forefathers' sin? Even if we accept that they actually committed a sin. So many, so many illogical, unsubstantiated "truths" that we are told we have to believe in. "God's ways are not to be understood by the limited human mind." Perhaps this is the main truth that everything rests on. But then how come so many organized religions, so many churches constantly tell us what God thinks, what God wants us to do, what God forbids us to do, feel, think. And here I come to the only reason for those organized churches — lust for power. Make people afraid, convince them that they are not capable of understanding, that they have to be humble, and you can manipulate them any way you want. Be it for money, for fighting, for submission. Power. The great drug. If you have power you respect yourself, you feel you are better than others, you are on top of your world.

Sometimes it seems that the struggle for minds is fought by two separate groups — one whose foundation rests on reasoning and logic of cause and effect, and another who believe that an all-powerful god guides and controls their lives, taking away

from them any responsibility for their independent actions.
Well, here I am biased. I should add that I do understand that a lot of people need a church. Sometimes just for socializing, for being part of a group, for not feeling alone and lost. Sometimes for being told what is good and bad, for giving them a reason to behave well, honestly, charitably. In this respect churches play an invaluable role for those who need it. I don't have this need. My parents did a pretty good job in bringing me up an honest, charitable person.

Am I always such? Of course not. I err, stray off the path, but I seriously try to get back on it, and always I try to be aware, not to lie to myself. Maybe that's the hardest thing to do. There is also that need of ecstasy in people, of the sublime feeling of happiness. The church with its traditions, rituals, mysticism helps many to get that. I do not need help in this. I get my ecstatic feelings from music, nature, poetry, from sensual pleasures like the feel of the sun on my skin, to say nothing of sex and the touch of the body of the man I love. But then comes the biggest question — why humans everywhere and always needed to create the idea of "God." And if I say that our minds are limited, I should not reject the notion that there is a powerful being creating all that we have and are, even if we cannot be aware of it. I should be more humble. Not believing doesn't necessarily mean negating. So, there I am. I know that I don't know.

I have read a fascinating book by Oliver Sacks, *Uncle Tungsten*. It is an autobiography of his childhood years. He had, among many other interesting family members, an aunt who was a mathematician. She liked to teach him about the beauty, the logic of mathematics. One day she told him, "God thinks in numbers." It shook me. What an idea! I immediately went to my room and wrote a poem. Here it is:

## NUMBERS

*"Numbers," I read, "are the way God thinks."*
*I struggled for long, how to reconcile*
*His goodness and Auschwitz,*
*His love and our pain,*
*Maimed children*
*And prayers in void.*
*Suddenly there's sense.*
*Planetary orbits,*
*The quantums, the genes,*
*Precision,*
*Plan,*
*Perfection.*
*He thinks in numbers.*
*We are not accidents,*
*Our feelings are.*

Maybe we are part of something much, much bigger. Too big to be comprehended by our limited, human brains. But then let's be consistent. Let's not pretend we know what is this much bigger entity. Let's not judge by our human standards and limitations. Let's learn as much as we can about our world, about our universe, about our brains, about ourselves, but always leave an opening for the unknown. Let's allow ourselves to create fables and myths, but not to mistake them for truths.

## JUNE 1, STILL ROME

Jan and Monika have arrived. We did some more sightseeing and as Jan knows a lot of good restaurants, we dined and wined magnificently several times. Tomorrow he rents a car and we'll leave Rome. Destination Venice, but on our way we plan to see several other places. We'll go west to the coast of the Tyrrhenian Sea, then north visiting Civitavecchia and spending the night hopefully in Livorno. But, as we are not on a strict timeline, if we are tired, we'll stop for the night before that.

## STILL JUNE, GARGONZA

We have spent several hours in Pisa. The town is very lovely, very old, very touristy. The leaning tower a total disappointment. So what that it leans? Big deal. A long line of people wanting to climb it. We didn't feel it necessary. In the same compound, Piazza del Duomo, now called Piazza dei Miracoli, a big church looked much more interesting. It is the cathedral — Duomo. We went there and were awed. I think it is the most beautiful of all the churches I have ever seen. The architecture quite spectacular. It was started somewhere in the eleventh century and as many of those very old buildings go, had been added to and refurbished several times since. Built in a Romanesque style it suffered a devastating fire in 1595. The fire destroyed most of the interior's medieval art. Only a few pieces of the old art survived. One of them is the tomb of Emperor Henry VII (1315), another is Giovanni Pisano's pulpit from 1302–1311, which has an interesting history. After the fire the renovators did not like it, so they dismantled it and stored it in a crate. Luckily for us they did not destroy it. It was rediscovered in 1926, reassembled and is a joy to look at it now. My eyes were drawn to the columns. It must be a common reaction, otherwise why the invention of columns, if not to feel uplifted, drawn towards the sky, towards heaven by their height and vertical reach. Yes, they are there for very practical purposes of supporting the roof, but their shape and markings, grooves, sculpted heads are not needed for function, they are there definitely for our emotional reactions.

Behind the cathedral, we visited the Baptistery of St. John. Small compared to the cathedral, but also an exquisite building. A jewel. It has such fantastic acoustics that one can harmonize with oneself. Any sound, once emitted, is supposed to last for over twelve seconds. Donnelly, of course, had to test it by some singing and yes, the effect was astonishing.

Finally, we left Pisa to go to Siena, our next planned stop for the night. We were very tired. After half an hour of driving, we started thinking of maybe finding some closer place to stop. Monika, a whiz on her smartphone, went into her organizational mode, and shortly found a place that sounded very attractive. Its name was Il Castello di Gargonza, a medieval village turned into a hotel. It did have some vacancies. We turned off the main road, went into the hills of Tuscany, drove up and up and up, and finally came to a walled-in village. Had to park the car outside the walls and walked in. The outer walls of the little cottages were unchanged from what they looked like in medieval times. The street was paved with uneven cobblestones, there was an old well in the center of a little piazza. We located an office, were shown available rooms and got two of them. The interiors of those old houses were quite modern — each of them had a perfectly functioning, and beautiful, bathroom. Tiles, mirrors, showers, bathtubs, you name it, they had it. Fantastic, old furniture, enormous four poster beds, but with new modern, comfortable mattresses. Each little cottage was surrounded with colorful, old-fashioned flowers. Some places by the walls of the village had chairs to sit in and enjoy views of the hills and valleys, of vineyards and orchards. We fell in love with it. Donnelly has even written a little poem about it:

> *The walls are silent whispers,*
> *lying stone on stone.*
> *They speak of hardened hands,*
> *calloused defenders, bent with purpose.*
> *With implacable firmness, they defy*
> *the assault of centuries,*
> *Capturing space, enclosing time,*

*empowering life,*
*To thread their way among*
*the gnarled roots of history.*

*Sunning lizards now breathe my air,*
*the birds my song.*
*Gone are the rough-hewn villagers,*
*whose voices crackled with industrious life.*
*Gone — the creaking olive press, rolling carts on stone paths,*
*the clanging anvil, squeaking well wheel.*
*Then a distant church bell,*
*perhaps they heard the same.*

*I place my hand on the sun-warmed stone.*
*For this moment I too am a villager.*

We were also shown the local restaurant — a renovated olive press just beyond the village walls. As usual with my kids, we dined and wined happily for a long time, then went for a little walk, and decided to stay longer than the planned one night. Tired as we were, we gave up seeing Florence. Can you imagine? Florence lost to the idea of spending two sybaritic, free of sightseeing, days in Gargonza. Instead of looking at palazzos, paintings, sculptures, we walked, lolled in the sun, read, talked and ate and drank. Florence can wait for a next trip to Italy. Tomorrow we are leaving for Venice.

After having an especially good dinner at the restaurant and seeing the gusto with which Jan eats and enjoys wine I was remembering Wojtek. Both my sons remind me sometimes very much of him. Then, when I went to our room I wrote a story about his appetite for good food.

## THE GOOSE

*Wojtek was twenty three or twenty four when I met him. An accomplished young man, freshly graduated from a good university, he was already working as a political columnist at one of the best newspapers in the country. Medium height, thin and handsome too. I was quite impressed the day we were first introduced to each other — with the long tweed overcoat he wore, the big black umbrella, and the fact that on this bitterly cold, rainy day his shoes were clean and shiny. We met often in the next few weeks. We could talk for hours, and I must have talked a lot about him too, because quite soon my parents invited him to dinner.*

*He came, elegant as usual, a pile of news faxes from the office for my father, roses for my mother, and a box of chocolates for me. The conversation took off easily, and after a short time we sat down to dinner. A typically Polish dinner — herring with finely diced apples and green onions smothered with a thick layer of crème fraiche and decorated with stripes of freshly ground black pepper, small glasses of ice cold vodka, and crusty bread and butter. Then soup. Then pot roast with wild mushroom sauce, beets, mashed potatoes, and salad. My father was a great cook. Wojtek seemed to like everything. He took a second helping of herring, didn't refuse a second plate of soup, gladly accepted a second of pot roast, helped himself to a third, and as he was reaching for the serving dish a fourth time, my father started laughing. "Do you ever reach a point of satiation?" he asked. Wojtek was totally unperturbed in the process of filling his plate. He seemed to think deeply about the question, then smiled and said: "I don't think so, if the food is really good. My mother says that I digest faster than I eat. But it is only if I really like the food. I think I could easily eat a ten pound goose." The whole family burst out laughing, and my father proposed a bet. He would buy and cook the goose and if Wojtek ate it, he would be invited to ten consecutive Sunday dinners. If not, well, shame on him for bragging. Wojtek accepted, the men shook hands and the next Sunday my father roast-*

ed two geese. One for Wojtek, the other for the rest of the family and some friends.

Appetizer, soup, and the big moment arrived. The geese were carried in. They were enormous, plump, nicely browned, oozing little rivulets of grease and juices. Their aroma filled the room. They were stuffed with nice, old-fashioned apples and surrounded with small round potatoes baked together with the geese. One of the birds was then carved into several portions — there were six of us in addition to Wojtek. The other was divided into four quarters, one of which, with a liberal helping of apples and potatoes, was served to him, the remaining three went back into the oven to be kept warm. A sauceboat with gravy, wrapped in a fluffy towel, was put on the table, and we all joyfully dug in. We were just starting to really enjoy our food when Wojtek asked for his second quarter. This he began to eat more slowly, adding gravy, drinking beer, even joining in the conversation. The third quarter went the same way. We had finished our goose by that time and sat back to witness what had to be Wojtek's defeat. He couldn't, no, he couldn't possibly... but here he was asking for the fourth quarter. No worse for wear. Actually enjoying himself. Cutting into the meat with gusto. One could swear he was salivating as he was piling the roast apples on top of a succulent piece of meat. Just looking at him made us feel hungry again. My mother was transfixed; she was looking at him with astonishment and getting giggly like a young girl. My father became speechless, and that was something! Our other guests tried to cheer Wojtek on. As if he needed it. He finished and scraped his plate clean, drank his beer, and with a charming smile asked about dessert. There were bravos all around. My father started making funny remarks about the dangers of betting and about the poorhouse.

It was after cake and coffee that Wojtek finally sat back, totally relaxed, and that was when, for the first time, I saw on his face this beatific smile of absolute happiness, total contentment, that I was to see so often in the next thirty years. After every good meal. After every good lovemaking.

## NEXT DAY

We saw a funny street scene in one of the small towns on our way. We got off the freeway to find a place for lunch. We pulled over to consult our electronic guide and noticed three policemen, or maybe they were *carabinieri*, talking to an old, visibly drunk guy. A bicycle was lying on the pavement near by. One of the policemen was talking on a cell phone. (By the way, the Italians call it a *telefonino*. I like that.) Shortly afterwards an old woman appeared on the other side of the street. As she started crossing to where the men stood, she yelled and waved her arms menacingly. On coming close, she grabbed the old drunk by the collar of his shirt, shook him and began to pull him back into the street. The policemen laughed out loud and one of them picked up the bicycle and followed the old people. What a way to deal with a drunk! Call his wife. Nothing they could do to teach that guy to behave himself would surpass what she could do. We had our lunch, then went on to another small town where we stopped for the night.

## VENICE, JUNE 7, 2007

So, here we are in the place I read so much about that I feel I've already been here. We left the rental car at Piazzale Roma, which we reached by a four kilometer long bridge. It is the last place one can get into Venice by car. That is where we were picked up by a water taxi from our hotel. Travelling with Jan and Monika provides us with luxuries we cannot afford on our own. It does feel great to be pampered in such a way. Luckily for us, we do not get spoiled, so going back to our normal frugal life is not a problem. Well, the hotel was quite a distance and we enjoyed travelling down the Grand Canal with its many beautiful palaces and bridges. Donnelly got so excited that at a certain point he stood up and delivered, full voice, the beginning of an aria from Tosca. The boat was just nearing a bridge filled with passersby who stopped and applauded wildly. What a moment! I was so proud of my man, and so happy for him.

The hotel was all we expected it to be, our room fronted a small canal where gondoliers, waiting for passengers, sang and chatted. Quite a show for the tourists that we were. After a quick visit to the bathroom, we went out. The hotel was maybe a two minute walk from San Marco Square, so we were immediately immersed into the absolute beauty of the city. As I said before, I had read so much and seen so many pictures, that I did not expect to be surprised by anything. Yet I was. The size, the proportions of the buildings, the magnificence of their walls fronting the Piazza, it all awed me beyond words. The only unpleasantness we found were the long lines one had to stand in to get into San Marco Basilica. Oh, these tourists! One gets so disgusted with their crowds, and the fact that we also are…

Not being able to get into either the Basilica or the Doge's Palace, we went for a fine walk around the city, enjoyed the absence of motorized traffic, were ravished by the views, and ended up having a fine seafood dinner.

Next day, we started early and got into the St. Mark's easily. I could have spent days inside just looking at the old mosaics, pictures, sculptures, and the proportions of the building itself. As it was, we spent several hours there. At a certain point my feet told me in no uncertain manner that I had to sit down, and then the thinking began. On reading the history of the church I found a lovely story about its beginnings. Apparently, somewhere in 828 the then Doge ordered the stealing, from Alexandria, of the body of Saint Mark and building a church to house it. It was built, next to the Doge's Palace, very quickly and consecrated in 832. Remember — one of the Ten Commandments says, "Do not steal." Okay, so there goes the saintliness of the whole enterprise.

There is more. After a few fires, some remodels, there came a time for a big rebuilding of the Basilica. It so happened that in 1204, a crusade (the fourth) started out to free The Holy Land from the Muslims. Knights came from all over Europe, filled with the holy fire of defending Christianity, retaking the sacred city of Jerusalem.... Well, the road to Jerusalem went through Constantinople, a very rich city in those days. When the knights saw all the gold, sculptures, jewels, etc., they couldn't help themselves from looting. They stole whatever they could, while in the process forgetting all about the holy goals; and so instead of defending Christianity they ransacked a Christian city. To make matters even more ironic, a lot of that loot ended up in Venice in the St. Mark's Basilica. Here we have the famous sculpture of horses, now in the church museum, while a copy adorns the façade. The horses have their own history in the historical thieving — they once beautified the Hippodrome of Constantinople, then were installed above the portal of the Basilica around 1254. Napoleon stole them from there and took them to Paris. Venice regained them in 1815, and that is when the copies were made, while the originals went to the museum. Even the main altar has a big part of it looted from Constantinople — the lower two thirds of the famous Pala d'Oro, The Golden Pall, were ordered by one of the doges from court craftsmen in Byzantium, the upper one third came from the infamous fourth crusade.

## NEXT DAY, VENICE

Today was the Doge's Palace day. In my life-long travels I have seen many palaces, churches, castles and museums, but never have I seen such opulence, such fullness of art at the highest level. Every ceiling, every wall, every floor was structured, painted, sculpted by people who knew and cared about beauty. Why, oh why do the rich of today not sponsor art? Why do they have, mostly from what I saw, in Beverly Hills for instance, such primitive taste? I will never forget the living room of a very rich couple, he a doctor, she a real estate agent, whom I knew on Long Island. They filled it with gorgeous antiques brought from their stay in Italy and Germany, side by side with a plastic Mickey Mouse and Donald Duck collection, and cute cushions in the shape of kittens and puppies on the sofa. Kitsch to the highest degree. Anyway, thank God for the old rich who sponsored the arts in the olden times, who felt the need to surround themselves with beauty, and who understood to what degree it is beneficial for them to awe people. Anybody who enters these chambers is awed. Still. Many centuries after they were built.

Supposedly our tastes have changed quite drastically — just look at abstract paintings, at modern sculptures, at architecture by, for instance, Frank Gehry (Disney Hall, Guggenheim Museum in Bilbao, to name just two of many, many others all over the world) or Jorn Utzon (Sydney Opera House, Kingo Houses, National Assembly in Kuwait). They are very beautiful, although totally different from what we have traditionally built. The proportions, perspectives, planes and lines of the buildings are very innovative. Many of the old ideas about beauty seem now outdated, even queer or outright ugly.

Yet when we are facing buildings like the Doge's Palace, they fill us with reverence, they make us marvel at their immediately recognizable beauty, they humble us. Those of us who visited many museums know the names of such painters like Paolo Veronese, Jacopo Tintoretto and of course Titian, and usually in a museum we can see only one or two of their works. If at all. Here, especially in the Sala del Collegio (the Grand Council Hall) the whole walls and ceilings are painted by them. The size of those paintings is staggering. In the council hall one of the walls displaying Tintoretto's vision of paradise is the size of a tennis court. Tintoretto painted it when he was seventy. Not my idea of paradise. Tintoretto made it crowded to the point of discomfort. The people pictured there are for the most part idle, only two or three of them seem to have some kind of book on their lap, a few have globes in their hands, the rest are just staring at God or the saints. But the picture is magnificent, the details done with great skill. The faces, the robes painted with such artistry that one feels their softness, as if we could touch and stroke the smooth cheek here, palpate the folds of velour or silk there. Well, *de gustibus non disputandum est* (one cannot dispute tastes). But great thanks to the doges, to the population of old Venice, for employing such masters to decorate their places of importance. Today I even pardon them for all the plunder, after all it was used to benefit us all.

To write about all the marvelous things in that palace, or in St. Mark's Basilica, would be to write a guide, so I'll stop and send the readers to the Internet or travel books if they want to have more. For this diary it will be enough that I fell in love with walking through the city, taking vaporetto along canals and viewing old palaces coming out of the water, visiting Murano glass makers and the freshly restored, after a fire, opera house La Fenice. When visiting that one Donnelly couldn't stop himself from jumping on the stage and singing to an empty theater.

Not everything is so fine of course. There are way too many tourists and businesses that cater to them in the kitschy way that obviously works for the businessmen who sell those memorabilia. The amount of gift shops with carnival masks (made in China), glass trinkets from the same source, the fast food places, is overwhelming and doesn't suit the art and history of the place. Maybe it is not so bad when we think of Venice as a living city and not a curio. Yet I cannot find any redeeming reason for allowing the monster cruise ships into the lagoon. The wake waves hit the walls of the buildings, the pollution changes for worse the water of the lagoon and canals. It is not bowing to the needs of life; it is vandalism.

On the whole, the week we are spending here will stay in my memory for always, I am sure. And for that my life will be richer, more satisfying, happier. Isn't this the real reason we travel to interesting places?

## June 13, 2007

I am sitting on this comfortable little balcony off our room. The day is warm, my stomach full of seafood risotto, and there is a pleasant wine-hum in my head. The singing of the gondoliers adds to the feeling of luxury. All of a sudden the memories of so many past travels invade me. They weren't usually this luxurious. When I lived in socialist Poland we were able to travel abroad to western countries easily if sent on assignment by our newspaper, or privately if we could show that we had enough funds to support ourselves. In those days the rate of exchange of our Polish *zloty* into western hard currency was such that our earnings, which in Poland were quite sufficient for a good life, were totally ridiculous in the west. The equivalent of one hundred dollars per month was enough for our family of seven to live on for a month. And we earned usually around twice as much. But if we wanted to go to the "bad capitalistic" countries? Well, I am glad to report that in a cunning way we managed to get quite a lot out of those trips. Usually the newspaper paid for hotels and an allowance for food. They would pay for air or train travel, and if we decided to go by car the newspaper often agreed to pay for gas. We usually went by car, for the simple reason that we could go together, even with some kids, on Wojtek's assignments. In the trunk, we carried cans with chicken or ham, dried fruit, crisp breads, etc.

How did we deal with spending nights in hotels? We would choose rather cheap hotels where we all could sleep for the price of a single room in a more elegant, bigger one. To accomplish this we always carried a few bottles of vodka and a few crystal trinkets. We would ask the manager of the hotel to make the bill for a single room instead of two doubles, or a double with additional cots that we really occupied. To facilitate the transaction if the manager was a man a bottle was given as a gift, if a woman — a nice crystal vase was produced. It never failed, and our children could see some countries that were beyond our ability to visit otherwise. Every trip we would go to a restaurant once in each country. Both Wojtek and I felt that it was very important for the kids to see how other people lived and ate.

Sometimes because of inability of making advance reservations we got into rather funny situations. One year there was a big industrial fair in Munich that we needed to report on. We took Jarek and Jan with us knowing that it would be very interesting for them. They were thirteen and fifteen at that time. Well, when we reached the city it was rather late in the evening, we were very tired, and quite upset when driving from one hotel to another we heard only "no free rooms." It seemed like the whole world came to Munich. I was close to tears when finally in one little hotel the receptionist suggested a place that might take us in, gave us an address and even called there to make sure they would have a room and two cots for us. The ground floor of the building was a cabaret, there was no hotel sign to be seen, but when we climbed the stairs to the second floor we were greeted warmly, shown to a rather small room with a double bed and two promised cots. We were relieved, and, if I remember correctly, within minutes were soundly asleep. Through the night I was woken several times by the music from the cabaret, but as I heard "La Paloma," a song I liked, being repeated on and on, I was not unhappy. In the morning we went to their dining room for breakfast. That was when we observed a queer thing — all the other people having breakfast were young, lovely women in dressing gowns. They looked quite sleepy but rather joyful, talking to each other and stealing glances at our table with obvious amusement. I finally understood — we had slept in a bordello. We had no qualms explaining to our boys why rather showy pictures of girls in negligees were hanging on the walls in the corridor. We all had a good laugh and were quite happy when we learned that if we wished we could stay in our room for the other nights we were to spend in Munich.

I am mighty glad that on our trips now we usually have rooms waiting for us, and there is no need to carry our food in the trunk.

Tomorrow we are flying back to Poland. This time, after only a day in Warsaw, we will go to Pluski for three weeks. Jarek, Jagoda and their son Mieszko will be there with us. Mieszko is my youngest grandson; he will have his first birthday while we are there.

## Pluski, June 16, 2007

It's the big day, Mieszko is one year old and it so happened he took his first free steps today. The first walk of his life was between his mother and me. She held him upright when I stretched out my arms toward him and he let go of her and walked to me. Oh. What joy for a grandma! Another fine thing — Donnelly wrote a lullaby for him as our birthday gift. Jan recorded it on his video camera and as the song is in English I promised to translate it. The lullaby is very tender, and is about a little boy and Pluski. I hope Donnelly will make a recording of it in both languages after the translation is done.

## June 20, 2007

Pluski is enveloping me, as usual, in its charm. The days are filled with the sound of lapping waves, singing birds, and fine conversations. Well, when Mieszko is not crying and yelling, which happens a little too often for my taste. He is mentally ready to speak, to communicate — he obviously feels the need to be understood, yet hasn't as yet developed the ability to formulate it all into words. Thus Donnelly and I go a lot to the forest to pick the wild strawberries, which are plentiful this year, or we take a boat for some rowing on the lake. The peace and quiet of those two places is incomparable to anything I know in America. The absolute beauty of the lake is partly due to the total ban of motor boats. Sailing, rowing, wind surfing add to the quiet enjoyment of the sounds of waterfowl and birds singing. Although, no, I forgot some of our hikes in the mountains in California and Oregon. Just some, for in the distance, even quite high, one often hears the freeways, or just plain commerce of everyday life, which includes so much machinery. Maybe up on Mt. Shasta at night we do have the perfect silence. Yes, when everybody else was sleeping we have, once or twice, driven as high as one can drive, which is around 9,000 feet, and then sat, wrapped in a blanket, enjoying the quiet and the stars.

There was another place of such tranquility in my past. That was in the total, unsullied wilderness in Siberia. The memory of it came to me yesterday while I was sitting on the shore of Pluski Lake, watching two preteen boys fishing, or rather trying to catch the evasive fish. It was so different from that day when my children fished in one of the small lakes in the taiga. But let's start with why and how we were in Siberia. It happened shortly before the end of our life in Moscow in 1975. On one of his journalistic trips Wojtek met and befriended Mr. Masyagin, the first secretary of the Party for a big part of Siberia. Now, hearing that we'd be leaving the USSR, Mr. Masyagin invited us to come and spend our last vacation with him and his wife. They lived in a small village, Erbogachon, over the Lower Tunguska river. As neither I nor the children had ever been to Siberia we decided to take the Masyagins up on their invitation. The first part of the journey was to be on the Trans-Siberian train to Irkutsk. Four days with four children age nine to thirteen. Darek was left at a summer camp in Crimea as we could not afford the risk of his compulsive stealing. He was quite happy about the camp and being on the shores of Black Sea. On the train we were assigned three compartments in first class, each having two comfortable berths for sleeping and a little table which when raised showed a nice wash basin and water tap. Two of the cabins were connected by a tiny, but totally adequate bathroom with a toilet and a shower. The carriage was some kind of a remnant from before the revolution, which meant beautiful wooden finish of the walls and quite luxurious porcelain and tile equipment of the bathroom. I was rather apprehensive as to how we could survive four days of bored kids, but it proved to be very easy. Not only they had books and board games, but the biggest attraction was the carriage assistant. She took to my kids with great joy, allowed them to help her with the daily tasks like preparing tea and serving sandwiches, but the biggest, the most exciting adventure was for them to get her hat and a little flag and be able to signal the train engineer that we were ready to leave the few stations that the train stopped at. The kids took turns in this important event and you should have seen how bursting with pride and self-importance they were. The stations themselves were an adventure. They were few and far between so each stop lasted around half an hour to give the staff time to refill water tanks, check the brakes etc. At the platforms babushkas were waiting with buckets of hot soup, big containers of freshly boiled potatoes, and *pirozhkis* (fried dough filled with meat, or mushrooms, or a mixture of hard boiled egg and carmelized onion). There was a restaurant carriage on the train, we took most of our meals there, but it was way too expensive for the passengers of third class. We visited those from time to time, they slept on hard wooden benches, their luggage in cheap cardboard suitcases often tied with string. There was even an old woman with chickens in a big basket. She let them out at each station. It was fun to watch and sometimes join in helping to get them back into the basket after their outings. In each of those carriages there was at least one man with a *garmoshka* (a small accordion) and people would sing and tell long tales about their life, war experiences, and where and why they travel. It was fascinating. They liked to be the center of attention, and having *innostrantsy* (foreigners) in the audience made it even more so. They were the main customers of the station babushkas, although we also tried some of that food. It was delicious.

I had prepared for those long four days by taking some wool and five crochet hooks and taught my children how to crochet little squares of different colors. The idea was that later on I would connect the pieces into an afghan. They made quite a big bag of the squares, it must be somewhere in the attic of our family home as I never did make that afghan. I am sorry kiddies.

Well after those very enjoyable four days we reached Irkutsk. Spent two days there visiting Lake Baikal and a museum of old Siberian artifacts, and then were taken by our host to a boat to go down the Angara, then Yenisei to where the Nizhnyaya Tunguska discharges its waters into Yenisei. There we changed onto a smaller boat that took us to Erbogachon the village where our host lived. It was very different from the days on the train, we enjoyed it very much, and after many hours finally reached our destination.

People like the very idea of time travel. Books are written, films made imagining what it would have been to be transferred back a few centuries, or how it would feel to wake one day in 2100. But we read the novels, watch the films comfortably ensconced in twenty-first century's armchair or a good seat in a movie theater. Erbogachon proved to be a kind of time travel in reality.

The village had, if my memory is correct, around 800 inhabitants. The Internet now tells me it grew to 1965 by 2010. The houses were built of wood, nicely decorated but very small. No plumbing, but outhouses and *banias* (saunas) in the backyards. The whole terrain was on permafrost, which meant that even in hot summers the ground thawed not more than around five to six feet deep. It had its good and bad sides. The good ones — people didn't need refrigerators. Every backyard had a little, low shed with two smallish rooms dug under it — the shed worked as pantry, the room under it as fridge, the one even deeper as freezer. My hostess, Mrs. Masyagin, told me that in the fall the men would go into the taiga to hunt for moose. The whole village would then freeze good meat for long winter use, and the parts of the animals not good for roasting were turned into thousands of *pelmieni* (similar to ravioli), which were packaged into daily portions and stored in the natural deep freeze of the permafrost. The bad qualities of permafrost, in addition to the inability of drilling for water, were few but important. First of all, the houses had to be built on low but deeply put stilts. Even a well-insulated house warms the ground it stands on and starts to sink into the mud. Why mud? Well, with the ground being always frozen those five to six feet below surface, the water produced from thawing had nowhere to go. Fine in summer, when some of it would evaporate, but for the rest of the year the ground, if artificially warmed by human activity, became more like a bog. So the only way to deal with it was to leave a layer of air between the ground and the house.

Another problem was transportation. In summer it had to be done by water or air. In winter the frozen rivers became roads for trucks. In between — there were only helicopters and small planes. And here our time travel became funny — on one side primitive houses, the need of locals to fend for themselves as the transportation was unreliable for long periods, on the other side helicopters used to go fishing on the nearest lake.

And this brings us back to the fishing kids. One day our hosts took us, in a helicopter, to a lake they used for fishing. A mere trifle, two hundred miles. The day was beautiful, warm, sky clear, flight over the taiga showed us how sparse are the trees in those northern forests, how very unpopulated the terrain. We landed on a fine meadow over a gorgeous blue lake, Mr. Masyagin took the children into the trees, gave them knives and showed how to cut fishing rods for themselves. His wife Elena and I started to collect wood for a fire. The pilot produced a dingy in which he and Wojtek went fishing for big fish. The children were shown how to tie lengths of string and hooks to their freshly acquired rods, how to dig for worms, how to put those on the hooks, and how to cast the baited hooks into the water. Jan told me not long ago, that on the first try the thing that he caught was the seat of his pants. Everybody was so intent on what they were doing that nobody noticed, but he was mortified and had a hard time unhooking himself. Anyway, in a short time, it seemed not more than half an hour, the children had a full bucket of perch and roach, and both our hosts and I had full hands of work with cleaning the catch and then cooking *uha* (fish soup) over the fire. By that time Wojtek returned with three enormous pike, which we cleaned, salted and wrapped in nettles to be taken back to the village. Yes, finding food in a lake that was left alone for most of the time was astonishingly easy. We in the so-called civilized parts of the world do not know places of such abundance. Well, maybe in some artificial pond that is created for the paying guests.

After a great dinner of delicious soup, boiled fish and bread (not to forget vodka for the grown-ups) we lazed around the fire and talked. At the edge of the forest there was a small wooden shed. A *zimovio* (a safe haven for winter) — Masyagin told us that there are many of those built in the taiga to give a shelter to hunters in winter. There is always a plank bed, a stove made out of an old oil barrel, there is always a pile of wood cut just right for making a fire in the stove, an ax and a box of matches. "Who equips it" — I asked. "Well, anybody who uses it has to leave it this way for the next person who needs shelter." — he said. "How often does it happen that somebody would use the wood and not prepare another portion?" — was the next thing I wanted to know. "It never happened to my knowledge" — came the answer. "It could mean life or death for a hunter who would maybe find the place at the end of his tether."

Jan told me, in that conversation when we were remembering Siberia, that what Masyagin said made such an impression on him, that all his life he has tried to think of the next person. "Mama," he said, "I always clean a toilet seat at a public rest room, even if it wasn't me who soiled it." Oh, the things we learn about our children late in life!

## August 2007, Ashland

On the eleventh, Jan, Monika, Oskar, and Ola came. Oskar is to stay here with us for a year, to go to school and improve his English. The others are just visiting. Ola is a niece of Monika. She was born with spina bifida, totally paralyzed from the waist down. She is sixteen, a pretty, bright, vivacious girl, confined to a wheelchair, and needing a lot of help with daily life. She says she has always dreamt of seeing America, of travelling. She had learned English for the purpose of facilitating it. Now Jan and Monika are fulfilling her dream. Good for them. They flew to San Francisco and showed her the city. Now after staying here for a week or so and taking her into the mountains, they want to take her to Los Angeles, to Las Vegas, and maybe some more places.

First though, Jan will take care of enrolling Oskar in the middle school. There is a problem there. Children can get a school visa only for high school and college. Oskar is middle school age. We do not want to sponge off American taxpayers; we want to pay for his school. The principal can enroll him because Oskar is our, mine and Donnelly's, grandson and will live with us, but he has no way to accept money as the boy doesn't have a school visa, only a tourist one. So after many deliberations the principal came up with an idea — Jan is going to fund some electronics that the school needs very much and has no money for. Great. Now let's hope Oskar will like the school, find some friends, and generally be happy. The only problem is that he will be attending school illegally. This is just one of the difficulties for people who want to live, or just stay in this country obeying the rules of the land. The laws do not allow them to do it in a legal way. Just think, why, if Oskar is my grandson, if we want to pay his way, isn't he allowed to do it aboveboard? These are the new, after 9/11 rules. In 1999, Magda, Oskar, and his sister Łucja spent a whole year with us in Mt. Shasta. The kids went to school, Magda attended classes at a local community college, and they did it on tourist visas. No problems. As the visa was valid for six months and they wanted to finish their school year, we applied for an extension. Motivated by the fact that they were attending schools, the U.S. visa office granted the extensions — everything was done aboveboard. Now are we so afraid of terrorists that we do not allow a thirteen-year-old Polish boy to stay with his grandparents? How sad.

## September 4, 2007

Today is orientation day at Oskar's middle school, a big day for him and for me too as today I become a soccer grandma. Oskar is very good at soccer, so he was accepted to a local team in his age bracket, and now I have additional duties — driving, attending games, etc. Fine. Something new for me. On one side I will somehow have to juggle my duties, so they would fit into the day. On the other I look forward to have Oskar with us, to be able to influence another young boy. I love the idea that he will remember us for so much longer than if he saw us only on holiday visits.

## November 2007

I try to maintain our life, Donnelly's and mine, as close to normal as possible, but even after this relatively short time with Oskar I see it will not be possible. The driving to school, to soccer practice, to soccer games, takes not only a lot of time, but also quite a lot of my energy. For the last month we had not stopped seeing friends, attending theater and concerts, and I already dream of some slow time, some peace, maybe even some boredom. I will have to limit our engagements. A pity. I do enjoy visiting with our friends — for instance Diana and Ron came for a few days from Los Angeles to celebrate their twenty-fifth wedding anniversary with us. And Jacquie is my good friend, and dinners at her house are such pleasure. We both enjoy the conversations with them. Her husband Jim is an interesting, well-educated and very well-read man. Last, but definitely not least, there are Sean and Mary, Michael and Joe, and Bob and Joy, who over the years have become our closest and dearest of friends. And then there are all those I call good acquaintances, people who might not be very close, yet who we like to spend time with and who, to our joy, like to be with us. A big part of our life is also music — we had three chamber music concerts, Camerata Nordica, The Miro String Quartet and Aspen Ensemble, a beautifully sung concert of Jacque Brel's songs, and a great performance by Tingstad and Rumbel. I don't want to miss all that. How to deal with the lack of time? I am sure I'll cope eventually, but for the time being it is difficult. In the coming days I am making a Thanksgiving dinner for ten. This is a very important holiday for me. After all it is I who should be most grateful for the life I created for myself here in America. Christmas, Easter I celebrate in our Polish traditional way. Thanksgiving I try to make as American as I can. It had been started as a way to give thanks by the Pilgrims. I am that Pilgrim now. I came to start a new life. I have not only succeeded, but my new life is happier than I had ever expected it to be. Thus the need in me to celebrate with Donnelly and my friends who give me so much.

## December 2007

I had a dream that shook me up. Had to cuddle up to Donnelly to calm down. So here it is:

> First scene is in a doctor's office. Donnelly and I, both in our late eighties, are sitting there awaiting the doctor to tell us the results of my lab tests. I am undergoing serious treatments for cancer and things are not going well. I am emaciated and very weak. The doctor reads from a file, and then sends me out, back to the lab to pick something up. Donnelly stays in the office. I suspect that the doctor wants to talk to him without me present there. Then Donnelly and I are at home, he is putting me in bed. Arranging it so I can sit in it. He goes to make tea for us. Then comes back with an enormous mug, like a big, ceramic beer stein. The bed, a big one, is in the corner of the room, and pillows are put against both walls, so that when Donnelly comes back he can sit with me in that corner, with our upper bodies separated but our legs intertwined. He takes a big swig of the tea, an enormous swig, filling his mouth to the max before swallowing. He passes the mug to me and tells me to imitate him. Which I do. I pass the mug to him and he repeats the filling of his mouth and swallowing the liquid. As he does this, I feel a fantastic relaxation, a big feeling of happiness. The mug is passed again to me and I take a second big swig. I see also that Donnelly seems to wilt, now not really sitting, but more lying in the pillows. I return the mug to him feeling this same kind of wilting of my muscles, and realizing with perfect clarity what is happening. It is not a regular tea, it is poison. I look at my Donnelly and say, "Oh, my dear this is the ultimate proof of your love. Thank you." He smiles and takes the third swig of the tea. I grab the mug as he is collapsing. I drink my third mouthful. I am so happy. And then everything becomes black and I wake.

What a dream! I wonder why it came. I do not feel ill, am not afraid of death, do not think that Donnelly should go together with me if I would be dying before him. Somehow deep down in me I must feel very safe about his love and loyalty. Yet, why now the thought about death? A premonition? I truly do not understand the roots of such a dream, yet it shook me badly. It happened three days ago, but it is still in me, I somehow cannot get rid of it. Maybe now, after writing it down, I will forget it.

## JANUARY 1, 2008

Another year, I wonder how many more I'll have. I don't remember when it started that I began to think about the fact that my life is limited. When did I stop planning for years to come? Funny thing though — it does not take away the pleasure of today, the pleasure of short-time planning, the enjoyment of everyday life. I think this is the biggest change that came on me with age: previously I always lived in the present with the future always connected to it. Every day was vivid, yet the future plans were always there in my consciousness. Now I still live very much in the present, but it is the past that is alive. No more longtime plans. Isn't it plainly visible in this writing? So many things that happen now immediately bring some memories. I heard somewhere that from the days of a small past and enormous, limitless future, we come to have this big, great past and a small, limited future.

## A FEW DAYS LATER

We had a very stressful day. Oskar was coming back from his Christmas in Poland. He had to change planes in Chicago. The border officer asked him why he was in Oregon with his grandparents, found out that Oskar was attending middle school, and even though the officer was informed that Oskar's parents had paid for it, he annulled Oskar's visa and told him he had to return to Poland. Then he put the boy in a detention place with some suspected criminals. A boy of thirteen! He wasn't even allowed to use a telephone to inform us in Ashland, or his father in Poland.

The stewardess who was supposed to take care of Oskar, while he was changing planes to reach the West Coast, notified the office of the airline he had the ticket from, and they (it was the Polish airline LOT) went to bat for the boy. They somehow got permission to take him out of the detention center into their office and they called both us and Oskar's father. The next plane to Warsaw was fully booked, but they found somebody who agreed to postpone his trip in exchange for some money. They called us so that we could pay for a new ticket for Oskar, although the airline paid the extra cost to put him on the plane that same day, fed the boy, and finally escorted him to the plane back to Poland. Oskar was in a terrible state of nerves, crying and shaking, but the pilots were so nice — they took him into the cockpit so that he could observe how they flew the aircraft. Of course, a totally forbidden move, but those were Polish pilots. Try to forbid a Pole. Not an easy task.

After they managed to calm the boy they saw to it that he went to his place and fell asleep. Still he was a basket case when Jan picked him up in Warsaw. What a fucking thing to do to a child. What harm can a boy do to this country by staying with his grandparents and going to school, for which he pays? A suspected terrorist? An illegal immigrant? He had a valid ten-year visa with multiple border crossings, he had been with us several times, never overstaying the visa, always going back home on time. Which is plainly documented in his passport. And in 1999, when he stayed with his mother and sister for a whole year in our house in Mt. Shasta, the immigration office extended their tourist visas, for which we had asked, basing it on the fact that all of them went to schools and were in the process of learning good English. I am so angry. I do understand a little better, why many people dislike America. And why my British friend Moira Cunninghame doesn't want to come visit us. We are always invited to her house in Cornwall, but she refuses to come to the U.S. after being exposed to the rudeness of officials at the border. She — a retired *Financial Times* reporter, born to an aristocratic family, a person well-travelled all over the world — she says she had never been treated as badly as the one time she came here.

Okay, I have to calm down. I cannot get angry at the country because of one guy. I have to remember all the things I love about America, all the fine people I know, and know of. I am just so sorry for what Oskar had to endure, and for the fact that from a boy who was in love with the U.S.A., he became a hater. He says he never wants to come here again. Let's hope it'll pass.

## FEBRUARY 7, 2008

We had a fascinating discussion at the Elastic Mind meeting today. The theme was "Whose Promised Land?," the books I suggested for reading were: *Palestine* by Jimmy Carter, *The Case For Israel* by Alan Dershowitz, and *Whose Promised Land?* by Colin Chapman. We had at least eighteen people in attendance. Dr. Robbins brought an interesting map of the wall that Israel is erecting to separate itself from Palestinians. Officially it is to prevent terrorist attacks, but the map shows a different picture — it shows that the wall takes into Israeli territory all the water sources, leaving the Palestinian villages, their orchards, without access to water. Dr. Robbins, a dentist, a Jew, goes to Israel and Palestine every year to work on the teeth of the poor of that region. He should, by now, know well what he is speaking about. There were several people who spoke very interestingly about the history of those lands. Some were definitely pro-Palestinians, some very much pro Israel, a few tried to be impartial. The discussion went over the allotted time as so many wanted to have their say. It was fascinating. This is why I do it. This is when I know how much people need a place where they can speak and hear others' opinions about serious matters. We have plenty of book clubs, but nothing for serious minded readers. Sometimes it is hard for me to read so much in preparation, sometimes I would love to just relax with a good mystery, but on a day like today I feel so happy, so appreciated. Although one person, a woman, went to the director of the library to complain about the anti-Semitic meetings. The director, Amy Blossom, asked some other participants, who, to a person, said that it was very well balanced. Well, there always has to be somebody with a prejudice. It will not stop me from taking on the serious problems of our times.

## MARCH 10, 2008

What a terrible thing happened! Colin Parker committed suicide. He was twenty. Such a fine young man, brilliantly intelligent, very sensitive. Too sensitive, obviously, to cope with the world, with life. Jacquie is devastated. I am going to Mt. Shasta to stay with her. I am afraid to leave her alone now. I can't even imagine what a mother losing a son to suicide has to go through. The horror of it defies my ability to perceive. Not only you lose a child, but your whole approach to raising him, to be in close relationship with him is put to doubt. What didn't you see? Where did you go wrong? Why he did not, obviously could not, reach out to you in the hour of despair? There is something about people who are very intelligent and sensitive that often leads them to self destruct. Be it by drink, drugs or as here — the ultimate — the suicide. The fact that they see more clearly what others have a hard time understanding? Does that lead to depression, to the feelings of alienation, of not fitting in, of always being alone, misunderstood?

He was brilliant. How do I know? He and his brother Nathan were homeschooled. Their parents were well educated and realized the necessity of giving their boys the best they could, or at least better than local, small-town school could give. The mother, a nurse practitioner, taught them science, a math teacher from the local community college gave them math lessons, and I was hired to teach them history, geography,

French and Russian. Donnelly taught the boys English. Both boys were exceptionally bright, but Nathan was older and calmer, whereas Colin was nervous, always prone to go his own way. Teaching them was pure joy. Such curiosity, such ability, such willingness to absorb what we could give them. A rare pleasure for a teacher.

Then came the private high school. One of the best, in Southern California. A good fit for Nathan, calm, collected, both feet on the ground, intelligent, knowing what he wants. A bad fit for Colin. He never could find a place for himself. Never could find a milieu where he would feel at home. Later, at the university, he studied philosophy, was praised by professors, yet changed schools, obviously was still looking for some place for himself. Then this. Why? We will never know. Although it does make me think about difficulties of those very bright. Are so many of them doomed to be always the minority? Always shunned by their peers? Never finding that person who could help them to access the hidden parts of themselves, to feel comfortable with being different from most? Somebody who would value their originality, uniqueness to the point of convincing them that they are valuable, lovable? In other words, a true friend.

In my youth, I very often felt a stranger. It could have come from early childhood, first a pampered rich kid, then, during the war, not being allowed to play with other children — because of the danger of saying something that could cost lives. After the war a foreigner in Egypt, part of the European upper class, so different than everything around me. Even after coming back to Poland I felt set apart. My colleagues in school were deprived of good clothes, of records with western music, of having seen the world. I had all this. I was envied. I felt comfortable only among grown-ups. I loved dancing, being among young people sometimes, yet needing to be alone often. And when I say needing I mean it — it was a painful need, a feeling I'll go mad if I am not left alone. I was also a bright girl and my father saw to it that I read serious books from early on. In my preteen years he would tell me not to touch a book by his bedside. "It's only for grown-ups," he would say. Enough for a precocious child of ten or so. That's how I read Michel de Montaigne, Voltaire, Balzac. Later he didn't need to use such ruses, I chose good books for myself. Luckily for me when I studied at the Politechnic and later at the University of Warsaw, I found many who were as bright, or brighter than me. I was also quite pretty and boys and men made me feel very special. I did find that place of belonging. But I do remember the days of alienation too well not to feel so very sorry for Colin. Such a terrible waste. So much pain he must have gone through. Poor boy. And now the pain of Jacquie, Jim, and Nathan. My God, what a living nightmare for them.

## April 1, 2008

I have spent several days in Mt. Shasta with Jacquie. Luckily she has friends, and even if not friends, people in a small town feel a need to help, to be with the stricken, so she didn't have time to fall apart, to do anything rash. Then we had a service for the boy. Crowds came. Many people, me included, spoke, Donnelly sang a song of his, a song that Colin had written lyrics to. And then we, the outsiders, all went to our own lives, to thinking about what's for dinner, to going to theater, seeing friends — just life as usual, as if nothing happened. Colin was, Colin isn't.

It is going to be the same when I die. It is the same for any of us. They say that a person dies three times: first when the body stops being alive, second when we are interred, and the final death comes with our name being mentioned for the last time. Is it the real reason why we try to leave something? Be it a book, a painting, an inheritance, or just a grandchild who might talk about us to his/her grandchild? In this idea Socrates is still not totally dead.

## May 10, 2008

A big day for me — a recording of an interview with me for the local television. The interviewer, Amy Blossom, director of our local library, asked about my writings and about Elastic Mind. A big chance for me to read some of my poems and a short story. It was so gratifying to see tears in the eyes of the camera woman when I was reading "The Summer Night." I had my TV moments in my previous career, in Poland, but here I never thought of becoming known through this medium. Well, let's not get a too big head — it is only local TV.

## June 3, 2008

Another dream:

*A grey room with two grey figures, not in focus — they and the background quite blurry. The only piece well focused and in vibrant color is an armchair and a girl, or rather a young woman sitting in it and in front of her there is a big TV screen. The girl is very lovely, dressed in colorful clothes, plenty of them — a frilly blouse, sweater, scarves and shawls; she has blond curly hair. Has a remote in her hand. The two grey figures, it is unclear whether they are male or female, are tending to her, wrapping her up, tucking her in, putting a stool under her feet, making her as comfortable as possible. The girl is smiling, look how free I am she tells me. I can choose from over a hundred channels. I ask her — can you choose to get out of the chair, the room? Why would I want to, she says, I have over a hundred channels....*

End of dream. What a portrait of America — as I see it. Sad, depressing. The more so, because I realize it is not only America — the whole world civilization is heading this way. Hi, Mr. Aldous Huxley — in the thirties you wrote *Brave New World*. How prophetic. Are we heading into your kind of world, a world divided into three main human masses?

One grouping, the smallest one, would be all the intelligent, well educated, creative people. The only limiting trait needed in order to belong to this group would be a selfishness allowing for disregarding the plight of others. The second group would be the workers, professionally trained, totally manipulable, not able to think critically, not able to see clearly any bigger picture. The third, those spurious, lazy, addicted to "the hundred channels" or games, or simply developmentally challenged, mentally ill. They would be allowed the comfort of the girl from my dream, until a better solution could be found. Better solution? Extermination? Castration? What else will they think of doing to the unproductive? Is that really the future? Have the writers like Aldous Huxley or George Orwell been prescient? Has Hitler shown us the way? I shiver at the very thought.

## END OF JUNE, 2008

Jan and Monika are in L.A. on business. They invited us to come stay with them for a week. During that week we'll celebrate Jan's name day (*imieniny*). I baked a big tray of Jan's beloved *babeczki*, pastry shells filled with dark chocolate cream, packed them in ice and we drove down. There were enormous forest fires in northern California, to the point that we had to have all the windows of the car closed without air conditioning, as the filters were not enough for the amount of smoke in the air. Very unpleasant trip. Once in the L.A. area, we were fine. Enjoyed the week, as usual with those two. In the hours when they were busy we went for long walks on the beach. One day as I was walking, I heard "you are a bitch and a cunt" coming from an ugly man biking past us in the company of a beautiful young woman.

Once back at the hotel I wrote a little picture of the scene.

## THE BIKE RIDE

*She was sitting on the seat of her bike, pedaling evenly, and a tiny little smile played on her lips. Ben was riding half a pace in front of her, talking, talking, once again furious.*

*— You are a cheat and a liar.*

*She jiggled the lever of the speeds of her bike. Ten or sixteen of them. She had lost count — but knew there were just as many as were needed to make the machine damn expensive. Smooth, dark wheels were going round and round, the silvery spikes sending flashes.*

*The sun today was lovely and the little breeze felt so refreshing. Ben was getting too disgustedly fat. She watched the flab above the elastic of his shorts. It was reddish and damp. She moved her eyes slightly to the left until she caught the sight of the ocean. Was it really blue? Was green prevailing today? She couldn't tell from that distance.*

*— You demean yourself by all those lies. You constantly pretend you are somebody much better than you really are...*

*Ha! This was quite amusing. Would it be better if she showed the whole world who she was? And what if in reality she was a cheat and a liar? His flab was once again in her line of vision. And the thinning hair on his sweat covered, reddish brown skull. Funny, the way hair moved in aging men, from the top of their heads to the interior of their ears and nostrils. She nearly giggled. Stopped herself just in time.*

*It wouldn't do.*

*— And the amount of money you spend...*

*Aha, here we go again. As if it could possibly matter. With the amount he had, he was just funny. Tried to be in control. That's what it was.*

*The breeze was a little stronger now. It was sweeping the abundance of her long, blonde hair from her face. She knew she looked great. Didn't need all the admiring looks from men passing*

her on the bike path, to tell her this. The little smile became more pronounced.
— *You are really just a bitch, you know…*
Ben was faster today. Did that mean that the rest of the trip was going to be quiet, or was he going to invent some new line of attack to keep them occupied? His thin, hairy legs beneath the jelly-like torso were positively nauseating. She was conscious, though, that the sun was doing great things to her skin. Her long slender arms and thin pampered fingers were getting browner and browner by the minute. She was glad she had put her golden bangles on, they looked so good against the tanned wrist.
— *Just throwing money out the window. You must have at least two hundred pairs of shoes, what the hell do you need more shoes for? A bitch and a cunt. That's what you are."*
It was still a good half a mile to where their car was parked. Her little smile got stiffer. She narrowed her eyes turning her face towards the sun. She was earning her keep.

## A BEAUTY OF A DAY IN JULY 2008

Please God, please God if there is an afterlife let me remember this moment. Not the ecstasy of first love, not the beautiful madness of sex, but this simple moment in time with my man — the blueness of sky speaking of purity of air, the songs, the chirps, the whistles of birds that say everything is fine. Even the distant sound of the freeway telling us of normal, everyday human life. And this slow, relaxed conversation which makes life so much richer. Oh, yes, I do want to be able to always recall this moment.

## AUGUST 2008

"One must dig deeply into opposing points of view in order to know whether one's own position remains defensible. Iron sharpens iron." Words of Francis S. Collins, author of *The Language of God*. It caught my attention as it is something I have always been acutely aware of. I love to be with people who are better educated or more intelligent than me. Or preferably both. Last night we were at dinner at a woman friend's and we met her new boyfriend. A fine man, a great conversationalist. I enjoyed myself very much. We talked about politics, history, literature, and joy of life. Our views were sometimes quite different, which made the conversation more interesting. As usual in such situations I rethink my positions, often finding them valid, sometimes though I have to accept that I am wrong, or just that my thinking has to be reevaluated, enriched.

I was surprised when Donnelly told me, upon coming home, that he was jealous. Yes, I had been more than usually animated. And the new boyfriend, Mike, obviously enjoyed talking to me. But jealous? I then realized that in all the years of my life with Wojtek I never saw, or heard, that he was jealous. And he would have had many occasions to be so. I loved flirting, I was very popular with men and liked leading them on. I derived great pleasure in getting them all excited, and then treating them to a cool eye. Even when I was still in my teens I discovered how men reacted to long hair. I joked that long hair in a woman woke the cavemen in them. You know, grab her by those tresses and drag her to the cave.

In the time of my youth, a young, to say nothing of older, woman with long hair did not show it unbound. It had to be braided, or put up in a bun. So if I had a date who would pick me up at my home, I was never ready on time. The boy had to wait while I dried my hair with a blower. My hair was dark, nearly black and very shiny. The effect was instantaneous. Another trick of mine if we were going to a dance, even when already married, was to put my hair up in a bun so sloppily that the first quick dance would make the coiffure disintegrate and I would dance with all that hair flying around me. That was even pre-Brigitte Bardot. Seeing the power of my body on males gave me a lot of satisfaction, especially when after arousing their hopes I would calmly go home with my husband. I once asked him whether he was jealous. No, he told me. He was happy when all that was happening, when he saw the others being captivated and knowing for sure, all the time that I am his, a faithful wife.

This flirting to feel my own power was something I most probably did (beside other reasons), because of what my mother told me. At around sixteen I very much wanted to cut my hair. When I told mother about it, she said: "Don't cut your hair, it is the only beautiful thing you have." I hated her for what she obviously thought of my looks. I had to prove her wrong. Now when I look at my photos from those days I see that although not a beauty in a classical sense, I definitely was quite attractive.

## NOVEMBER 2008

At a dinner at Mike's we met a couple of his new neighbors, Tom and Cynthia Stauffer. He, a retired music professor from San Diego University, a cellist; she, a pianist. Fascinating conversationalists, well read, widely travelled, thoughtful. I think we will enjoy them very much.

## DECEMBER 2008

I was just looking through my notes, if I wanted to put here all that caught my interest, all that made me happy, or frustrated, the book would be enormous. I do not want it to become so. Let those who read it feel thirsty for more, not satiated to the point of boredom. So I'll still omit big portions of my life. After all, my goal is not to write a detailed history of me. In addition to the history of my family, my intention is to show how relative our memory is and how rich a life experience can be if we only allow it to be so. If we only open ourselves to the outside as well as to what is happening inside us. If, to use a metaphor, we do not resort to pain pills every time something hurts.

But certain parts of life are too important to be omitted. One of them is how come I am in the U.S.A., and married for the second time.

Well, it all started in 1986. Towards the end of the year I began to feel weak, to lose weight, which at that time I could hardly afford. Doctors, tests, and the diagnosis that we all fear — cancer. Cancer of the uterus. In March of 1987 I underwent a total hysterectomy. The doctor was optimistic that he had it all out. I opted for no radiation or chemo. If it really all went out, I didn't want to go through the shocks to my body of those preventive measures. If some of the cancer was left somewhere to spread, I didn't want to live through more surgeries, etc. I felt I had had a good life and wanted to end it on my terms, not my body's.

In April of 1987 my father died. I felt very unhappy, very depressed. Wojtek took great care of me. I already wrote how good he was in caring for me. But it was always in his own way. He knew when I should go to sleep, and when to wake. He knew, and acted accordingly, what I should read, eat, drink, think… There was no more fight in me. That is when the realization came what my future was going to be like. Vegetation. Eating, defecating, sleeping, doing chores that others expected of me. The body was recuperating nicely, the "I" who inhabited it was dying. I knew I didn't have the strength to withstand Wojtek's goodness. I seemed to be lacking even the ability to think, to want, to feel on my own. With the last crumbs of my old self I drove to Pluski. Alone. With a stash of sleeping pills. I went for a long walk. I sat at the pier and watched a family of swans. I drank some cognac. And I thought of my children. How much I loved them. And I understood that I could not do it to them. It didn't matter what I felt, the only thing that mattered was my kids. I packed my belongings, pills included, and went back home. I knew I could not stay with Wojtek. He was too overpowering for me. I decided to go somewhere, start a life on my own. See whether I could, whether I had the gumption of dealing with my life independently, whether I could lead what was left of life for me without fighting. To finally have some peace, and to do things that were the result of my own decisions. I had never in my life lived on my own. Only if I tried, would I see whether I was capable of taking care of myself. And if the cancer returned, the stash of pills would still be with me. Then the children would understand. I would be able to explain.

Wojtek was surprisingly understanding. It helped that for several years I had been telling him how unhappy I was. This time I told him I would come back only if I found myself incapable of taking my life in my own hands, like a dog returning with its tail between hind legs. I got a visa to the U.S. relatively easily after sending to the consulate my previous newspaper writings about American education. I contacted Vitold Tchaikovsky who lived in Los Angeles and was a brother of a good friend of mine, Wanda, asking whether I could crash with him and his wife for a few days. Bought an airplane ticket to New York, and a Greyhound Bus ticket for tourists, Ameripass, which gave seven days and nights, unlimited mileage on their buses. It gave me the ability to interrupt my trek any time and any place I felt I wanted to, and take another bus to wherever was my pleasure. I flew to New York, spent a night there, and the next day after sending my luggage to L.A., I went on that big unknown adventure.

I got off the bus for a few hours in Columbus where I had a fine walk; in Saint Louis where I visited the Arc and for the first time saw poverty and slums in the U.S.A. It was in St. Louis that Greyhound won my undying respect. When buying the ticket, I was told that they will always take me on a bus of my choice after an interruption of the trip, I thought — ha, ha, promises, promises, I wonder how it is going to be if the so called bus of my choice would be full. Well it so happened that after seeing all I wanted to see in St. Louis when I came to the depot, the bus to New Orleans, which was my next intended stop, was full. I, and another man in the same situation, were the only people left out. The Greyhound personnel apologized that we'd have to wait another hour as they needed to find a driver. In even less than an hour we were invited into an empty bus which took us on. At the next stop, we were joined by some of the passengers from the previous vehicle which allowed both buses to go on roughly half full. That way I arrived in New Orleans not tired at all and enjoyed my stay there very much. I spent a day and a half in the city, stayed at a hotel, had a good shower, changed clothes, and enjoyed the music and general atmosphere of the streets. New Orleans gave me my first taste of how varied, how very different parts of this country can be. I fell in love with the free, joyful behavior of the people in the streets. What I didn't like was the steamy air. Not enough moisture to open an umbrella, too much of it to be able to stay dry.

Then came another long trek through Texas and New Mexico to Phoenix, Arizona. What a way to get to know a country! Hours of travel make people talkative. Where else would I have a chance of listening to a life story of a black, retired truck driver? As usual with old people, he was very happy to talk, reminisce about his childhood, young years, marriage, retirement.... Explaining to me all the details of being black in America, of the famous sixties, of the enormous changes they brought into his life. Of course I knew from the newspapers about the presidency of Lyndon Johnson, about the civil rights movement, about desegregation. Yet, in his telling of it all, there came colors, feelings, human perception. So different than a newspaper article.

I had also several hours of listening to a nurse, who told me about the healthcare problems of the poor, about hospitals, about being a single mother of three. There, in that bus, I met also four young men travelling to Las Vegas from Puerto Rico to spend the money they earned over the summer. They were nice enough to give me one of their travel pillows. I suppose I reminded them of their grandmas. That is also when I had my first marriage proposal in America. A guy in his sixties, a Texan from Corpus Christi, a veteran travelling by bus to a health checkup in a veteran's hospital, after telling me about his life and widowhood, was so enchanted with my ability to listen that he very much wanted to marry me. Tried to entice me with photos of his home and boat. Was quite unhappy when I thanked him and said I would not marry him, as I was married already.

In Phoenix, I again changed buses and went north to Flagstaff to fulfill my great wish to see the Grand Canyon. I was very short of cash and quite happy when the motel man in Flagstaff told me they had neither electricity nor heat (it was snowing outside), so if I agreed to stay nevertheless, he'd just charge me five dollars for the night. Of course I stayed, had a great night's sleep under a pile of covers the owner gave me from other rooms. After a bracing cold water shower in the morning I went by bus to the canyon. I spent the whole day there, duly awed.

Finally took the last portion of the trip to L.A., where I was met by my friend's brother. It was Saturday evening. Feeling very smug about how much I knew now about the country, I bought the *Los Angeles Times* the next morning, looked at the "Help Wanted" ads, and by evening had a job as a housekeeper. Yes, I know, illegally so, as I was not supposed to work on my tourist visa.

I don't know why I took this one. I had interviewed for three, one of which was with a couple who needed a nanny for their two lovable children, six and eight. It included a trip with the family to Hawaii, staying at their vacation house there for the whole of winter, taking care of the children in the garden or on the beach. Paradise. Yet I took a job with Mr. and Mrs. Franklin as a housekeeper cum nanny for two boys, six and nine. Cleaning, cooking, driving the kids to school and back, doing shopping — a lot of work, no beach in Hawaii. The family of Franklins proved to be very decent and lovely. Patty, the wife and mother, was in her thirties, a beautiful woman. Howard, the husband and father, was a lawyer and writer. I knew I had found a good family to live with and work for when just a few days into my life with them I had a fine conversation with Howard about reading poetry, in which I mentioned that John Donne was my beloved poet, and started reciting the song he wrote: "Go and catch a falling star, / get with child a mandrake root, / tell me, where all past years are, / or who cleft the Devil's foot, / teach me to hear mermaids singing, / or to keep off envy's stinging, / and find what wind serves to advance an honest mind…" and then I couldn't remember the further lines. Next Sunday, which was my first day off, when I came back to the house, I found a new copy of John Donne's poetry on the pillow of my bed.

Yet, it wasn't a bed of roses. In a couple months Patty was diagnosed with cancer. In six months she was dead. The six months were pure hell for the whole family, me included. I came to care for her very much. Seeing her in constant deterioration and pain was extremely hard. Then there were the boys — Matthew and Nicky. I tried to make their life as normal as possible. I allowed Matt to teach me baseball, I read lots of little books to both boys to take their attention away from what was happening around them. I served as a sounding board to Howard, who desperately needed somebody to talk to. In later months, when Patty couldn't sleep because of pain, I would sit at the foot of her bed and do acupressure on her feet, which ameliorated the pain so that she would fall asleep. The minute I stopped she would wake with a moan, so I sat for as long as I could. Wasn't easy. Howard maintained that fate had sent me to them. He was highly superstitious; I believe he still is. Patty didn't want morphine, she still believed in a possibility of a cure and, having an addicted to drugs sister, was afraid of becoming addicted herself. She only spent the last two weeks in a hospital and on morphine. She died in the middle of May.

In the meantime, Howard hired an attorney to get me a work permit and, the so-called Green Card. It necessitated an ad in a few newspapers, looking for a housekeeper that would be a citizen, or at least a permanent resident, to explain the plea for making me a legal worker. Well, the attorney wrote the ad — it said that Howard is looking for a domestic, speaking at least four languages, with a European university degree, and citing a pitiful wage. Of course nobody answered the ad, so the attorney could truthfully state that I am the only possibility for Howard to get the kind of help he needed. It worked. I became legal.

My role in the household changed. I had all the responsibilities of a housewife, without the benefits of one. There was a fine friendship between Howard and me, yet, luckily for both of us, we did not develop a man-woman attraction, so the friendship could stay pure and uncomplicated. I was often taken, with the boys, to a bowling alley, to a restaurant, to a movie. We ate together, and most evenings, after I put the kids to bed, Howard and I sat and talked or read our new poems to each other. It was then that he changed the dining room into a study for me and gave me an electric typewriter for my writings. He was such a generous, understanding man.

What I saw though was a fear in his family that he might fall for that housekeeper. Can you imagine? Of course she would want to entrap him into marriage. He a millionaire — and she, a poor housekeeper from Poland. It was quite funny for me to observe the little humiliations they tried to inflict on me. I looked at their behavior with amusement. I felt beyond their reach. That was when I found that nobody could humiliate me without my consent. I felt so impervious to their attitudes, I just pitied them for being so primitive and insecure. The only person in that family with education, sensitivity and tact was my employer, the rest resembled the caricatures of the primitive, filthy rich. Well, maybe not his father who was very polite towards me, and Patty's mother Arlene, who treated me always with respect and showered me with gifts.

That was the time when I felt very secure in knowing I could take care of myself, I could envisage a new life without a man at my side. My plan was to save enough money to redo the Pluski house, to make it a year-round proper house, to go back to Poland, move there into the village I loved so much, and live alone doing translations for money. In winter I would visit Wojtek for some theater and concerts, in summer he, my kids, and friends would come to enjoy the lake. Everything was planned nicely. That was when I met Donnelly.

## April 2009

We had such a fascinating line of Elastic Mind meetings: Hitler, Stalin and Hoess — the Juxtaposition of Good and Evil; Slavery; Informed Electorate and Manipulation; Is Compulsory Schooling Harming Us; Crowds and Power. The people who come to the meetings are obviously starved for a possibility of intellectual conversation, of hearing what others think and of being heard. I feel so needed on such occasions. The difficult parts are sometimes how to, tactfully, shut up somebody whose need to be heard is limited to their personal life, to their grandchildren's lives... We also had a woman come faithfully to every meeting who was fascinated with *War and Peace*. A fine book for sure, but she talked about it no matter what the meeting's theme was. Tiring.

At the meeting about good and evil we had a good discussion about how it was possible that Stalin, who was born in Georgia, was a poet (pretty good at that) in his youth, studied theology, wanted to become a monk, and only after being disillusioned about the church's honesty became a revolutionary. How Hoess, the commandant of Auschwitz, loved animals, tended roses, and played Chopin on his piano to relax after his hours at the concentration camp sending thousands of people to their death. What does it say about humans? How can we combine poetry and murder? How can we trust our friends, our families, ourselves that given certain conditions of life we would not become cruel? And yet luckily we do trust. But through the whole history of our civilization we tried, and still try, not to allow the development of such dangerous conditions that would awake the beasts lurking in us. We just relegate them to the culture of war, and even then try to curb the cruelty if it becomes excessive. And by excessive we usually mean not getting the wanted results. We do not call it cruelty, if it achieves what we planned for. We speak of necessary tragedies of war. The innocent dead become collateral damage.

Difficult discussion, everybody aware of the evil that might be lurking inside anyone of us. It is easier to see the world in black and white. It is much easier to portray the villains as monsters, devoid of any feelings except anger or hatred. The fairytale ogres and bad witches. But that is not reality. Discussions like this are immensely important, just so we never forget how much evil lurks in seemingly normal, decent people.

In a few days we'll fly to Switzerland. What a change of mood!

## May, 2009, Zurich

We have arrived here on a beautiful, sunny day. Łucja, Fritz, and Olaf greeted us at the airport. The kids have given us their bedroom and moved to the sofa bed in their living room, explaining that because Fritzie leaves for work early in the morning this was going to be more comfortable for him. Ha! Believing it or not, we received it gratefully. The bedroom is roomy, the king size bed very comfortable, the window looks out at the common green. Peaceful, flowery, what not to like.

Immediately after settling in we were taken for a walk to the lake. What a fine place they live in. A big city, yet they bike to work and in the evening they can relax and swim in the lake, with its surprisingly clear water.

Fritz is great at planning, Łucja has fine ideas and organizational skills, so we bought totally into their propositions as to how to spend the two weeks we'll be with them. After five days we are to go on the Glacier Express — a train with viewing windows that are not only on the sides of carriages, but also in the roof — to Zermatt, a little town closest to the Matterhorn. Of course we want to see Matterhorn, which we know from so many stories and photographs. Then west to Geneva, Lausanne, and finally east to Ascona at the other end of Switzerland, before we come back to Zurich.

## A WEEK LATER, GENEVA

Matterhorn was impressive, and the three days we spent in Zermatt would have been a pleasure, but Donnelly woke the first day with a high fever and feeling bad. He never complains, so if he says he feels bad, that means we have to treat it seriously. When we were leaving America, there was this scare of swine flu. People died of it. Fritz called the local doctor who on learning that the patient is an American, immediately came to our rented apartment, took a lot of time in checking Donnelly's symptoms, gave prescriptions for several medicines and told us that if the patient doesn't improve in the next twenty-four hours to please take him to the hospital. He did improve. The medications, as well as chicken soup Łucja and I cooked, helped. We just delayed our departure for Geneva for another day. Which was very lucky, as there was so much to see in Zermatt.

In Geneva there is the beauty of the town itself, plus my memories of my staying here with my father in the winter of 1947. Also, so many international organizations are located in this city and what goes with it: there is a very racially mixed population. The city is mainly French speaking, with great French food and, what I was especially waiting for, French bookstores. I bought several books. My French has become quite rusty, so I am looking forward to going back to reading in that language. It's a pity it is so difficult to buy books in languages other than English in America.

Here in Geneva another surprise awaited us. Łucja and Fritz have a friend, Hubert Niewiadomski, a Polish physicist who works at CERN (European Center for Nuclear Research). He was waiting for us to show us the inner workings of the Large Hadron Collider. Of course it's an exaggeration in saying, "the inner workings," what we could see was part of the twenty-seven mile-long circular tunnel under the city, in which the beam pipe is set. We have seen the control rooms. But most important was that our host explained to us, in general terms, how the whole collider is supposed to work.

It was so simple when I was studying physics in my high school in the 1950s. Matter was built of atoms. They in turn consisted of protons formed into nuclei, around which electrons were circling. There was Isaac Newton and his theory of gravity, Galileo and his telescope, Keppler and his laws of planetary motion, Faraday and electromagnetism…. The explanations were relatively simple, I felt I understood how the world around me was built, how it worked.

This brings to mind another funny quirk — so many nations teach their children a twisted history of scientific discoveries and inventions. When in Moscow I heard that most of such were done by Russians. In the U.S., to my amazement I heard that the discovery of electricity is attributed to Benjamin Franklin. Well, in my young days I learned about the amber rubbing in ancient Greece sometime between 600–550 BCE (the word "electric" comes from Greek "amber" and was coined in England in seventeenth century), then Franklin connected lightning to the idea of electricity, but it was a pair of Italian physicists, Galvani and Volta, who created a battery, a means of producing electric current, by submerging zinc and copper in salt water. Then at the beginning of the nineteenth century Michael Faraday, a British scientist induced electrical current by moving a copper wire in a magnetic field, which gave the beginning of generators and electric motors. Finally a British physicist Joseph Swan invented an electric bulb in 1860, which later gave Thomas Edison the idea of transmitting electricity via cables to homes to provide light. He used the direct current, available at the time, which meant a lot of power was lost through the resistance of cables. His coworker, Nicola Tesla, a Czech, developed a new kind of generator producing a current that switched directions many times a second — the so-called, alternating current (AC). Despite fierce opposition from Edison, AC was eventually adopted and is used to this day. See what I mean about nationalism in teaching history in general, and in this respect the history of science? But let's go back to CERN.

So here that whole fine feeling of mine that I understand went out of the window. First of all, the language used has changed drastically. Names like electronvolt, muon, nucleon, graviton and several others, were totally new to me. I already had been in some doubt whether I properly understand quarks, the quantum theory, and the time warp. Now I became sure I know next to nothing. Not the pleasantest feeling, yet it fills me with such awe for the development of science, that on the whole I am happy with it and am looking forward to learning more.

And talking about learning — I have to pay more attention to my languages. Although I still can read French novels, newspapers, poetry, I have a great difficulty in speaking. There is this thing about passive knowledge and active use of it. Even if one's passive use of a language, or for that matter any other acquired skill, is kept alive, the ability to use it actively does not necessarily follow. When we came here to the French speaking part of Switzerland, I had a hard time in speaking, finding words and sentence constructions fast enough to be able to communicate easily. After spending three mortifying days of "hmm…er…," I did start to be able to speak, slowly yes, but speak nevertheless. Now in our fifth day here I am more or less capable of using my French. Hallelujah! Maybe in Ashland I could find somebody who, for money of course, would converse with me in French. We'll see.

## Ascona, a few days later

Łucja and Fritz's car is too small to carry four grownups and their luggage, so we travel separately, most of the time Łucja, Donnelly, and I in trains, and Fritzie in the car with all our luggage. There is quite a lot of it, as we had to be prepared for hiking at high elevations, which means cold air and warm sport clothes; then in the cities with their good restaurants, museums etc., we need more elegant attire; and finally the south where we were told to expect very warm weather, so Łucja and I wanted to have a summer dress or two, and our men needed shorts and tees. It has worked very well. The three train travelers enjoy public transportation, especially when unencumbered by suitcases, and Fritz loves driving. Then upon reaching our destination we spend all the time together.

After leaving Geneva we stopped for two days in Gruyere, a lovely little town famous for their cheese. What I like most in travelling around Europe is the combination of beauty and history. Gruyere is a small, old town, the most important parts of which are cheese factories. Of course they get their money from making and selling cheese, but found a good way of augmenting their income by allowing tourists to watch the preparation of the main product. There are lots of people who want to see how it is still made in small artisanal places, in traditional ways. So we looked, learned, tasted, enjoyed.

Then we saw the castle — quite a beauty, and ended the day at a restaurant eating raclette cheese. A chunk of raclette is heated on one side in a little grill on each table, and then the diners scrape the melted part off onto their plates. So much more convenient than melting it in front of a fire, like it was done in the olden times. The cheese was and is accompanied by freshly boiled small potatoes, gherkins, pickled onions, and dried meats. It was delicious, we were hungry, the company was fun to be with, the result a gross overindulgence. No one could sleep in the night. The heaviness in our stomachs kept us tossing and turning.

We're now in Ascona, which is on the shores of Lago Maggiore, a beautiful, long lake. We'll try to stick to fish and vegetables. And a lot of walking. The town is such a relaxing place to be in — a vacation-time type of town, with lots of fine architecture, plenty of trees, an abundance of bougainvillea and roses. The fences, gates are made of very artistic wrought iron, which combined with the multicolored roses, hydrangeas, phloxes, jasmine, and vines in the gardens behind them create an unforgettable picture.

When we travel to different continents, or even on the same one but to different countries about which we know that they have widely different languages and history — say like U.S.A. and Mexico, or Sweden and Italy — we are prepared for, so called, culture shock. But Switzerland? A country of a little over eight million inhabitants (Oregon has four million), with an area of less than 16,000 square miles (Oregon has 98,000 square miles). And yet that little country has four, yes that is not a mistake, four official languages — German, French, Italian, and Romansh. The east is mainly German speaking, the west French, the southeast Italian, with the southeastern villages speaking Romansh. The most interesting for me was to see how each of those different language speaking regions has a different feel.

In Zurich I felt much more like in the well organized, always punctual, easy to live in Germany. In Geneva the feel of the street was very much French, artistic, international, more noisy, crowded. Ascona? As I described above, much more like Italy, although it could have been the result of it being such a vacation place. Yet in all those towns, cities, and villages, there was a unifying trait — orderliness, peacefulness, friendliness, punctuality. Everything was working the way it was supposed to. Everything seemed to be easy.

Oh well, if I only had the money I would love to spend my later years in Switzerland. No wonder so many writers and artists choose Switzerland as their home for retirement years.

Tomorrow we go back to Zurich, then Poland for three weeks, and then back home.

## July, 2009, Pluski

So once again we are in Pluski. Jarek and Mieszko and Martynka are with us. Jagoda will join us in a week. The children are very well behaved when with their father, they start acting up when Jagoda joins the family. I suppose that it is quite common with working mothers who feel, maybe subconsciously, guilty that they spend so little time with their offspring and when they are present start to make up for it by spoiling the kids. Luckily Jagoda is such a good person, the children do not seem to be too unruly with her. Just showing some capriciousness.

While here with Jarek I spend a lot of time on talking to him, on listening and on reminiscing about his childhood. Which he remembers very differently from what I remember.

I like one of my memories from the time he was very young — maybe two — anyway before he was comfortable with speaking. I asked him how much he loved me. He stood for a minute or so in deep thought and then reached his arms in front of him, joined his hands together, then separating them reached behind him and also joined them. He knew, even at that age, the sense of a closed circle being the emblem of a whole. I was astounded and so proud.

His thoughtfulness, his sense of responsibility was very much above of what we expect from a child. We could always leave him in charge of his siblings. It was much later, when he was already a grown-up, that he told me how he resented being treated as reliable, as sensible and serious. He said: "Mama, I always felt that I shouldn't make any mistakes, and that was a heavy load for a child."

We have so much to talk about. He, just like Łucja and I, loves to read and always has opinions on what he read. He also has a great sense of humor and gives me links to Russian comedians whose jokes we appreciate very much. It is interesting how we are incapable of finding anything funny in the humor of cultures that we are unfamiliar with. In my first years in America I could not, for the life of me, find anything funny in Garrison Keillor's jokes and stories. Yet after spending something like ten years here I started to laugh out loud whenever I heard him. Although I have never lived in England I find their jokes outrageously funny. Maybe because I have always been so immersed in the English culture through books and films. Anyway, I find Russian comedy very funny, and I think that the meatiness of Russian swear words and phrases surpass any in the other languages I know.

## A FEW DAYS LATER, STILL PLUSKI

Jagoda is here. I enjoy her company very much. She is such a sensible, down to earth person. Calm and loving, accepting people for who they are even if very different from her. There seems to be no meanness whatsoever in her. Pure goodness and tolerance. Maybe that's why the children try to push her? To see the limits? Just like I did with my mother? But they show a lot of love for her, which I didn't with my mother.

The conversations now are different. She reads mostly

fiction, has quite a few recommendations for me of what would be interesting in the new Polish literature, and I appreciate it. It would be too difficult for me alone to know what is happening in the literary world of Poland when I live so far away. She and Monika are great advisors in this respect.

## STILL PLUSKI
The three weeks here have passed way too quickly. Now we are starting to think about home and what is waiting there for us.

## AUGUST, 2009, ASHLAND
So, after spending a fine time in Pluski and Podkowa we came home in July and learned of our friend Al German's death. It is very hard to say goodbye to people who became part of our lives. It is hard to accept that never again we'll have a chance of hearing his voice, of getting into, so often fiery, discussions, of eating dinners together, of being a foursome with him and his wife Margot, who is I am happy to say, still with us and in perfect mental ability. She is seventeen years older than I, yet I sometimes feel like she is my younger friend. Oh, to be that bright when I am her age! For now it is quite hard to lose our friends and acquaintances who became such an important part of our lives.

My mother, in her later years often complained to me "it gets empty around me." She died at the age of eighty-eight and was quite senile by then. When Donnelly and I spent a year in Poland (1992–1993), we visited with her twice a week, and every time, after talking to Donnelly for a few minutes, she would turn to me and ask: "Who is that charming young man?" I would duly answer that he is my husband Donnelly. To which her response was: "Oh yes, of course, and he is charming, isn't he?" In a few days the scene would be repeated. I wrote a little story about her.

## A VISIT

I visited my mother yesterday. She was very happy to see me. Throughout the visit she kept mistaking me for her sister and marveling how young I looked. "I can't believe it," she wondered repeatedly, "you are only three years younger than me, yet look at you, walking without a cane. And here I can hardly move." Then she told me a story of the times when she lived in India. It was quite an interesting story, although I didn't like her definitely racist attitude towards the Hindu people. The only problem was I knew well she had never been to India. Not even for a short visit. I was sitting there, looking at her, so calm, so happy, and so far away, beyond my reach. Beyond any possibility of reach. I was listening without listening, just nodding my head, and smiling from time to time. All of a sudden I remembered the time reversed, when it was she who was listening without really knowing what I was saying, and I was inventing stories, pretending I was reading a book that I held in my hands, sometimes upside down. She called it "blahblahing," this habit of mine — creating stories about kids alive in my imagination and their adventures which could not have taken place in our country tortured by war.

I was four or five at that time. A very lonely child. My sister three years younger and sickly couldn't provide the companionship I needed and craved desperately. So not having it, I invented it. It was only logical that I had to pretend I was reading. After all everything interesting and safe in my life came out of books read to me by my mother or father. Yet, they didn't have much time for me, there weren't many books available, and anyway I couldn't yet read on my own. So I would take in my hands a book, any book, and I would create for myself what I needed so much. My stories were long and colorful. The weather in them was always sunny, the kids in my stories sometimes fell ill or their adventures took them into dangerous situations, but one thing always remained the same — the grownups in my stories knew what to do and did it. The grownups were all-powerful. The grownups were never afraid. They were in control. It must have been hard for her to listen, while she was cooking our meager food rations or washing clothes with a small piece of harsh soap, to the stories of a four year old. And now here I was, smiling patiently, pretending to listen, knowing full well, that even if I heard what was it that she needed, I would not be able to give it to her. Just like she hadn't been able… All of a sudden I realized that something has changed. She was looking at me in a different way. She knows who I am!!! She is here with me! She reached out, put her hand on mine, and with a warm, tender smile said: "Here I am telling you all those old stories, you must have heard many times, while you say nothing. Do you write still? I do remember, you know, your blahblahing. Wasn't that fantastic? I always knew you'd be a writer. There was one thing though, that I never understood. Why the grown-up people in your stories were always so strong? Usually children want to imagine themselves in positions of power. You were quite rebellious in many ways, yet here in your stories it didn't show…"

She was really concerned. After all that time she was still bothered by the fact of not understanding her child. I was looking at her helplessly. Should I? Would it bother her? To hear now that I had considered her too weak to be trusted? Could I say it now, in the state she was in? When one never knew whether she comprehends what is being said? This was too much for me. "I don't know, mother." I heard myself say. There was pain in my chest. A panic. Like I lost something valuable. Something that would never again come my way. Her eyes became distant again. "Do you think they'll give me my dinner soon?"

– You have just had your dinner, mother.

– Oh, did I? You know I want to tell you about that time I lived in India…

## September 29, 2009

What a month! On the fifteenth Donnelly had his seventy-fifth birthday. For a long time he was planning to celebrate it with something akin to a swan song — singing a recital for our friends and acquaintances, before his voice went away. When we counted those we wanted to invite it came up to nearly sixty people. When we measured our living room we decided that even after taking out all the furniture and renting chairs, we couldn't fit in more than forty to forty-five. It was hard to cross out some of our acquaintances, but what can one do, the walls are not of rubber. Well, we did put in some heavy lifting and moving, rented the chairs, hired a caterer, got a good friend who happens to be a great pianist to accompany the birthday boy, and on Sunday the thirteenth we had our bash. Donnelly sang his beloved opera and musical arias for forty-five minutes, after which we had an intermission, then another forty-five minutes, this time of his own songs. He was fantastic. His voice held fine, he made people laugh, and sometimes have tears in their eyes. He is such a good performer.

The whole show was filmed by Sean Curry and he promised us to make it into a DVD, as well as put some of the songs on YouTube. Everybody had a good time and there was a new romance started between two of our single friends. Hurrah!

Another good result of the concert was that Donnelly has finally been convinced that his own songs are really worth recording. When he saw people's reaction — all that laughter, all the tears in their eyes - he at last believed in what I kept telling him for years, namely that he has to record them so that more people can enjoy his poetry and singing. So that those songs will be there for others even after his voice will be gone. Now he promised me he was, for sure, going to do it.

Organizing the day was difficult for me, physically I mean. I suppose I am getting a little too old for entertaining on such a big scale. There was also not much of a rest afterwards, as a week later, when the house was barely put in order we had a big forest fire not far from our place. We had to evacuate. Luckily after my wartime childhood I do not panic in such situations and I know without having to think twice what has to be packed in a hurry into our cars: cat first, then diplomas, documents, memorable photos, and last if there is still space in the car - valuable art. Donnelly was out of the house at the time when the fire started and the police came to order the evacuation. When he came back my car was already fully packed, I left to leave it with some friends in town, but when the friend, Brian, tried to bring me back home to help Donnelly decide what to take into his car, we were not allowed to enter the evacuation zone. I just got out and knowing back paths ran home. We finished packing and were able to leave before the police shooed everybody out, no matter how ready they were. We were lucky, only one house, quite a distance from us, burned, the firefighters got the blaze under control and by late evening we were allowed to come back. It took some time and effort the next day to clean the patio and driveway of the accumulated ash. By the end of the week I was totally exhausted.

## OCTOBER, 2009

I have been ironing today, all of a sudden I started to think about Darek. Whenever I think about him I have such feelings of guilt. Yes, at that time, in his years with us I didn't know any better. Now I do, hence the guilt. Too late. Like so much in our lives. When we gain some wisdom it's often too late for many of our mistakes to be corrected. I already mentioned the saying "can you blame the lame for limping," yet it is in my brain, not in my feelings. So, let's talk some more about Darek.

He was a few months shy of seven when we adopted him. A lovely, sensitive, intelligent boy. Curious about everything he had no knowledge of, yet with a bad heart which prevented him from running, but otherwise didn't seem to give him much trouble. When we took him to Moscow he seemed to thrive on the newness of everything. One of our first moves was to take him to a doctor. The man was optimistic. He prescribed antibiotic injections to be taken once a month for at least a year, and told us that nature, Darek's growing, will take care of normalizing his health. Fine. What was not fine was the fact that the injections hurt badly. Poor boy was crying and yelling every time he was given the shot, and eventually was shaking with fear on the day of the visit to the clinic. But, it was supposed to heal his heart, it had to be done. What didn't have to happen was my yelling at him to stop this hysterics. To tell him to be a man. It didn't hurt that much. As if I knew. Now, I suppose I would be taking him into my arms, trying to calm him, then — well, there are plenty of excuses. I was in the process of organizing a new home, with all of a sudden five children instead of three, in a country where everything was difficult, even buying bread or milk. Wojtek was organizing his office, visiting government officials and other newspaper and TV offices to introduce himself, he could not be of any help at home. We had to obtain a special permission to be able to enroll the kids in a regular Russian school and daycare, and it took time. So in the first weeks of our life there I had to drag all of them every time I went shopping for food. A ten minute walk through our apartment buildings settlement, then crossing a very busy street, with five children between three and seven. Add to it that I did not have a washing machine and all the laundry I did by hand in a bathtub, and then hung on the two balconies of our apartment. Yes, I suppose it was only normal that I was overworked and stressed to the max. But this I know now. Then I felt a superwoman. To the point that I was enjoying guests often in the evening after I put the kids to beds. After all Wojtek's new acquaintances had to meet me, see how we lived etc. I could cope, things were OK.

They weren't. The children were paying the price. A stressed mother has no time for their small needs. Cannot pay attention to their feelings. Yells often. Spanks when she cannot cope otherwise.

Jarek, Jan, and Łucja seemed to be fine. It is only now, when they are grownups that they tell me of many resentments they had then. Especially Łucja tells me how she missed being held on my lap. Now, they remember the furious mother of their childhood. Interesting that in my memory there were many fine relaxed moments of joking, of my reading to them, of our outings. They hardly remember those.

Iwonka, when she joined our family, was thought to be retarded. At four she hardly spoke, never asked a question. I sometimes joked (well, it wasn't a joking matter), that if a pink elephant with blue dots all over entered the room, she would not become curious, she would not ask "what is this?." She just quietly played, preferably alone, somewhere in a corner. And as I mentioned before, if she cried she did it like an old person. Without a sound. Here I had good instincts — I sat with her for hours on the floor, trying to talk to her, playing with her, trying to develop her brain. I remember buying a bunch of greeting cards with pictures of animals. She liked them. I would take one and cut it in two and show her that in a certain position we could see the animal, but when we put the card together in a different way there is no animal. She became fascinated, she tried to regain the beloved creature on her own. It would take a lot of effort, but the joy of finally getting it right was great. It took us several days to arrive at a point when I risked cutting the card into three pieces, then four… A year later she was assembling twenty-five piece jigsaw puzzles. It took a lot out of me, but by the age of seven she could count to ten, at eight she went to school. She spoke two languages, she could read and write in Cyrillic alphabet. Then after we came back to Poland she learned the Roman alphabet, that is used in Polish, quite easily. At fifteen she graduated from an elementary school.

She got a good profession in dressmaking in a trade school. She is a married woman, with two fantastic children, Ula and Marcin. Not long ago, she decided to get a regular high school diploma, she was embarrassed to have two children studying at a university, and she not having a high school education. She did it. I am so proud of her. She reads a lot. She is still developing. If only she didn't have to work so hard. But, sorry to say her husband Jurek is not a reliable provider.

I consider her my greatest achievement in life, I love her very much, same as my blood children.

With Darek the story was totally different. The first notion that we might have a much bigger than anticipated problem came when we went in Moscow for our first social visit with the children. A couple of Polish journalists, parents of a girl roughly our kids' age, invited us to dinner. All seven of us. My aunt Helena called such invitations "proof of suicidal tendencies." When we came to their apartment I was impressed by the wife's organizational abilities. There were two tables set, one for the parents, one for children. We got a gourmet dinner, the kiddies got what all the children love and eat without fussing — a pizza. Homemade at that, as there were no pizza places in Moscow at that time. Yet their table was set as beautifully as ours. Even their soda glasses were like our wine glasses. We, the grownups, enjoyed a leisurely, relaxing dinner. The kids were allowed to go play as soon as they felt they had enough food. The evening was a total success, or so we thought. Later, when children started to show tiredness, the happy Kubicki family went home. Imagine my shock when on undressing them I found, in Darek's pocket, a gold chain with a lovely gem incrusted pendant. The next day, while Wojtek took care of the rest of them, I drove to our new friends with Darek. He had to apologize, to promise that never again, to see how humiliated I was, listen to a lecture on honesty… I really thought it would be enough. Oh, the naivete of a young woman. I was sure that through love and showing good example, through making a kid feel secure, I could change the influence of first years of his life with his birth mother, or maybe even genes, who knows. When probed for answers he told me once that when he was small his mother took him to shops and occupied the personnel with talking while he was supposed to shoplift. But my doubts are now, not then.

That visit with our new friends happened in late spring, the summer we spent in Pluski, in September both older boys went to school. Jarek to second grade, Darek to first.

It was shortly after the school started that Jarek began to behave strangely. Normally a happy, serious, loving his school boy, all of a sudden he tried to find reasons not to go to school, became moody, didn't want to play with his siblings. After our long conversations with him, trying to find what was wrong, he came up with a confession: on their way back from school Darek was throwing money into garbage cans, or digging little holes and burying money in the ground. Another big conversation with Darek. Does he need money of his own? Where did the money come from? Well, he was quite forthcoming, the cash he stole from other kids' pockets or bags. He didn't need money of his own. He didn't know why he did steal. He will never ever do it again. The "never, ever" lasted a week. This was when I lost it for the first time. I told him to stick out his butt and beat him to the point of my hand hurting badly. He cried, he once again promised to never, ever... And then he became very loving, relaxed, as if that beating was something that he waited for, accepted as a show of — yes, she cares. I was ashamed of myself, but at the same time relieved with his reaction. This time we had peace for a longer period. We really tried to show him love when he behaved well, and anger when he misbehaved. I don't know whether I was right in surmising that if I do not punish Darek for such gross crossing the line it would be a bad example for the other children. What's more I promised Darek that he would not be punished if he owned up to his mistakes, but that he would be punished severely for lying. I kept my promise, but to no avail. The stealing and lying went on. The beatings continued. The promises of "never, ever" also. And after every beating Darek was like an angel for some time. In those days he was a joy to be with, he did well in school, and I believed that some day he would see how pleasant life can be if he behaves like the other kids. I am sorry to say but the spanking started to go on with the others too, although not often. I suppose I found that it relieved the feeling of unbearable stress that my new life had put me in. When my children wouldn't obey, when I would talk, then shout and they still kept on doing what I wanted them to stop, I started hitting them. I know, although it was never to the point of bruising, I am very ashamed of that period in my life. There came a day when Iwonka was particularly obnoxious and I grabbed a wooden stick, which was part of a toy she played with, I hit her on her bottom and — the stick broke. It made me stop. I was terrified of what was becoming of me. Next day I went to a doctor and got a prescription for Valium. It did help. With me. Not with Darek.

As I mentioned before, my father liked a French saying *"Tout comprendre c'est tout pardonner"* (To understand everything is to forgive everything). I do not agree with it. I do understand the weight under which I lived in those long ago years. The amount of purely physical work, too little of intellectual stimulation and satisfaction, the need inside me to have the apartment always clean and lovely to look at, the ambition to have food that was delicious and nutritious at the same time, although buying the ingredients was so difficult, the problems with Darek that seemed to be unsolvable... Yet, I cannot pardon myself. Maybe one of the reasons for this is that I still was greedy for life of my own, that I could not, did not give up on all the little things that made life pleasurable for me. Even after days of hard work, I found time and energy to entertain, to talk, to dance, play bridge late into the night. No wonder I had no patience for children and their needs. When deciding on five children I didn't take into account the necessity of changing my own life, or at least my priorities. And this inconsistency is why I cannot pardon myself.

But, back to Darek. In 1975 our time in Moscow ended. We came back to Poland, moved into a new big house which we had been building while abroad, sent the kids to a new school. Not easy for them. Now they had to read and write in Latin alphabet, learn new names for math functions, get to know new teachers, new colleagues. Four of them adapted very nicely.

Darek a few weeks into the school year was caught stealing his teacher's money purse from her bag.

I started to home-school him. He was not to go out of the gate without either his father or me. I was afraid what this kind of house arrest would do to him. Well, another surprise. He was happy. Helped at home, did his lessons very well, was nice and relaxed. Wojtek took him for long bike rides, I taught him everything he would have been taking at school, there was peace, normal family life. At the end of the school year he took official tests and passed them with top marks. Once again we became hopeful. Now, for sure he understands how it pays to be good. Summer in Pluski. Lots of swimming, biking, sailing. Freedom. Such a happy time for everybody. Then back home. A new school for Darek. A school where nobody knew about his stealing, a school with very good teachers. Darek was well prepared, started with good grades, was liked by the teachers and kids in his class. It lasted until December, when he was caught with some outsiders drinking vodka in a little copse of trees by the school playground and then kicked out of school. Once again at home. This time we added horse riding to his homeschooling. He absolutely fell in love with horses. He rode them, talked to them, cleaned and fed them. He would do any household chores, any amount of learning just so that we would take him to the stables. Other children were lukewarm, except Jarek who took to that pastime with the same vigor. So the two boys were now spending a lot of their free time together. Jarek was already in high school, Darek was to enter one. His dream was a school that would teach him not only caring for, but would also prepare him for breeding horses. We did find such a boarding school, 200 miles away, with just the kind of program he was dreaming about. Peace lasted into early spring when Darek and another boy from his class stole a car and went travelling. They, of course, were caught soon, sentenced to a reformatory school, and sent away. He did well, teachers liked him. Although the sentence was for two years, the school informed us that Darek improved so much that we would be able to take him home at the end of that first school year, in June. Well, at the end of May he and one of his friends ran away, stole a car and when gas ran out, stole another, were caught after third or fourth. This time he was nearly eighteen and went to prison. He learned a craft there, started a life on his own when finally freed, got married. We were all at his wedding, accepted him and his new wife back into the family. And then they vanished. Moved, did not leave an address, never called. We know he is alive, we know they divorced, we know he is an alcoholic with frequent problems. We respect his decision not to contact us. Basically so convenient for the family, isn't it? Yet, that is such a thorn in my side. I feel guilty, disappointed, I still love that boy who has created hell in my life. I still think that had I been wiser, more patient, more attentive to his needs... Such a bitter feeling of failure.

## February, 2010

Did I write in September "What a month!"? I think I still live through some very interesting, although taxing times. At the end of October I had foot surgery. Nothing much, but I was laid down for a few days and then was slow in regaining my strength. OK, I thought, normal for an aging person. After all I had anesthesia, which I remembered from my previous surgeries always affected me unpleasantly. Then at the beginning of December I began to feel pretty bad, tire easily, get short of breath, and somewhere in the middle of the month came chest pains. Nothing new for me. I have had chest pains always before a big weather change. What was worrisome now — there was no weather change. I went to the doctor, he sent me to a cardiologist. They gave me a stress test and sent me to the hospital where I was to undergo a coronary angiogram, which showed one of my arteries blocked in 90 percent. The doctor put a stent into it, they kept me for another day in the hospital and then sent me home telling me to take it easy for a few days, and then come back for cardiac rehabilitation. Which I am still doing. It is a fine exercise program that one does while monitored by a nurse. It helps very much in knowing when to slow or even stop, but also gives courage by showing how much one can exercise without fear of having a heart attack. I feel much better now. I also know that my difficulties in September, with getting so tired, were not resulting from aging. It was my heart trying to tell me something.

 The stay in the hospital, my first in the U.S.A., the prettiness of rooms, the ability of choosing what one wants to eat, the telephone by the bed, TV, private bathroom with the entrance from the room, in other words luxury, brought to my mind other hospitals I stayed in, the hospitals in Poland in the days of our so called socialism. In the years of socialism we did not pay taxes, they were automatically taken out of our earnings. The factories, offices, schools, hospitals and such were owned by the people, which meant by the government. It was the government which decided how much we should earn, it was the government which paid for healthcare, education, and all the other national needs. The socialist economy was failing so there was never enough money for all the needs, but I am glad to say that whatever bad we might say about people in the ruling class, they never skimped on education, culture and the real health needs of the population. The real needs — so the doctors were very well educated, the nurses also, but the state of the hospital buildings, bed linen, food were not considered to be of great importance. I often lay in rooms with peeling paint on the walls, with bare electric bulbs under the ceilings, with food that was enough to nourish a sick body, but was barely edible. And telephone? TV? It was enough that they were usually one to a floor. It went on like that for quite some time after regaining independence from Russia in the late eighties. The country's tax system had to be started from scratch, people had to learn that it was their responsibility to pay taxes, and that was not easy. You know, for two hundred years of Poland being partitioned, then the years of war, then feelings of being under occupation by the Soviet Union which lasted for over forty years people considered cheating on the government a virtue. It was practiced by nearly everybody. So now it was hard to change. Anyway, in 1993 when in Poland, I broke my leg. It was a very bad, complicated break. The bone above my ankle was shattered into twenty something pieces. Small pieces. The doctors were at a loss what to do. The pieces were too small for surgery and putting metal pins. But here is what I meant that we had such good doctors — they came up with the idea that the muscles have a memory of the bone, so if they put me in bed with my leg in traction tied to a stick of metal drilled through my heel and told me to nearly all the time flex my foot, the muscles would set the bones in their proper place. It worked. I was in that bed on my back, flexing and flexing the foot for five weeks, after which the leg was nicely set and could be put in a cast to heal. And the naked bulb for light? The absence of TV or telephone? Well, I have a perfectly functioning leg, and although not being a Polish resident at that time, which meant I had no insurance, I paid five hundred dollars for those five weeks. So, my dears what is more important? Inexpensive health care or TV? And we never had to wait for a doctor's appointment. It makes me laugh when I hear here the fear of socialized medicine. And it makes me quite angry when I have to pay through my nose for any doctor's visit and see the lovely buildings, the comforts, the plants and pictures and then the doctor doesn't have the time to examine me properly. But to be fair, here in the Asante hospital in Medford the doctors were marvelous and I did not mind having the telephone by my side. Have I never had bad experiences in Polish hospitals? Oh yes I had. You know a school is just as good as its teachers are, a hospital as its doctors. My worst experience was when I went to the hospital with birthing pains with my first child. As my waters hadn't yet burst, I was put in a big room with several beds separated by curtains and filled with women in a similar state. A group of doctors was coming through, stopping at every bed and examining the future mothers. After they saw my neighbor they were still talking about her when they stopped at my bed. A male doctor said "Shouldn't we do a caesarian? The baby's pulse seems weak." A woman doctor, oh I remember her to this day, a heavily made up redhead, responded with "Are you silly, our shift ends in half an hour, let the next ones take care of that." They examined me, everything was OK, they went. An hour later another group of doctors came. The neighbor's baby had no pulse. After I heard what happened to the baby of my neighbor, my contractions totally stopped. I got up, called Wojtek to come pick me up, and as he had only a raincoat in the car, I, naked underneath it, barefoot, went home and called my beloved Dr. Fitkal to tell him the story. As we were talking my waters broke. He told me to go back to the hospital, he would be waiting there for me. He was, and after sitting with me for several hours he performed a caesarian, Jarek was born, and I was taken great care of by Dr. Fitkal who told the others not to touch me. I never went to that particular hospital ever again. I never witnessed another such gross negligence.

## A FEW DAYS LATER

While in bed, resting after the surgery, I needed to lighten my mood, to take my brain off the seriousness of the situation. I started to write a funny little piece. Here it is:

### A CONVERSATION

– *Well. So you love him, you say.*
– *I said no such thing.*
– *You implied. Everything you told me seemed to point this way.*
– *How queer. I thought I had been rather efficient in describing the whole situation, in explaining the complexity, the intricacy of the relationship, and yet the only thing you can come up with is "you love him." A label. Yes or no. Black or white.*
– *That's how I see it. Either you love somebody or you don't.*
– *Oh, no. Come on, you know better than that. There are so many kinds of love, and so many shades in each kind. And I suppose the whole palette is different for different people.*
– *This discussion leads us nowhere. Now you exaggerate. Do you really mean to say there are five billion different "love palettes"? Don't be silly. Love is love. Most people love the same way. Look, there are so many love songs, love stories, films about love, and they are so popular because people see themselves in them. They see their own feelings portrayed, slightly embellished, slightly dramatized, but basically their own. They usually can identify with the hero or heroine. That's the beauty of it.*
– *You used the right word "basically." Yes, I agree. But on this common base we build our personal structures. Sometimes quite simple, sometimes very complicated. Some of the structures are hideous, but some are extremely beautiful. And most, of course, fall in between.*

– *And this is what you wanted me to see? How beautiful this structure of yours is?*
– *Yes, I suppose I just wanted to share the beauty of it, its uniqueness. You know how it is, all happiness is a little more alive when shared. But I think I also wanted you to understand that together with all this, there are other feelings making this particular relationship so much richer, and so much, much more difficult than just "love."*
– *As if love wasn't difficult enough. Would you like another cup?*
– *Yes, I'll have one more. Although John tells me I drink too much coffee. I suppose he is right. I often sleep poorly nowadays.*
– *It should be "nowanights," shouldn't it?*
– *Yes, funny, how certain things never got round to having their own names.*
– *Aha, and certain names never spread enough to be of real use. There is a word "fortnight," most people I asked do not know what it means. Do you?*
– *No, I don't think I do. Something to do with tennis? I seem to connect it with Wimbledon…*
– *It is fourteen nights. It is commonly used in England. That's the only connection with Wimbledon. I know it because of all the British novels I like to read… Have another piece of cake. Or does John also comment on your waistline?*
– *As a matter of fact he does. And this is one of the reasons I am not sure of my feelings. I love spending time with him, but do I love him? Do you understand?*
– *Yeah, I think I did see it from the beginning. I really contradicted you for contradiction's sake. You love being with him, yet you do not accept him enough, and he doesn't seem to fully accept you. The only difference between you two is, as I see it, he wants to change you, for your own good, of course, while you would rather see him stay the way he is, only at an arm's distance. Did I get it right this time?*
– *Perfect. I knew you'd understand. You might see it all even more clearly than I do. You look at it from the side… By the way what do you see "from the side"?*

– *Well, I see love, my dear.*
– *Here we go again! Why?*
– *Because love and acceptance do not often go in tandem. They usually don't. Don't you see? Of course you do. Only you would call it love if it were perfect. As it isn't, you want to call it a hundred shades of something. Why shy away from the word? Afraid? Still deep down believing in existence of perfection? At your age? Now it is my turn to say — come on, you know better.*
– *Yes, I do. Of course I do. Has it ever occurred to you, that I never fully accepted my children? And yet I love you all so very, very much.*
– *We never talked about that. You pretty well hid it from us, but I felt it anyway. Did you ever think why?*
– *Yes and no. Meaning yes, I thought, yet I never really tried to get to the core. There was no pressing need. You don't have to accept totally, as you said, to love. And not accept fully doesn't mean reject. Does it?*
– *Oh, God! Mother! Now we are back at the beginning. Only roles are slightly, I would say, reversed.*
– *And it doesn't matter.*
– *Doesn't it? Really? What does then?*
– *The fact that we could discuss it this way. Or any way for that matter. And know what? Give me another piece of that cake. It is delicious.*

## MARCH 2010

I am still doing the cardiac rehab. As I have to spend an hour on treadmill and similar machines, I do quite a lot of thinking. Today it came to me, that all my life I have been a spectator. I love music, yet never felt the need to play an instrument, always preferred to listen to records, then tapes, now CDs, and I often go to concerts. I have always been reading tons of books, never (before) tried to write one. I worked as a journalist, which was active, of course, but what I wrote was the result of observing not participating. OK, OK, so it wasn't totally so. I didn't observe raising five children, building a house, or sailing, I did it. Yet, as can be seen in what you are reading right now, I realized that after taking in so much, at the prospect of aging and the realization of the inevitability of death, I started to feel an enormous need of putting out at least some of what I had taken in. In Donnelly's opinion, I am an inductive thinker and he is deductive. I don't know. I do not like such generalizations. For sure I am a critical thinker. Once again it comes from my father. He loved playing the devil's advocate in our conversations, so that I never could just take for granted what he was telling me. It is plainly visible in how I read the political news. Always asking myself what is hidden behind what is said on the surface. Sorry to say even in conversations with friends I always try to hear more than just the spoken words. The why the person says something, what might be hidden in the choice of words, how the speaker tries to manipulate my understanding of the situation. Manipulation. I think this is my biggest fear, to unwittingly allow somebody to manipulate my thoughts, my feelings. That's why I hate advertisements and propaganda. That's why I sniff it all out suspiciously. Am I sure I am not being manipulated? No, there cannot be any such assurance, after all I do read the newspapers, magazines, books; I watch TV and listen to the radio. How much do I take in without being conscious of internalizing, without criticism, what somebody else wants me to think or feel?

It was especially important during my life in socialist Poland and USSR. We, the journalists, had to learn to write between lines. So that the censors could not delete, yet the readers got the meaning. Wojtek was great at that. I remember when Salazar, the Portuguese dictator died, Wojtek wrote about him, criticizing his despotism in such a way that readers in Poland understood it as criticism of Gomółka, the first secretary of our communist party then. The censors could not even show that they understood it, that they also saw how much our own government resembled the despotic rulers in "bad capitalistic countries." The readers were overjoyed reading something that was so much like what they were thinking, talking among friends about, yet what officially was a taboo. Letters were coming with congratulations and asking for more. Sometimes though, this writing between the lines could be misunderstood. I remember once after a fine article criticizing governmental intrusions in church life he got several letters calling him a clerical footman, and a few accusing him of being a Jewish slave. Well, he said after reading those, either/or, I cannot be both at once.

I remember getting once a frightening letter with threats. Wojtek must have offended somebody grossly, the letter told us in detail what that person intended to do to our children. We did put up a strong fence with an electrically operated gate, and we got a big fierce dog. As far as I know nobody tried to do anything to our kids. They just wanted to frighten us, I suppose. Mostly though, Wojtek was very popular in Poland and on Thursdays, when his opinion page article was appearing, the newspaper sold many more copies than on other days of the week. I was very proud of him.

My writing was quite innocent by comparison. I mainly wrote reportages from our travels and interviews with important people, one of whom was Andrew Schally — an American endocrinologist, Nobel Prize winner, of Polish origin. It was fascinating to work freelance; it gave me time for my kids, home and the translations which were much better paid than journalism, yet allowed me to write when something interesting was happening. Like Schally's visit to Poland in 1977, for instance. It was such a change from my everyday life to be able to travel with him and a few of our best doctors and scientists to Kraków and Wieliczka, an old salt mine changed into a sanatorium, with underground chambers for salty inhalations. The whole of the big mine was made useful and at the same time beautiful, as it is filled with salt sculptures. Even lamps, mostly candelabras, are sculpted in rock salt. That was an adventure for me, the hard working mother of five, laundry woman, cook, cleaner, translator, teacher — all of a sudden transformed into a career woman, elegant, with a Dictaphone, travelling with these intelligent people, listening, sometimes speaking and having them listen to me. It always gave me a surge of self confidence, of happiness, of knowing that I still can, I still haven't lost it.

I said I still read newspapers. Yes and no. Until three or four years ago I read them every day, I felt I wanted to know everything that was happening in the world. Then, when I discovered in reading French, Polish and Russian news on the Internet (in addition to our own, American) how much we are misinformed by our journalists, I decided to go on reading only facts, no opinions, on those several different websites. At least now I often see how all of them lie, but each in a different way, and about different events. No pundits for me. The ease of spreading opinions is creating a cloud obfuscating the reality. The language the pundits use, the slogans, the truisms become their reality. I refuse to be mired in it. I want to be free to see the world as it is, with its existing problems, and make my own mind about them. Do I succeed? I have no idea.

Some words of Thomas Jefferson come to mind: "The man who reads nothing at all is better educated than the man who reads nothing but newspapers." So the level of newspapers that we have now is nothing new, is it?

## April 2010

When Donnelly was starting his business of counseling high-school students, helping them to choose and then apply to colleges, and working long hours everyday, I told him we do not need all the money he thought it was his duty to provide. I said that I would prefer to live with him in a shack, but have him as a companion, as compared to living in a beautiful house that we had and seeing so little of him. Well, then he thought he was a superman. He actually enjoyed the feeling that he was doing something good, something worthwhile. He basked in the praises his students and their parents lavished him with. He was very successful. Now he gets tired much sooner, allows me to talk to him about cutting the amount of students he accepts to work with. Hurrah! But it was easy to speak about that shack, now when I started counting how we will be able to live on his retirement I discovered that we'll be able to afford a two-bedroom apartment. And my mood definitely sobered. Shack it ain't, but the idea of having no space for my own study, or of having college students with their loud music, with their partying, for close neighbors, is not appealing. Yes, the garden we have is too big to be maintained by just us. But no garden at all? Yes, the house we have gave us a lot of space to enjoy together or separately, but it is a big house to clean, keep warm in winter or cool in summer. But an apartment? With an air-conditioner in the window? Ha! OK, I will need to lower my expectations, I will have not to show Donnelly my doubts, I will have to adjust, get realistic, find all the good sides there are to be found. I am usually good at that. Life is calling my bluff.

## May 2010

Łucja has come up with an interesting idea. She called me to ask whether we think about moving now that Donnelly is considering the idea of retirement. Yes, I said, we are, but with the money we have we most probably are going to rent an apartment. Well, she said, Fritz and she were thinking how they could invest pretty safely some of their money. Both of them earn good salaries, she also has an additional income from her little Russian Language School, and they thought about maybe buying a house in Ashland. They wouldn't move here, of course. They are very happy in Switzerland. They thought maybe we would want to live in that house and take care of it.

The time is right with the prices of houses so low in the U.S. What do we think about that? Neither Donnelly nor I want to live off my children. But we could go half and half with the down payment, then pay half of the mortgage, which would be roughly the same as the rent for an apartment. Then, after we die the house would go to them. That would give us a sense of independence, and them an incentive in seeing their investment grow nicely. So we all agreed that I should look for some houses in our price range, which would suit the living needs of the old couple. Very soon we decided it should be a townhome. Very small, easy to keep garden, common greens taken care of by homeowners associations, nice, quiet neighborhood. I am glad I have a sensible girl for a daughter. The first such house I found was absolutely lovely – three bedrooms and two bathrooms upstairs, downstairs a separate dining room, a nice livingroom with a fireplace. Up on the hill, far from freeway. Price just right. Łucja very tactfully asked me do I remember my age. "Can you imagine one of you in bed with flu, or heaven forbid broken hip, and the other running upstairs with every cup of tea, or just to check on the bedridden? And, Mama, you already have problems with driving in the dark, yet there on the hill you would have to drive everywhere. You know, shopping, doctor, a concert, anything." A bucket of cold water on my head, but she is absolutely right. So, let's look for something with master bedroom downstairs, and preferably walking distance to the shops, bus etc.

July 11, 2010
Remember that old Polish saying about man shooting and God carrying the bullets? All the talk about houses went out of the window. Łucja and Fritz had a terrible motorbike accident. They are alive, thank God, but very badly hurt. Both have serious concussions, he has a leg broken into several pieces, some internal bleeding; she has an arm broken so badly that a

part of her arm bone is missing. The concussions are severe, so the doctors are worried. They are both in hospital in Lucerne where the accident happened. Apparently, and I know it from Olaf, her son, they were stopped in front of a red light when an SUV ploughed into them. They were thrown around thirty meters from the bike. They were unconscious, others called the ambulance and the police. And it is from those others who had seen the whole accident, that we know what happened as neither Łucja nor Fritz remember anything. Their story is that they stopped in front of a stop light and then they were in hospital. Apparently it was an old woman driving that SUV. Ironically she was an American, visiting Switzerland, looking at signs, not seeing the red light. I am so tense, it is hard to be so far away. I considered going there, but Olaf convinced me that I couldn't help, I would just be in the way, and he (a medical student) is staying with them and he promised to call us every day. So be it.

## NEXT DAY

They are conscious today. They were put together in a room with two beds, so at least they don't worry about what is happening with the other one. Both had extensive surgeries but the doctors seem to be very positive today. She had a piece of a bone cut from somewhere else in her body, pelvic bone I think, to replace the part that was missing from her forearm. He had leg surgery and an opening drilled into his skull to lessen the pressure and drain fluid. It is going to be a long hospital stay. Luckily, Switzerland is known for a very good health care system. No insurance companies that want the patients out of the hospital as soon as possible. There is nothing we can do to help. Just wait and try to calm down. I started to take sleeping pills, otherwise I would lie awake for hours.

## Two Weeks Later
There is quite an improvement in my kiddies' health. Their doctor told Łucja that she could go home if she wanted, but as Fritz needs to stay in the hospital for longer, she could stay with him if she chose to. Can you imagine? Staying in the hospital so that she would not be alone at home with a broken right arm? Worrying about her husband who was to undergo two more surgeries? And the insurance paying for it? Would be totally impossible here. Even after my heart procedure I was sent home the next morning. Nobody asked me whether I have somebody at home to take care of me. Well, different approach to healthcare, here it seems to be all about money, there about the health and nerves of the patient. I am impressed.

## Two More Weeks Passed
So they are at home today. They were taken home to Zurich in an ambulance and told that their family doctor will visit them every day, a nurse will come also every day to give them their injections and change dressings. The insurance will be sending a house cleaning person, every day, you guessed, to clean the apartment, disinfect the bathroom and kitchen, do the laundry, ironing and shopping. As Łucja's right arm is in a cast, the help would also cook, but as Fritz has both arms usable and is in a wheel chair, they declined. They will enjoy coping with cooking on their own. It'll give them something to do, and will be a welcome challenge. What a relief that it all ended in a relatively painless (?!!) way. We are on the telephone daily, so, judging by the hours that Łucja can spend talking to me, I can rest assured that everything is going to be fine. No more need for sleeping pills.

## August 29, 2010
My life is kinda busy. Yesterday Monika, Jan and Oskar came. Oskar will stay with us for a year or two, this time totally legally as he is now of high school age and thus could get a school

visa. Enough time has passed since his bad experience with immigration officers for him to be once again open to live with us in America. He will be a junior in high school in Ashland. I will again be a soccer grandma, a driver, provider of food, clean clothes and generally "*in loco parentis*." We'll see how it will go. For the time being I am quite excited. When the kids stay with us I give up my study, that is the only "guest room" we have; and if the stay is as long as it is supposed to be this time I am really deprived of my beloved solitude behind closed doors. There is always a price to pay for everything we want to do. I know that the boy needs it, what with his mother Magda's new married life and Monika and Jan working so much and travelling so often for business. A teenage boy needs a stable home, which it seems, right at this moment, only we can provide. How that will change our life, the future will show.

## September 13, 2010

For the time being everything is going smoothly. Oskar proved to be a good student — he, a foreigner has been accepted to two AP (Advanced Placement) classes, English and U.S. History.

Łucja called and she wants me to resume looking for a suitable house. My God, what a difference between the U.S.A. and Switzerland. First of all they haven't been charged for any of the care they got after their accident, no copayments or deductibles. Second, although the doctors predict they will not be able to go back to work for several months, their jobs will be waiting for them. Then there is a third — they are and will be paid their salaries throughout their time of recuperation, no matter how long it'll take. But this is not all, Łucja in the last three years was the owner and the only teacher of a registered school of Russian, with very small classes of three to six students per class. At first she didn't charge a lot, but seeing how popular she had become, she raised her prices considerably. Now she learned that the insurance is going to pay her, her lost wages for

July and August, and starting in September they, the insurers, counted by how much her earnings grew from year to year, and will add the same percentage to what she will get from them. Ha! Not only will they not lose any money, but considering that they are not able to enjoy many costly entertainments, like theater, eating out, skiing etc., they will end up better financially than they were. Oh, if you are to have an accident, try to have it in Switzerland.

OK, so out I go again on the lookout for a residence that would fulfill our many needs.

## September 15, 2010

Today Donnelly turned seventy-six. How time flies. Every year seems much shorter than the one before. Understandable? After all each year is now less than 1/70 of our lives, whereas when we were ten it was 1/10 — 10 percent of what we knew as life. Now it is around 1.3 percent.

## October 3, 2010

I have seen umpteen houses, each of them had some plusses and some important minuses. One which I liked very much was too close to a busy, noisy street; another had no garden, another had other houses on all four sides, no open view at all. I found one that was a possibility, but Donnelly didn't like it. Finally, finally I chanced on one that I fell in love with. It belongs to a very nice single man, a musician.

It is very well kept, a townhome, semidetached, master bedroom downstairs, two other bedrooms and a bathroom upstairs. The downstairs bedroom has its own bathroom and a walk-in closet. The WIC, as we started calling it, is a first for me, but also for Donnelly. I like the idea of a little room for all our clothes, for having space to dress and undress in, for a bedroom that is unencumbered with the necessity of keeping our clothes in. For now, upstairs is going to house Oskar's room and Donnelly's study. Eventually I will regain my place after Oskar leaves.

There is a very small garden space in the back. Half of it is paved, half covered totally by weeds. That will give me some joy of getting rid of what is there and planning and planting everything from scratch. I will want to have a pergola type roof over the paved part, giving us some shade while we eat or read. Also inside we will get rid of the carpet in the living room and put hardwood floor in. We will have to add shelves in the closet, in the pantry, and some cabinets in the laundry, but a bigger job is awaiting us with the downstairs, so called, powder room. The one that is in the house is totally ridiculous. What did the architect think when planning it this way? The door to it is right by the only place where one can put a dining table!! Can you imagine the embarrassment of those who have to pee or even more in the middle of a dinner?

I do not have a good opinion about this architect, not only the powder room, but one of the upstairs bedrooms has windows looking out to a space of maybe five or six feet that separate our house from the next one, while he/she put a closet on the only wall with a beautiful view towards the mountains. Well, how stupid and uncaring one has to be to bungle one's job in such a way? It would be difficult and very costly to move those windows, but the door to the toilet will be moved for sure. (When I was eleven or twelve, I once entered a WC in the presence of an old Great Uncle. I had a lecture later on from my Great Aunt, "My dear, a lady never enters a bathroom in the presence of a man." I am far from that kind of "manners," yet to have it next to the place we eat is a no-no.) Another big plus is that the little garden abuts two fenced-in pastures with some trees and bushes and plenty of birds, giving us a feeling of space and allowing for a lovely view of the mountains.

Of course, with time, somebody might build a whole colony of houses there, but knowing the time needed for change of zoning from agricultural to residential, and then getting permission to build, I am pretty sure we are relatively safe. Today, as I looked at the property I saw two horses grazing peacefully. The house is also within a walking distance from a food market, a pharmacy, our bank and a YMCA. No hills in between! What could be better for a couple of old codgers? (Donnelly asked me whether a woman can be called "a codger," I said I don't mind. We settled on "codgerette" for me.) All we need now is a loan.

## OCTOBER 20, 2010

The loan situation is quite complicated. The banks here do not want to give a loan to Łucja and/or Fritz. No matter that they have very stable and well paid jobs. No matter that they have no debt whatsoever. No matter that the house is here, so although they live in Switzerland, if ever there would be a problem with mortgage payments the banks could easily requisition the property. Strange isn't it? So the only possibility is a loan for Donnelly. The fact that he is retirement age, with minimal savings, doesn't seem to be a problem. Queer. The loan guy tells us it will go through. OK, so we are working on it. The owner of the house, Michael Mish, is agreeing to wait, and we are in no hurry, so everything is fine.

## NOVEMBER 3, 2010

We have contacted Tim O'Donnell, who had put a very good hardwood floor in our previous house, to come and give us an estimate for the work we would like to have done for the house we hope to buy. He is a fine worker, and very honest, as we have seen on that previous job. After he finished laying the floor in the Greenmeadows house, he came with his bill which was less than the estimate he had given us, and to which we had agreed. Of course we asked why, and imagine our surprise when he said that the work took less time than he had expected. That was a first for us. Usually if there is a change in price it is in an opposite direction. So now, with all the work that we envisage on the Brooks Lane house, we decided he would be the best, and wanted to have him save some time for us. Another surprise — previously we had to wait for a couple months before he was free to begin work, now with the economy tanking he is totally free. Nobody is building or remodeling anything, people are waiting for better times. Good for us. He promised to start as soon as we have the ownership. Tomorrow he will look at the house and start planning for how and when he'll do it, and what materials he'll need. Mr. Mish is fine with us behaving like owners.

## November 6, 2010

I am very busy going through our possessions and trying to decide what to keep, what to give away, and what to simply throw out. And that in addition to being the housekeeper and soccer grandma. It does occupy all my time. But it has to be done before we move. The new house is quite lovely, yet much smaller than the one we live in. It is also three bedrooms, with two-and-a-half bathrooms. But on Greenmeadows we have a separate dining room, whereas in the new home the living room will have to accommodate a dining room table, in addition to the sitting and TV arrangement.

We'll have a one-car garage instead of a big two-car one we have here. Both Donnelly and I love to have our books around us. It's like having friends at arm's reach. Whenever we want to visit, to revisit, to enjoy — they are available. But in the new place we'll have less shelf space. Even our beloved enormous, made to order bookshelves will have to be cut to fit the walls. As I counted roughly we have around three thousand books. The novels are mostly negligible. Whenever I was truly fascinated with one, I would send it, after both Donnelly and I finished reading it, to either Łucja or Magda, so those standing on the shelves and taking up space are the ones we didn't like very much. Ironic, isn't it? So I'll be able to pack them up and donate to the library. The nonfiction ones are a different matter.

Some, like my beloved *Encyclopedia Britannica*, which was Donnelly's gift to me on our wedding day, I am not going to part with — for sentimental reasons, but also because I, quite often, prefer to look up things in it rather than go to my study, switch on the computer and Google the needed information. Just to hold a tome in my hands, to know that the info I'll find there is 100 percent reliable, gives me such pleasure. Then there are those books that I might want to use when preparing an Elastic Mind theme, and those that we keep to compare their, be it political or economic, prognostications to what happens later in reality. And the art books — how many times we pick one of them to remind ourselves about the beauties that were created in years, in centuries past. So which of them we can part with? Difficult decisions.

I have moved a lot in my life. My parents, sister and I never lived longer than two years in one place until I was sixteen. Quite often, especially during the war, we moved two or three times a year. Either the building had been bombed, or simply for safety reasons because of my father's involvement with the underground. In those days I never allowed myself to be attached to a place or to things. It would have been too painful to lose them so often. Later our moves were simpler, but I still remember the one from Cairo back to Poland when my mother decided, without consulting me, to leave behind my bicycle and tennis racket. Bicycle I can understand now — the heaviness, difficulty to pack, but tennis racket? I never pardoned her. When we returned to Poland in 1951 there were no bicycles or rackets to be bought. Peak of Stalinism. It was difficult to buy food, even simple things like bread, milk or eggs. Meat was a rarity. For all the necessary things we got coupons, and even with them we had to stand hours in long lines. Anyway, there were no tennis courts anywhere near where we lived. But a bicycle? Luckily my uncle Tolek, aunt Helena's husband, loved creating things. He managed to buy at flea markets quite a few different bicycle parts and put them together into an ugly but very serviceable bike for me. As a matter of fact, I never had another bike and I still rode that one in 1992 when Donnelly and I lived in Poland for a year.

People react to the same circumstances in such different ways. So after the war I never attached much importance to possessions. Well, when a bicycle could not be replaced, and being a teenager I desperately wanted to go biking with my new friends, it was a different matter. It took me years to start treating things in a possessive way. Even when I decided to leave my husband, I left with only two suitcases, one of which contained clothes, the other was filled with books and music tapes. Yes, there were no CDs then.

Wojtek's reactions, attitudes were very different. Every single thing he owned was a prized possession, he was constantly afraid that somebody might steal it, damage it in some way. Even when we managed to buy a newly published and hard to get, at that time in Poland, encyclopedia, he forbade the kids to touch it (!) because they were quite sloppy at that time and, horror of horrors, they could dirty the pages with greasy hands. I had to find a way of obtaining another copy. I put it on a shelf in my study and told the children it was theirs to use whenever they felt like it.

So I left him the house, the car, art, furniture, my jewelry, simply everything we had. I thought that because I was reneging on my vow "till death…," the least I could do was not take what he cherished so much. And it was not a problem, I did not miss the fine house we had built, which I designed, organized, lived in. I had the whole world to find a place for myself. That was enough. In 1993 when Donnelly and I were leaving Poland after the year there, Wojtek insisted I take my share of things. Finally, after many conversations, I agreed to take those things that came from my parents and those that were Wojtek's gifts to me. Which were many, so we took a container and filled it with a nineteenth century secretaire he gave me as a birthday gift, an Arabic table I got from my father as a gift in 1949, some pictures, sculptures, an old kilim which came to me from my grandfather, plates of old Meissen china for twenty-four people, etc., etc. That was as I see it now, quite an unusual divorce we had. Normally people fight for possessions. "This is mine!," "Oh, no it is rightly mine"... Here we tried to accommodate each other, he even put in writing that 40 percent of the house belonged to me. Not half because in building it we used the money from selling his Mother's house, in addition to our own savings. All the children were told that in case he dies before me, they are to sell the house and give me my part before dividing the rest between themselves. And it is after my telling him that there would be no property division because I was leaving everything to him. This shows his character very well. A good and honest man, what a pity so difficult to live with. Although, as Donnelly once said, had Wojtek been easier to be with, I would have never met Donnelly and we would not have the happiness we enjoy now. The unexpected consequences.

We often hear about abused women that they lose self-confidence. That they feel they are somehow in the wrong. I suppose it may be true in many cases. In my case, although I shudder at calling myself an abused woman, I also did start at a certain point to feel that all the quarrels, the inability to accommodate to each other's tastes and ways, might be my fault, that I am incapable of living with another person. Yet, after coming to the U.S. in 1987, and after a few months of living with and working for the Franklin family, when I was liked, listened to with interest, I started to feel that after all, I might be easy to live with. And when the second family of my employers, the Oster family, became my dear friends, I knew for sure that my inability to live peacefully with Wojtek did not stem from any fault in my character, rather from an incompatibility of our personalities. Now, after so many years with Donnelly, I see how important the ability to communicate freely with one's partner is. How easy it is to live with a person who listens and hears what is said. And how that quality of his makes me softer, allowing to hear the spoken words and notice those unspoken, but visible if one wants to see, feelings.

## NOVEBER 26, 2010

We had a traditional Thanksgiving feast yesterday. As usual twelve people sat at the table, I roasted an enormous turkey, made a Waldorf salad, roasted yams, green peas, Brussels sprouts, cranberries and freshly baked rolls. Donnelly made two chiffon pumpkin pies. We drank wine, beer, and later on coffee and tea. The mood was fine, conversation lively, everybody seemed to be enjoying themselves. I love those American Thanksgivings. Tonight we'll go to the street lighting ceremony which, here in Ashland, is always quite spectacular. Then the Christmas season is officially open. For me this year it is the season of packing and moving that will open.

## DECEMBER 5, 2010

The loan came through. We'll take possession of the house on the nineteenth, Tim can start working on the twentieth. He is quite happy about it, as he says that will make it possible to have a real Christmas for his family. So many people are hurting financially because of the recession. An enormous number of homes are being foreclosured. People who thought of themselves as owners are becoming homeless, moving back to parents, or sofa surfing with friends. Prices of homes went down drastically, which of course is to our benefit, but still I am very sorry for those in dire straits. Yet, it is one more of the cases of "let's pretend" that is pervasive in the life of Americans.

Everybody says, "I own my house" — well, this is not true in most cases, we just rent-to-own from a bank. The biggest chunk of the price of the house comes not from our pockets but as a loan. It is enough to fall on bad times, to have the bank repossess the property, kick the so-called owners out, and remind them who the real owner is. I have a big problem with this culture of false fronts, the modern equivalent of a "Potemkin village." And yet I am happy that I'll live in a house that will belong jointly to my children, Donnelly and me, and the bank. At least there is that assurance that as long as we pay, we are not going to be evicted. Potemkin or not, it is a little better than a plain rental.

## CHRISTMAS DAY, 2010

Our last Christmas in the Greenmeadows house. The tree is big, a good five feet in diameter, and touches the ceiling which is here quite high by American standards. All our decorations are hung on it. That is going to be another hard decision — we'll have to get rid of some of them, and yet they are all holding memories — some are from Donnelly's childhood, some we bought on memorable trips, some have been made by little Łucja and Oskar when they lived with us in Mt. Shasta. Tomorrow, on Boxing Day, a second day of Christmas for me, as it is celebrated in Europe, several of our friends will come for a festive, traditional Polish brunch. We'll have trout in aspic, four kinds of cold meats — roast pork, smoked ham, turkey and a Polish kind of sausage, that I had sent to me from a Polish shop in New York — vegetable salad, pickled mushrooms and pears, cranberries and hard boiled eggs with curried mayonnaise. It'll be paired with wine or beer, whichever one would prefer. Then, after moving to the living room we'll enjoy tea or coffee with a fruitcake. In Poland we usually do not have a big Christmas dinner, as everybody is so stuffed with food at breakfast time. Debbie and Brian and Chris, Cynthia and Tom, Mary and Sean are going to be with us, so we'll sing a lot of carols.

I know we won't be able to have such parties in the new house. There is so much less space there. It'll be a hassle to get used to only small groups at the table. I like to feed people, I like to see my friends enjoying each other, I like to have animated conversations at a dining table. Good food with plenty of good wine opens everybody up, allows for uncensored opinions, forgetting that mania of "I want to be liked by everybody," which is often inhibiting.

For a long time I had a problem with women here. They seem to be raised to be pleasers. Always agreeing with everybody. I have a problem with them, but they also have a big one with me and my outspokenness. Men usually like me, women often do not. For the first four or five years in America I tried to keep my tongue in check. I wanted to hear what the locals think, how they perceive the world. Later I decided that it was more important for me to have friends than to hold my cards close to my chest. And you can have a friend only when the other person knows you well and still likes you enough for friendship. I am glad I have quite a few such friends I can count on now. Especially the women who not only are able to cope with me, but who have become quite close. It gives me a lot of happiness.

## January 10, 2011

Ten big boxes of books have been delivered to the library, two were sold at a used books store for credit on my future shopping sprees. It was hard. I had to stop myself several times from retrieving a book or two from the already packed boxes.

Now the decisions about furniture, kitchen stuff, cutlery, crockery, clothes. I have already started taking boxes of small stuff down to the new house in my car. As soon as Tim finished the floor we moved the big bookshelf, although we had to cut it down a little. The ceiling in the new house is lower than the one here. The cut piece Tim is going to remake into a TV stand.

Nothing wasted. I hope to have the house organized before we have the last big move of large pieces of furniture — table, beds, armchairs, etc. Donnelly is working all the time, Oskar has school, so I use them only when I need a pair or two of strong arms and healthy backs, but as the new place is five minutes drive from the old, I carry some books several times a day and immediately put them in their places on the bookshelves. It feels good not to pile unopened boxes in the garage.

I bought the first thing for our new house — three little pots of violets to put on my future bathroom's windowsill.

## JANUARY 29, 2011

Yesterday was the big move day. Donnelly rented a truck, Tim, Mariana (our house cleaner) and her boyfriend, our friends Tom and Geoff came to help and we transferred the rest of the stuff to the Brooks Lane house. A big job. Everybody had a part in it. I was impressed with Oskar handling the carrying of the desk and the big sofa upstairs. I am sure it was borderline too much for him, but the manly spirit didn't allow him to show any weakness. Donnelly is astonishingly strong considering all the time he had been spending at work in his study. Obviously the gym keeps him in good shape physically. I too ran up and down the stairs multiple times. Good that I had prepared the house for the moving day and preplanned how everything and everybody would work, so when we finished the house looked lived in, and we could sleep in our properly made beds, in well appointed bedrooms.

While we were working, a nice woman stopped by and asked me what our plans were for dinner. I was very surprised, and told her that we had no plans whatsoever, to which she said: "Come and have dinner with us, we live down the street." Well, I was stunned with her kindness, told her we would be way too tired to be good company, but thanked her very much. She then said: "I understand, but please do not think about any preparations, I will bring a dinner to you." Which she did. As soon as we finished and Donnelly took back the truck, she brought a tray filled with food and drink. Even desert was there. What lovely neighbors we are going to have! Her name is JoAnn. I am looking forward to getting to know her better. Such a good beginning of a new chapter of our lives.

## FEBRUARY 5, 2011

Pride goes before the fall. How true! I was so proud that I still could be a super woman, packing, moving carrying, running up the stairs, never complaining. Ha! On the second of February I had my yearly check up at the cardiologist. Dr. Dauterman, who in December 2009 put the stent in my heart, listened carefully to its beatings, took an EKG, talked to me, and then told me he needed to put me in the hospital and give me some more serious testing. And it's pretty urgent, he said. He put me in a wheelchair and pushed it, right away through the grounds separating cardiology offices and the hospital. The doctor, a specialist, pushing a wheelchair himself! That did frighten me. They gave me an angiogram which showed that the stent is still fine, and no new blockages were formed, then a USG, which told them that one of my valves is not functioning 100 percent. With it not doing its job properly and the amount of work I made my body do, the result was not good. They kept me under observation for two days, then Dr. Dauterman gave me a lecture how I should behave in the future if I don't want to have another surgery, and allowed me to go home on the condition that I take life very slowly in the next week or two. I promised, and now, lying comfortably on my sofa I do "take it easy." The silver lining is that I have now lots of time to read which I was not able to do for quite some time.

## February 7, 2011

I am rereading Ezra Pound's *ABC of Reading* and marveling at how he managed to put so much meaning in such short paragraphs. Well, he himself wrote that ambitious fiction and poetry are "language charged with meaning to the utmost possible degree."

When I was in school in Cairo, the Saint Clare School for Girls, I had a magnificent English teacher, a nun, Sister Barbara, who always taught us that the shorter our writing is the better. She used to say, "Language is for communication so try to communicate in as succinct a manner as you can. Just remember that it also has to be beautiful." And here in Pound's book I find him saying, "One definition of beauty is aptness to purpose." And Sister Barbara's "to be short, full of meaning and beautiful" I think, are other words for "aptness to purpose." It surprised me when I went to a Polish high school upon our return to Warsaw that my Polish teacher made fun of me when I turned in my first written paper. "What is this? Two pages? You are lazy. Go and rewrite it, I expect at least four pages!" And this before she read what I wrote. Of course I rewrote it by adding meaningless clichés, by padding it with redundant descriptions. After all I had to have a good grade. I never respected this teacher afterwards, and in my own writing I always tried to be very succinct. It was valued by my editors at the newspapers that I wrote for later on. So there.

Another piece of Ezra Pound that I find fascinating is his division of poetry into: 1) melopoeia — poetry as music; 2) phanopoeia — poetry as picture; 3) logopoeia — poetry as idea or argument. I love reading poems aloud to hear their melody and rhythm. I admire the expressions used for descriptions, especially of nature, and I am pulled into the poems that give us an idea, an original idea that makes me think, or even rethink my own views. He also says, "…verse should be as well written, as exact and natural seeming as prose."

And then I take *The New Yorker* and try to read the poems

they decide are good enough for printing and most of the time I find none of the above in them. Why does anybody consider that medley of mindless clichés, of words put together without any sense or beauty to be poetry? Originality for originality's sake? Modern? Just because nobody wrote such drivel before? Then I take books by my beloved David Whyte, Sharon Olds, Leonard Cohen, Wisława Szymborska and several other contemporary poets and I immerse myself in the feelings they evoke in me, and am happy that these poets exist and keep writing. I am, for instance, in love with one of the poems by David Whyte. It is called "Sligo Glen" and consists of two parts. The first, "Walking into Silence," speaks of getting into a place of "…exuberant exclusion of human sound." The second, "Walking out of Silence," takes us back to hearing "…the sound of the road and the machines and the blank cries of everyday commerce…." Then come the words that are so very important to me:

> *"…and then you could practice*
> *leaving and*
> *returning in your own body,*
> *through your own breath,*
> *inward and outward,*
> *descending and*
> *entering and reentering the silence*
> *and shelter of your own*
> *narrow valley of aloneness,*
> *from interiority*
> *to conversation*
> *and back."*

When I read those words for the first time, I realized that all my life I tried to be able to do exactly this entering into and exiting out of my inner silence. Now when I read it again and again it tells me that I am not alone in my pursuit of this inner peace. That it's all right to need to withdraw from "everyday commerce." And the poem does so with a beauty that never gets stale, no matter how many times I read it.

I have found today, in looking through my old papers, a poem that I have no memory of writing, yet when I went to my books, surfed the internet, asked people, I could not find it anywhere. It seems to be too good to be mine. Yet if I cannot find it anywhere should I assume I did write it? The more so that it is crossed out and corrected several times. I'll risk it. Here it is:

> *A stranger to myself, distrustful —*
> *Will the tongue say*
> *What the head thinks*
> *Will my feet take me where the heart pulls,*
> *I stand in front of a mirror.*
> *I don't know this lady.*
> *Mine until not long ago*
> *Today somebody else's face.*
> *Yesteryears' hands agile, dancing feet,*
> *Today only memories*
> *Enliven my day.*

I am often afraid of rejecting something just because I am incapable of understanding. There is this way of receiving something as art only if we are ready, prepared by our previously being exposed to art that was in a certain way leading to the new. We know from history that many artists, musicians, writers were at first rejected and ridiculed because they were "before their time" as the saying goes. The impressionists, Stravinsky, Kafka, James Joyce, Ibsen, to name just a few. So who am I to say that what others consider to be poetry — isn't? What qualifications do I have to reject rap as music? Why do I dare to say that an untouched-by-paint piece of canvas, a kitchen gadget enclosed in a see-through box, have nothing to do with art? Alyson Renwick, an art teacher at the Ollie classes whose knowledge of art and quick wit I like so much that I sometimes think I could listen to her every day, tells me that if something is created honestly, not because the creator does it for money or fame, it is art whether we like it or not. But then weren't Michelangelo, Caravaggio, Raphael painting what they were told to paint by their sponsors — popes, princes etc.? As far as I know, it was only in the late nineteenth century that artists started to create what they wanted to create, and try to find customers afterwards. And does that mean that if some lady is honestly moved to paint cute little kittens playing with balls of yarn — we should consider it art? On the same level as "Guernica"?

Too many unanswerable questions. So I like to read those who are historically accepted as great and who thought the way I do now. That validates my opinions, gives me courage to form my own judgments and not to feel too much of a dunce. Yet I always try to read also the ones I do not readily understand and try not to reject them on first approach. Just to be on the safe side. Just so I do not miss something big.

## A FEW DAYS LATER

See what happens when I am bedridden? Yesterday I had picked up a book I was sure I had never read before, yet after perusing the first chapter I not only realized I had read it at some time past, but also I remembered the plot and that I didn't like it very much and why. And then a thought came — if I forget what I read, is the time spent with the book a wasted time? And I realized that no, I cannot think of it as wasted. Even if the book seems to be forgotten, even if I have no conscious memory of what I read, it has lodged itself somewhere in my brain, or it wouldn't have come back so easily. I see also a second reason why the time hasn't been wasted — while I was immersing myself in the text, in that time long ago, it was influencing me. It was changing some of my attitudes, creating questions, the answers to which I later pursued, it was giving me new words, or reminding me of words I knew, but hadn't used for some time. I suppose that is why I go on reading such diverse books. Great literature, or just mysteries, history, economy, politics or religious debates. I feel this insatiable thirst to constantly expand my brain. Although it hit me now, that barring senility this brain is going to grow, grow, grow and then within a second it will die, and a short time afterwards it'll disintegrate, become a rotting piece of proteins, a nothing. Just think how many memories, experiences, feelings vanish from this earth every second. Well, so be it, but for now I want more, more, more…

## MARCH 2011

Well, I got more. The only minus is, it was more of pain and trouble. Kidney stones. Visits to the emergency, doctors, crushing the stones, days of misery. Not exactly what I had in mind when I asked for "more." This time I didn't even have the strength to read or think. We are so dependent on our health, to say nothing about the world in general, or weather in particular. Funny? Sometimes. And at other times depressing.

There is also a new development with Oskar's school. His counselor, in looking through Oskar's school reports from the school in Warsaw (it was an American School with an International Baccalaureate curriculum) saw that the boy could graduate at the end of his junior year if he took a senior course of English online, managed to do his senior project, and maintained his grades. Oskar got very excited, immediately went online, registered for a course at the University of Utah, and sat down to hard work. He also signed up for classes preparing for SAT (Scholastic Assessment Test). This way he'll gain one year, and we will gain our freedom one year earlier than we thought we would. Now comes the real test for him. Can he work that hard? We are going to help in any way we can. Donnelly started to check which good colleges will still accept applications.

## JUNE 5, 2011

So Oskar has shown us, and most importantly himself, what he is capable of. The day before yesterday he graduated from high school. One year early. With pretty good grades. He has been accepted to college — Wagner College on Staten Island, New York, just as he had wanted. The celebration in Lithia Park was magnificent. Seeing him in the cap and gown was very moving. I had tears in my eyes, a normal grandma reaction I suppose. We are so proud of him. He showed that if he wants something he can forget watching films way into the night, drinking with his friends, doing all the stupid things young boys love to do. It was very impressive to watch how he managed his time and achieved everything he wanted to achieve. Yesterday we had a party for him. All our friends came, he got a ton of gifts, then went out to be with his friends. Next week he leaves for home. And I am regaining my study! Maybe I'll manage to write more often.

## JUNE 25, 2011

Having my study back, having much less work is paying dividends — I have read several fascinating articles and two books, *The Astonishing Hypothesis: The Scientific Search for the Soul* by Francis Crick and *Incognito* by David Eagleman. Francis Crick was an English molecular biologist, biophysicist and neuroscientist. In 1953 he co-discovered the structure of the DNA molecule, together with James Watson. He won the Nobel Prize for Physiology and Medicine, and in 1994 he published a book titled *The Astonishing Hypothesis* in which he says that a person's identity, joy, ambition, sorrow, memory, free will are nothing more than the result of actions of nerve cells and their interconnections. In other words, there is no immaterial soul — all our thoughts, feelings are created through chemical or purely physical actions.

David Eagleman, a neuroscientist and in my opinion a genius of clarification, starts with a citation from Pink Floyd's song, "There is someone in my head and it's not me." Although the whole book is about brain, how it works, how its physicality affects all our thoughts and feelings, it leaves a slight doubt about whether there is nothing more. There is always this uncertainty about how our brain conceives of a thought, idea, feeling, even before we are conscious that we want to think about it. All the seemingly automatic ways our brains work. He calls it "brain on automatic pilot."

There had always been in me this feeling of uncertainty as to whether we know everything about the world, and especially about humans, that there is to be known. And I don't mean in the realm of science as we have it now. Of course we haven't reached the limits. What I want to say is — are there parts of us, of our world, that we have no idea exist and thus we cannot formulate questions to which research would give answers? A hundred years ago, we didn't know about the existence of TV waves. Two hundred years ago we had no idea about x-rays and a possibility of actually seeing our bones without cutting the flesh. It is only in discovering how something we are conscious of works, that we see some unknown-up-to-now phenomenon, which then we start researching. We have all learned in school (or so I hope) about Galvani dissecting a frog and discovering bioelectricity, or Maria Curie Skłodowska who discovered radium and polonium, and in the process found many new things about radioactivity. What she didn't expect were the results of being radiated and she died a painful death of aplastic anemia, after having worked on, and even carrying in her pockets, radium without any measures of safety. All those discoveries led to deep research into previously unknown fields. Marie Curie directed the first world studies into the possibility of killing tumors with radiation. Galvani's

discovery led Alesandro Volta to build an early electric battery.
It seems that in our tackling the world of science we can build only on already known foundations. Yes, there were throughout history some singular geniuses who were able to leap forward because of their superior imagination. Two come to mind immediately — Leonardo Da Vinci, with his idea of a flying machine, and Albert Einstein. In the case of Da Vinci there were no similarly gifted peers to follow and develop his ideas. Einstein was luckier — after some strong opposition, quite a few mathematicians and physicists started working with and achieving success in his, at first considered to be ridiculous, pronouncements.

Eagleman doesn't go into totally new fields. He bases his book on well-researched brain studies and speaks very convincingly about how a tumor in the brain can change our character, how a peaceful, happy person can become a violent murderer, yet after the tumor is removed the patient goes back to his previous personality. Just think what this might mean for the justice system. Can we in good faith convict as a murderer somebody who was changed by a tumor? On the whole, his book opens us up to so many new realizations. In light of the nearly constant advancement of knowledge, we need to continually reevaluate what we think is true.

The theologian Mascall wrote that the biggest difficulty people experience today is in convincing themselves that they have a special assigned status in the universe. The more we know, the more difficult such a conviction or belief becomes, doesn't it?

In May I decided to title the July meeting of Elastic Mind "The Philosophical Search for Soul." Now I think I'll make the August meeting about how scientists seek the answer to this always bewildering question about whether the soul exists. I'll suggest people read Eagleman's *Incognito* and maybe *Human* by Michael Gazzaniga, which is another engrossing book about the brain and what makes us human. The discussion should be fascinating. I will love to hear what others think about it all.

## AUGUST 2011

Yes, both meetings were everything I hoped for. Discussions were lively and learned. People were so intent on talking and listening that after both meetings ended, we went to Pasta Piatti, a local Italian restaurant, for lunch and a continuation of conversation about "soul." We talked about an article, brought to the meeting by Jerry Simon, about an Australian Nobel Prize winner, neurophysiologist, John Eccles who believes in the existence of "vis externa," what others call the soul. He asks important questions: What makes the brain work? How does the brain think without a person's command to do so, and even how is the command initiated? Questions that have bewildered people for ages. Questions that contemporary scientists try to answer, but the more they know, the more there is to be answered. The fact that Eccles was such an accomplished researcher makes it rather impossible to outright reject his postulations.

Well, what is left to us laics is to wait for more and more research and not to become too sure too early. I am fascinated with the need of so many people to believe in the existence of an immortal soul. Yes, I know, if the core of what we are is immortal, then, whether we believe in heaven and hell, or not, we still do not have to fear death. If the soul is eternal then death is not the end, it is just a transition. But a transition of what and to what? If the "soul" is just some energy that powers the activity of our brains, then that would suggest that no memories, no experiences are transitioned to whatever is happening with the "soul" next. Unless we still know so little about energy, that we cannot even imagine that it is capable of storing memory. And if the "soul" is reincarnated, as many believe, then why talk about transition if we have no indication of memory of our soul's previous lives. My thinking leads me to a conclusion that as there is no scientific proof of any immaterial part of life, we still should not reject a possibility of its existence, we should just wait for more and more scientific revelations. Be open to all eventualities.

Meetings like these two make me so happy.

## SEPTEMBER 2, 2011

After a long telephone conversation with Łucja, I began to think about why I am not a feminist. Why the feminism of today angers me. The short and obvious to me answer is that in my opinion both sexes, although physically not equal, should have the same opportunities, same rights, same treatment, except for the period of pregnancy and lactation during which a woman should be protected. After all, the safety and health of mothers and babies is in our interest, as a nation and as a species.

And here is something that I feel very strongly about — the attitude of politicians and the voting population in general, that can be simplified as caring only about short term, about the near future, the next election. Yet so many political decisions, although favorable in the short run, are disastrous in the longer time span. Yes, it is good for businesses, especially small businesses, not to give a maternity leave to mothers, or give them just a few days, a couple of weeks.

Yet in the long run, looking at it from the point of view of the whole country, it is a disaster for which we pay a very high price. Both financially and morally. Financially because we have such a big percentage of developmentally harmed children, and later on, such a high prison population. Morally because children raised in day care, in preschool, that are often run by inadequately educated people, do not develop the kids' brains to their full potential, to say nothing about the possibility of strong family attachments, or family values. So much in the development of a person happens in the first two, three years of life, when a child learns about life through imitation.

Is the difference in the length and availability of maternity leave between European countries and the U.S. part of the reason for the enormous difference in the prison population in them? That also brings to mind the percentage of children born to addicted parents. As statistics show us there is a baby addicted to opiates born every hour in the States. All those children most probably would not benefit with a longer stay with their mothers. But with free health care for pregnant women, with free rehabilitation centers for those women, that problem would be much lessened, although probably not totally erased. Yet the most dangerous opiate pain killers have to be prescribed by doctors. So? Is there a way to influence the medical practitioners to give those medications only in really dramatic situations? How come thousands of generations lived without them? And then the most often heard argument is that small business owners cannot afford to pay for maternity leave, yet how come countries like Germany, Switzerland, Sweden or Poland for that matter, not only can afford such leaves, but also have thriving economies. Well, now that I feel American it pains me very much to see this damaging the future of our nation.

But, *revenon a nos moutons*, as the French say. Let's go back to our feminist argument. Most of the feminists I know or read about behave as if a woman is something very special and a man is the enemy. A woman goddess. Long ago it was the male who created the idea of a goddess, a sex goddess. Like Marylin Monroe. Now that goddess is the women's creation. Meaning what? A perfection? An untouchable, indestructible being? Somebody to adore and obey? I can't stand it. Maybe because in my long life I have known too many women who were ignorant, outright stupid, irresponsible. Same as men. I remember during the 2008 primary between Hillary Clinton and Barack Obama hearing from women around me that they voted for Hillary, in her quest for presidency, because she was a woman. And it didn't matter what she stood for. The voters might not know and might not care what the candidate professes about her attitude to the world problems, or even to our own country's problems — the only important thing seems to be that she is a woman, and it is high time to have a woman as president.

But, I am sorry to say, I do not think this is the only reason I am so disgusted with feminists. The deep down foundation of my feeling might be that I was always closer to men in my life than to women. As a young girl, a young woman, I never had a real girlfriend. By real I mean the person to whom I would confide my innermost feelings, with whom I would like to spend most of my free time, whose opinion about boys, fashion, likes and dislikes would be important to me. My friends were always boys, later on men. Of course it all started with my father. Then came Wojtek, then Donnelly. The three important men in my life. Very different men and their influences on me were also very different.

## A FEW DAYS LATER

My father was of course the one who formed the basic me. After all, I grew up with him. He was my love, my idol, my friend. I wanted to imitate him in so many ways. I learned to look at the world and form my opinions like he did.

My mother, whom I never wanted to imitate, was in her youth quite a beautiful woman with a softness, an elegance deeper than just the clothes she used to wear. An educated woman, an accomplished equestrian, yet she lacked self-assurance. She tried to please everybody around her, even her little daughter. It must have been very difficult to do the latter. I was extremely stubborn and much stronger than her. Early, very early as a child I learned that Daddy was somebody to admire, respect, love and listen to. Mommy on the other hand didn't have to be obeyed at all — what for? With her I was always the pushy me, with her I did what I wanted to do and she acquiesced, and instead of loving her for that, I held her in contempt, never respected her. Maybe I didn't feel safe with somebody I considered weaker than me? If she obeyed my wishes, she would obey anybody's wishes. And then there was that problem with her inability to see things as they were. She was often creating her own imaginary world.

It is hard to know why I did not like her very much. The more so that from time to time she really went to bat for me. Once, it was in 1941 I think, my mother, sister and I were spending vacation time in a rented apartment in Otwock (Otfotsk) when late one evening I came down with a very high fever and had difficulty breathing. It was way past the curfew imposed by the Germans. If they saw anybody in the streets after that time they shot without asking for a reason. A doctor lived a few blocks from us. To get to him my mother went through our garden, climbed over a fence, ran through another garden, climbed over another fence and so on, risking being seen only when she had to run across a street, until she got to the doctor's house. On hearing my symptoms, the doctor decided it could be diphtheria. Luckily he had the needed antitoxin and agreed to see me, retracing my mother's route through backyards and over fences. I was saved from an illness that in those days was nearly always fatal.

In my case it had damaged my heart to a certain degree, so the doctor decided I had to convalesce without much movement. I spent quite a long time in a deck chair out in the garden wrapped nicely in a blanket. The kids from the neighborhood were coming daily to play by the side of my chair, and one of the little boys became quite a sensation with all of us, when we discovered that, because of some medications that he had to take, he would piss one day red, and the next day blue. We always wanted him to piss near us so that we could see this fascinating event.

Yet, instead of being grateful for my mother's care, I hated her nervousness. For instance, when travelling, I tried to stand away from her at railway stations or airports so that nobody would know that I was with this visibly nervous woman who constantly counted the luggage, and was very upset by my not being in the closest proximity.

With my father it was only when he became very old, disillusioned, bitter, that I saw where strict realism leads us. Yet throughout my formative years I trusted him totally. Although I knew well he wasn't perfect. He was a heavy drinker, a womanizer, idolized Winston Churchill, whom I could not pardon since he, together with president Roosevelt, sold out Poland to Stalin, and last, but not least, my father considered people en masse to be poor idiots. But he allowed me to have my own opinions and to argue with him about them, while at the same time being absolutely immovable if he considered something important enough. Which meant big things like his involvement in the war, but also small ones like teaching his daughter responsibility. Example — my sixteenth birthday party. He allowed me to invite whomever I wanted, to plan the food, the dancing, choose music, dimmed lights, etc. The only thing I had to agree with was his imposing the time limit. It was to end at ten o'clock. Fine. I did promise ten was the limit. Yet when ten came we were all in such a good mood, the dancing was enchanting, the feel of boys' arms around our bodies, the rhythm, the nascent romantic feeling... And then my father appeared in the door, beckoned me to join him and reminded me of the promise. He told me we are allowed to dance to the end of the running melody, and then I had to tell everybody that it was the end of the party. I returned to the dance floor. The music ran out. The next melody started, I went on dancing... My father calmly came into the room, went to the record player, switched it off, and started to put the room in order. I was so humiliated! I hated him, I again hated him.

Well, the guests had to leave and I went to my room where I burst out in tears. He came in and told me to consider that this whole humiliation was of my own choice. An agreement is an agreement. A promise has to be kept. He kissed me good night and left the room. That was it. No discussion.

I remember one day when we talked about sexual infidelities, he told me that he pities the man who has only one woman. "He is," he said, "like that farmer who ploughs his one field, no matter how big, but always the same, and doesn't know of the existence of so many other fields, soils, weathers, views." To which I responded, "yes, but your farmer who leaves his one field for another doesn't know about the seasonal changes, the changes in light, in the birds that accompany him while he works, about how different the forest by the side of his plot is in spring or summer or winter." "Yes," he said, "you have something here, but what about the farmer who leaves his field after many seasons?" Well, I suppose that's exactly what I have done with my life.

By the time I was big enough to be critical about his views, he was, as I said before, a bitterly disappointed man. Before the war he was an idealist, believing in honesty and goodness at the core of people. After the war, after the incarceration by the Soviets, after Poland was again not free and his idealized Churchill and Roosevelt had as good as given away Polish freedom, he was a very unhappy man. I know that having me to talk to, to influence, to build up was important to him. It gave him a purpose in life. My mother was not the partner he needed. Her reaction to all the terrible things happening to the country in general and to her in particular, was a flight into an imaginary world. She was a good, honest woman and firmly believed that everybody was like her, refusing to accept facts that could contradict this belief and fleeing into the fictional world of novels. She read profusely, but only books divorced from the realities of the contemporary world. Agatha Christie,

John Galsworthy, Romain Rolland were her companions of preference.

My sister was too sickly to keep up with him. I was, most of the time, healthy, strong, and curious about everything in the world. Just what he needed. I internalized this need of his to create order and beauty around us. His attitude towards food, cooking, feeding others became mine. My mother couldn't care less about order and she was a terrible cook. It was my father who hung pictures on our walls, who tended to potted plants embellishing our apartments, who made all the good dishes and tried to get me interested in cooking, tried to make me help him in the kitchen. Sorry to say without any visible result at that time.

Only when already married did I discover how lovely my man was after a good meal, and how his mood changed to nasty when hungry or dissatisfied with his food. Seeing this I started to pay attention to what we ate. Of course, at first it was not easy. I remember several disasters with salting, frying, not knowing which cuts of meat to use for what dish, etc. But very soon I found the pleasure in creating something that was so quickly praised as success, and that also gave me such pleasure in eating. My father's example became a strong incentive to go on exploring, then inventing combinations of tastes, textures, even colors in what I was serving. It came very handy when I started to work as a housekeeper. My employers loved my food. To the point that when, still working for Howard Franklin, I wanted to invite Donnelly to dinner, Howard and a friend of his asked me if I wanted Donnelly to marry me, because if yes, then I should serve — and here the gentlemen disagreed — Howard said I should cook beef stew with Polish style dumplings, whereas Chris maintained that it should be pork chops with potatoes and cabbage. Well, I did not want to remarry, I do not remember what I served, yet Donnelly and I married and he loves my cooking.

Well, back to the men influencing me. When I was twenty, I met Wojtek. He had my father's hunger for knowledge, curiosity, and a very good encyclopedic memory. Even at his young age of twenty-two when I met him, he was impressively well educated. His past was very different from mine. He lost his father in 1939. In one of the battles with the invading Germans his father Wacław Kubicki was taken prisoner and died in a POW camp. Wojtek was five in 1939. Up to that time his parents were relatively well off, his father, a brilliant chemist, was named the CEO of a big newly built chemical factory producing ammunition for the army. His mother, a stay-at-home mom, had a little summer house in Podkowa Leśna, a small town fifteen miles from Warsaw. They owned an apartment in the city for the winter.

Stanisława, the mother, and little Wojtek were spending their summer in the vacation house when the war started. The place was rather primitive — two rooms and a glassed in verandah, but without plumbing and with the kitchen located in a separate building in the garden, so as not to annoy the masters with the cooking smells. The kitchen was well equipped and had a tiny bedroom for the servant. The garden was Stanisława's hobby and joy. Long before the whole idea of eating local and organic, she was happy being able to feed her only son with the produce from her own garden. It had everything — potatoes, vegetables, a little orchard and lots of herbs. But, of course, all the beautiful furniture was in Warsaw, not there. And when they spent the summer days in Podkowa they had only summer clothes with them. Basic jewelry, some money, maybe a sweater and a light jacket for cooler days. She was an elegant woman, so she had there one good dress and a fur jacket for cool evenings when she would go to a theater.

As it happened, one of the first bombs that fell on Warsaw destroyed their apartment in the city. Everything in it was lost. Germans closed the banks. Wojtek and his mother were left penniless, without winter clothes, without heavy shoes, in a house not prepared for winter.

Stanisława had no profession, yet, she had all those vegetables and acquired some hens and rabbits, so by being frugal they didn't starve. For wood to make fire in tile stoves in the two rooms of the house she would take Wojtek to the nearby forest where she would cut a small tree or two and then they would drag it two or three miles back home. The only problem was — there was a curfew, so if they were caught they would have been shot. And as it was stealing the wood, they could not do it during the day. What's more, she had to choose rainy or snow storm nights because in bad weather the Germans didn't like to patrol. After all they were human, weren't they? Wojtek told me about his fear on those nights. He remembered how difficult it was to drag the heavy trees, and how, although it was easier to pull them on snow, on snowy nights while his mother pulled the trees he had to run behind with a branch smoothing the path so that nobody would see the track that the tree was making. After the war ended, when he was barely twelve, he started to go to the train station to earn some money by unloading the cars. He had his first clothes in a proper size then — previously they were always way too small or too big when somebody took pity on him and gave him some discards. He worked through his high school years, he worked through university. Luckily with the soviet-style socialism came free health care and free higher education. He also started to get some monthly payments as a war orphan.

All that time, I had my father to take care of us and love us. And although we were quite often hungry, although the food was terrible and not very nourishing, I didn't have to worry where my next meal was going to come from or if at all. And after the war, as I wrote before, I had several years of plenty. Great places to stay or live, fantastic food either at home or in fine restaurants, clothes of good quality and of my own choice.

Travelling, meeting interesting people, learning languages. Even when we came back from Egypt in the years of Stalinism, in the years of empty shops and fearful people, we still had some savings from those times when my father was working. And after 1956, when life in Poland became more normal, my father got a good job and once again we lived well.

When Wojtek and I met, in 1956, he was an elegant young man, working in the best newspaper and taking very good care of his mother. Finally, Stanisława could relax, although they could not change the place they lived in. The housing situation in the country was terrible. So much had been destroyed during the war. Right after it ended people felt lucky if a family had a room to themselves. The government was building full speed, often using bricks salvaged from ruins, creating big apartment buildings in the cheapest way they could, just to give shelter to the homeless. So Wojtek and his mother stayed in the little house. Happy that they had it.

It was surprising how well-mannered he was. Obviously his mother, even over a plate of potatoes for dinner, paid attention and taught him good table manners. And how after years of wearing bad clothes he knew how to move unselfconsciously and elegantly still baffles me. Genes? Anyway, when we met we discovered so many similarities in our world views, ambitions, dreams and ways we planned to fulfill them. I was studying at the Warsaw Polytechnic to become an electrical engineer and I started to realize, that although the studies were fascinating — I loved math, physics, and discovering how the physical world around me worked, yet the work of an engineer didn't appeal to me at all. I got to understand this during summer practices at electric plants and factories producing electrical machinery. I also realized that had I wanted to stay in the academic world of Polytechnic, I would have to spend most of my time on my profession, whereas I loved theater, concerts, travels, reading literature and not so much books about engineering. Wojtek studied at the Warsaw University — in the school of economics and the school of journalism. Just to spend more time with him I began to accompany him to his lectures. In the school of economics he had lectures and seminars in history, geography, law, logic, math, philosophy and, of course, economics. At that time, we as a country were opening to western thought, which meant that there were lectures in socialist economy, but also in capitalistic system. My God, what riches of knowledge. What fantastic professors. I became fascinated, left my studies at the Polytechnic in the middle of the third year and enrolled at Warsaw University. Wojtek also convinced his editors at the newspaper that they needed a weekly article about what was happening in technology in America. And what better way than employing a woman he knows who is fluent in several languages and in technical matters. Thus, I became also an employee of his newspaper.

Life seemed to be offering us all the possibilities to achieve what we wanted. Studying together, working together was close to paradise. But Wojtek had to keep his mother fed, clothed and warm, and though my father was working after nearly five years of unemployment (after all he was the enemy of the people, wasn't he? A prewar officer, landowner, oh my, what could be worse?), yet the family needs were great so we were only too happy that I could take care of my own needs.

Late 1950s, the situation with living space still tight, my parents, sister, grandmother and I lived in a three room apartment. There was a divan in the living room which served as my parents' bed at night, another one in the dining room, that one was for grandma, the third room was my sister's and mine. No possibility to get a husband to move in. We became lovers. Luckily, our newspaper needed us to travel, so hotels were our only possibility to be really alone, together. Then Pluski, a rented room at a farmer's house, spending days on the lake, evenings writing or studying.

In summer of 1958, my grandmother, whom I loved very much, died. My sister moved out of my room, I could get married. Talk about ambivalent feelings! I grieved and was happy at the same time. As soon as we were able to organize things we had a wedding. Tenth of January 1959. The day before we had a big snowstorm, the night sky had cleared out, freezing temperatures accompanied it, so our Big Day was exceptionally beautiful. Blue sky, sunshine, everything around white, all the little twigs on trees were covered with rime glistening as if the branches were covered with jewels. Neither Wojtek nor I were church goers, so we were married in the local city hall. The official who pronounced us husband and wife gave a little speech wishing us a life as beautiful as the day was. The two of us plus our families and two friends who were to be our witnesses walked to the hall, and then back to the house where my father, the best cook in the family, prepared a feast. Both my parents loved Wojtek, my father even insisted that Wojtek married me just so that he could have him as a father-in-law.

My mother-in-law's attitude was, sorry to say, different. She seemed to like me, yet as she later told me, our wedding day was the biggest tragedy of her life. She also told her son that unless we had a church wedding she'd refuse to take any money from him. Some blackmail, we could not say no, as she didn't have any means to live on without Wojtek's support. So, okay, we went to the local priest, he agreed to marry us, but told us we had to present a paper stating that we did confess our sins. We both went to Warsaw, found a church where there were priests in confessionals and tried to do what was needed. I told my confessor the whole story and asked could he please give me such a report. He was very understanding, talked to me about the value of faith, and asked me to promise that I would consider coming back into the fold, and that I would not stop my children from attending religious classes if they ever would want to. I did promise, and in the years to come fulfilled my promise. Wojtek was not as lucky. The first man of God didn't want to hear about a confession certificate without actual confession and a follow up of coming to church. The second one was more amenable, but asked for Wojtek to confess his sins. One of the questions he posed was: Did you have sex with your fiancé? Yes, Wojtek answered truthfully. To which his confessor came up with: "Be sorry!" And Wojtek couldn't stop himself from saying: "If I were, I wouldn't want to marry her!" That was another complete failure. Finally, a third one was magnanimous and gave him the needed piece of paper. We did marry in church, in a private ceremony, with only my mother-in-law present. Talk about hypocrisy. What is the worth of doing it in "front of God" in whom we do not believe? Well, she was satisfied. And I, personally, was very sorry for her. That also explains, I suppose, why I never could like or respect her. Although I was "a good daughter-in-law." Her words. When later on she was dying of liver cancer I took care of her and she called me her angel.

So, as I said, I didn't like her very much, yet I learned a lot from her. The first and most important trait I wanted to emulate was getting dressed right away after rising from bed and washing. She used her dressing gown only to go to the bathroom. That was so different from my mother who sat in her dressing gown, drinking strong tea, smoking cigarettes and reading murder mysteries, until early afternoon when she would jump out of her armchair with, "Oh my God, look at the time, Father is going to be home soon." Then it was a rush to make the bed, do some slapdash cleaning of the house, washing the dishes, etc. As a matter of fact, the normal state of the dishes in our home was dirty in the sink. A big pile. If I wanted to have some food in the middle of the day I would dig out a plate, wash it, use it, leave it on top of the others in the sink. My father was very tidy, so she really tried to wash them before he came, but often did not succeed.

Stanisława was very much against armchairs. "They make you lazy," she would say. Well, both Wojtek and I were all for having them. When you read a lot, when you spend time just sitting and talking, there is nothing as good as a fine upholstered armchair. But her attitude about not wasting time on just plain lazy lolling around got me to thinking and moving more than I previously used to.

I think that Wojtek, who loved his mother very much, found in me quite a few of her characteristics plus so many of those that he missed in his life with her. He idolized me. It was very difficult for me, as I had to constantly try to live up to that image of me that he had. I had to? Well, when I was meeting his expectations he was so happy, so loving, so nice to be with. When, on the other hand, I fell short, he would become quite unpleasant. So, I had to, you see? And to a certain degree it served me well. I worked hard, I kept looking at life in a sunny way, I read a lot of valuable books, so that he would admire my intelligence and so that I was always up on world events, on science, on art. How did I manage? Today when I look at those years I do not understand how I could have managed. Maybe I was a genius as he maintained. It was much later, as I already wrote, that trying to be that "genius" became too difficult, too limiting. I once told him how it made me feel, hoped for him to understand. I remember I said that I am that bush trying to grow towards the sun, with the wind, spreading my branches whichever way they want to grow and no matter how it looks. And he is the gardener with big clippers, cutting me to shape, to a beautiful shape, snipping off any twig which loves to dance in the breeze. I needed to be free, he needed me to be beautiful and great. It couldn't work. It didn't. After thirty years of trying. That's when the third man in my life entered. He gave me freedom, he gave me understanding. For the first time in my grown-up life I was, I am able to show my weaknesses. For the first time since Father, I am loved for who I am. It was one of my conditions I made clear to Donnelly when I agreed to marry him — that he will never put me on a pedestal. No more thinking of me as ideal. I want to have freedom of making mistakes. I have it. And I have something else that I never knew that I missed — the tenderness. Donnelly changed the fighter in me into a calm, peaceful woman. I don't have to fight anymore. Everything can be discussed, both sides rethink their attitudes, neither side is afraid of compromise. As I put it in one of my poems, there is "submission that doesn't mean defeat." Part of it may be because we are so different. There is no, or hardly any, competing. He is an artist not very interested in the small particulars of daily life. I am much more down to earth, to the nitty-gritty of our days. He is definitely a people person. He needs to do things with others, be among others. I am a mixture of introverted loner and joyful extrovert. But the latter occupies no more than 10 or at best 20 percent of my personality. I was always happiest when alone. I liked to joke that when alone I am in the company of an intelligent and interesting woman. Maybe it's not a joke, after all. Yet from time to time I need, I enjoy being with other people. Thus my involvement with the Elastic Mind group, my many friends and dinners with them. But it is always my choice of how much, how often etc. In my past life with Wojtek and the children, I had periods of intense need to be alone. Luckily, Wojtek understood it and would take the kids biking or skiing so that I could spend some time in the peace of an empty house. With Donnelly I do not feel that need. I do not feel any pressure from him. Life became so easy.

Yet it boggles my mind how we have come to this point of compatibility. He was born into a middle income family of intelligent, well-educated people. His father was the first to graduate from college in his family, his mother left college after three years to get married. They started from very little financially, they achieved a nice, comfortable situation. Never rich, but also never hurting for money. Donnelly's childhood was peaceful in a happy home of loving parents. He had two sisters — one his twin and the other two years younger. At the age of seven he started to sing in a boys' choir. So — peace, comfort, good schools, choir, church, enough food and southern California sun. The choir he sang in was so well known and respected that it was employed in singing for several Hollywood films and Capital Records albums, to the point that Donnelly had enough money saved to pay a big chunk of his college expenses. Occidental College, a fraternity, his own car, summer jobs in the mountains above Los Angeles, with water skiing, flirting, created a life nice to remember. In those same years I went through war, bombardments, seeing death, experiencing hunger, fear, cold, no schooling. Then a total change — affluence, good hotels, restaurants, museums, elegance, sophistication, finally a good school. Then again a big change — Poland in the years of Stalinism, surrounded by oppression, deprivation, a good university, but the necessity of political correctness, standing in long lines for food, not having good clothes. Then again after 1956 a relatively free country, plenty of work, good money, but a problem with spending this money as the shortages continued. For Donnelly, finishing college meant a satisfying, steady job teaching vocal music, a marriage, a new house, two children, a safe life filled with contentment, with being appreciated in his job, loved by his wife, his family.

Yes, loved by our spouses, family, and appreciated in our work was something we had in common. Maybe the only common thing in our two different lives. Although Łucja told me that as she looks at us, she sees we have one, the most important, quality in common — values. I think she is right.

In the hard years of socialist economy even such a simple, unimportant thing as where our food was coming from was difficult and stressful. With enormous shortages in shops, and having five children at home, Wojtek devised a way of procuring meat in a totally illegal but very satisfying way. We would find some friends who would like to join us in sharing the meat and expenses, and then Wojtek would go to some village to look for a farmer who had a cow, or a pig he was willing to kill and sell. Which was risky for the farmer as legally he was obliged to sell his animals to state-owned slaughterhouses. Then on the day of the killing, Wojtek would drive to the village to pick the animal, which was also risky as the police would confiscate the meat if they ever discovered it.

Some cunning was involved in that. We would strap a table, upside down on the roof of the car. Strap it with ropes in such a way that was secure, yet allowed the table some movement. It saved our contraband one day when a policeman stopped Wojtek to check what was in the car. Wojtek got out of the car to open the trunk, yet looked at the table and started lamenting: "Oh, my God, how lucky I am that you stopped me, look — this table could have fallen off the roof. Will you help me to retie it? Thank you for stopping me." The two of them secured the table and doing it together, joking, sharing a smoke, became friendly enough that the policeman wished him a safe trip forgetting totally to ask about what was in the trunk.

I don't think that Donnelly had to think about where his steak came from. His wife, Louise, also had no problem. Just time to go to a shop. On the other side of the world, both geographically and lifestyle wise, I stood at the kitchen table cutting half a pig, making sausages, curing ham, cutting, cutting, cutting. I remember a day when I had enough, I sat on the floor of said kitchen and started crying and yelling, "Is this why I studied for eight years, is this going to be my life?!!!" I was miserable.

And then to both of us came a similar dissatisfaction with our lives. Donnelly, as he said it himself, had to go crazy to get out of a life that was too comfortable, too confining for him. There comes such a moment in many people's lives in their forties or fifties. A midlife crisis. He left his wife, fell in love with a very young woman, moved in with her, bought a red pickup truck, stopped teaching, started working on his own music, singing solo and in a country trio called Sierra Highway. He joined the Los Angeles Master Chorale and L.A. Opera Chorus. I, as I already wrote, came to Los Angeles to see whether I was capable to live on my own. I took a job as a housekeeper and had two days totally free for myself for the first time in my grown-up life. That's when I started to write poetry and stories. Things I so much wanted to do and never before had the time for. After all earning money had been imperative and as we know poetry doesn't pay.

That's when Donnelly and I met. By that time, he was again single. I knew that, yes, I was able to live on my own, I was even happy with this. He, a freshly retired educator (he could afford it), I a housekeeper for some rich people. I wrote a poem about the first months of our getting to know each other:

### DANCERS

*A formal dance, a bow, a turn,*
*Three steps towards, two in reverse,*
*A bow, a turn — and all with words,*
*Ideas dance, opinions fence,*
*Like eastern merchants spreading fare,*
*Attracting, drawing, catching in a net.*
*But then the rhythm quickens its pace,*
*The dancers hop and skip and go*
*Pirouetting madly through past untold,*
*Unfolding scenes that dazzle hearts,*
*Evoking dreams that give them strength.*
*And round, and round the music leads*
*Into a magic superbly theirs,*
*While with those words they spin and weave*
*A tapestry shimmering with shades of joy.*

*And soon they go through hopeful trembling,*
*Awakened need of touching hands,*
*Transmitting lips and eyes that say*
*What speech might trivialize and kill.*
*Afraid of words in this domain*
*They let their bodies take the lead*
*And tumble headlong into the thrill*
*Of a night that smells of love.*

With all that talking and circling, we recognized each other as the other half of the proverbial apple. How come? How such different pasts could have created so much compatibility? Why do we have similar tastes in everything important? Why our differences seem to us not only unimportant, but even enriching our lives, our world views, our days? We'll never have answers to all those hows and whys, but we don't need them. We are still in love with each other. We are happy.

## September 10, 2011

In three days Łucja and Fritz are coming. They haven't yet fully recovered from their injuries but are able to travel and enjoy life if they take things slowly. He will stay for two weeks, she for over a month. While Fritz is here we will do quite a bit of walking, relaxing at our lakes, eating, drinking and talking, talking, talking. I am so happy. They come at this particular time so that they can celebrate Donnelly's birthday and later Łucja's birthday with us. I have always considered my kids' birthdays to be my great days too. After all it was me who on that day, after a lot of pain, gave them the world. I wonder why it is not a common attitude among mothers.

We will also spend a few days on Diamond Lake, where Donnelly reserved a very nice little vacation house for the four of us. Then we will come home the long way through Roseburg so that they can see the beauty of Oregon forests and waterfalls.

It's a gorgeous highway which I discovered on my first trip north from Los Angeles.

After Fritz leaves, we plan to do quite a bit of theater and socializing. I love to show my girl to my friends. I am so proud of her charm, intelligence, sophistication. She will again come to an Elastic Mind meeting. This time the subject is going to be on why empires always fall. History is one of her passions so I am sure she'll have a lot to say. We often talk about how history views the past; we quite often disagree. Of course facts should not be disputable, but who can truthfully say they know the facts? We are constantly fed lies. Either outright falsehoods, or lies by omission, by twisting the truth with opinions, by playing with it in depriving it of context. I went through the German occupation of Poland, through Soviet, should I call it also occupation, or just influence, pressure in all important facets of national life. I became suspicious, maybe even cynical, I always try to understand what lies behind the information I am being given. Never, or hardly ever, do I take what I am told without the proverbial grain of salt. She has less life experience, is more academically minded, more trusting the books. And books are written by people, with their limitations, biases, loves and hatreds. To say nothing about their need for justifications of their own, or their tribal, national deeds. Are my opinions sometimes based on my own biases? Quite possible, so I love those long telephone conversations I have with her and how they make me think, rethink my attitudes. In the long talks she also asks quite often about the past, lately we spoke a lot about my mother whom she loved dearly. Of course, she has totally different memories of her, as she was a beloved granddaughter. Mother used to take her for overnight visits, which Łucja adored. She, the youngest of five, was the center of loving attention there. Attention that only now I know she craved, which I was always way too busy to give her.

In one of my conversations with Łucja I remembered my last, very bitter for me, serious talk with my mother. It was when I received the diagnosis of cancer. I was devastated. I phoned my mom. Who else was I to call? She listened to my crying and telling her of my problem, to which she responded, "Oh, my dear how terrible, so now both my daughters are sick. Isia has such a terrible cold, you know runny nose and...." I told myself then — no more confiding in Mother. No more thinking that she loves me. I just quietly put down the receiver. That was it. I was alone.

OCTOBER 21, 2011

Łucja left yesterday and as usual I already miss her presence. The house is so quiet. When she cooks or does something else with her hands, she always hums some melody. It can get on my nerves this constant hum. Yet every time she leaves I miss it.

In the evening, Donnelly and I went to a poetry reading of Eavan Boland, the Irish poet, now a professor at Stanford, whose poetry I have loved for quite some time now. It is beautiful, both in choice of words and the melody when read aloud. And I was sorry Łucja wasn't with us. Eavan Boland wrote quite a lot about how women were and often still are not recognized as poets, painters, composers just because they are women. The soft, feminine touch is fine in a male poet's writing. In a woman's — it is considered too feminized. I am glad that has changed to a certain degree in the last decade or two. At least here in America it has — I don't know how it is in Europe. Have to ask Łucja. See what I mean that I already miss her? Anyway, moved by Boland's readings I thought about my own writing, and then I wrote:

## *WRITING*

*I juggle words*
*Experiment*
*Experience*
*Trying for size, for color, for smell*
*Move up and down*
*And in and out*
*I turn and knead*
*I pinch and stroke*
*And in the process*
*Greedily discover*
*Shades unperceived*
*Sounds filled with meaning*
*Meanings void of feelings*
*And feelings I didn't know exist.*

I also looked through my older poems and found one that perfectly describes how I saw Southern California and Beverly Hills, especially in the first months of my life there. I wrote it in 1989. I was feeling very isolated, I knew I didn't fit in the culture that surrounded me. Didn't know how to speak to all those, whose life experiences were so different than mine. When I talked with a Beverly Hills person about hunger, I thought of the food deprivation of the war years, they thought of the pangs of hunger they felt when on a slimming diet. My ideas about social class were about difference in culture, education, manners, taste. The people surrounding me were sure America is classless. They do not see the difference in wealth as a class difference. They do not see, maybe do not want to see, how in America the money brings an enormous difference in availability of good education, of travel, which, especially in young people, opens minds, creates tolerance, teaches to think critically.

Yes, some rich kids grow up to be worthless playboys or

girls for that matter. Same was in Europe. Sometime in the nineteenth century somebody coined an expression "salon idiot" for all those who could be charming, knew how to behave at a salon gathering, yet had educations limited to a foreign language or two, the knowledge of a few big names in arts or literature, and were generally stupid and lazy. Our "salon idiots" here do not have even this. It's enough that one is rich, lives in a mansion and is seen on the screen or mentioned by the media. Look at the whole family of Kardashians. See? Even I know about them.

It seems to me, we have an even bigger class division, and definitely harder to breach. With the cost of higher education, with the need for young boys and girls to earn their own money, the slogan "equal opportunities" becomes meaningless. Just think about such a simple thing as lack of reliable, always accessible public transportation. No young person needs to have a car in any European country — there are buses, trams, trains. Here a car is a must. And the lack of equality I am talking about is not the fact that a rich kid has a BMW, while a middle class or lower one has a second-hand Toyota. The lack of equality lies in the fact that the BMW is usually bought by parents, the used car has to be worked for by the young boys and girls themselves.

Here is this poem, here is how I saw the world I came to live in:

### TWO WORLDS

*Words, words, words spinning a tale.*
*Pretending words, drugging words,*
*Words that conceal, create, lie,*
*Words that give us roles to play.*
*Maybe I am part of another world,*
*Another world where things are serious,*
*Where love is deep and missing hurts,*

*And to give is much more than to take.*
*This world of façade is not for me.*
*I abhor words like "cute" and "sweet."*
*The icing pink and shimmering veil*
*Won't do for me, won't light a spark.*
*'Cause everything has a core and a skin.*
*The core is life, the core is truth,*
*Though often rot and worm infested,*
*This is what counts, this is what stays.*
*Maybe I am part of another world,*
*Where pain is pain and hunger kills*
*But where to deal with evil things*
*We look them straight in the naked face.*

As time went by I met, befriended, and was accepted by several magnificent people. I found that there is a "real" life here just as well as in my Europe. There is another class — all the intellectuals, musicians, artists. There are working people who have quite an impressive knowledge of life, who are good, honest and courageous. They just do not live in Beverly Hills. There is one small, but for me important, remnant from my days working for the millionaires — I pay off my credit cards at the end of the month never having to pay interest. I am not going to fund the bankers, the wealthy, their life style. I wonder how many people acquiring credit card debt think that they work for the mansions, the yachts, the casino visits of the billionaires.

When working as a housekeeper for one of those super rich I one day cleaned a waste paper basket out of which a letter fell. I knew I shouldn't read somebody's mail, yet the temptation was too big when I noticed the name of the sender. It was a casino in London. They were informing my employer's father-in-law that during his last visit a mistake had been made in the rate of exchange. Because of that, the casino owed him five thousand dollars. They were inquiring whether he wanted them to keep it in his account for a next visit, or send it to his bank account. Can you imagine how much money the man had to exchange if a mistake of five thousand went unnoticed? Just on the side, my employer's mother always gave me a Christmas gift — it was always a calendar or notebook that is sent to people as an advertisement. How generous of this millionaire's wife!

A certain aspect of that feeling of alienation persists in me to this day. Just yesterday in the morning, while still in bed Donnelly started to reminisce about little things from his childhood. He told me about the time he and his father were at the Union Station in Los Angeles to meet his grandmother coming by train from Arizona, and how enchanted he was seeing a gift she brought, which was a napkin holder in the shape of a man. Then he went on with some other memories — a Mickey Mouse watch he got for Christmas and then lost at the playground, a plastic pseudo film camera showing a little movie, his joy when as an adolescent he earned, by selling newspapers, enough money to buy for himself a pair of Levi jeans. He was deep into his young years, I was lying by his side and a heaviness landed on my chest. Every memory of his was met in me with a quiet thought, I didn't know about children's watches, I didn't know about the existence of films, about thinking of clothes, about choices. I cared only about being alive, about my loved ones returning home from wherever they went. The heaviness grew until I stopped him saying, "How is it possible that with such totally different childhoods, with such an enormous abyss between what you remember as important, pleasant parts of your early life and what created my memories, we came to understand each other? Not only understand, tolerate, but receive with tenderness."

But, of course this is a question without a possibility of an answer. It is marvelous to love so much somebody so different from me, not only in how he is now, but also how he was. And not to resent the happy, peaceful life that created the grown-up man I love. And how come he understands me so well. How he is able to see and appreciate, respect the end result of this life so far from what he knew as life. And how come I, who usually look at people without big, difficult experiences as necessarily shallow in their understanding of life, do not see him as shallow at all. On the contrary I see his sensitivity, his wisdom. Well, I think I am repeating myself in saying — the longer I live the more I know and the longer I live the fewer answers I have.

## DECEMBER 2011

Oskar came for his winter break. He is not happy with the college. Finished his first semester with quite decent grades, yet says he is very disappointed. "It is not worth the fifty thousand dollars per year that my father agreed to pay." He wants to go back to Poland. I suspect there is more to it, but the idea of going back and applying for the University of Warsaw makes sense. He will have a lot of work, as Polish high school is quite much higher in education than what he had here. He will have to catch up with Polish literature and history for sure, but maybe with some other subjects too. The European school system is very different than American. Both medical and law schools accept kids straight after high school mainly because the kids already had achieved in the high school a level comparable to at least two years of college here. Oskar wants to apply to a law school at the university. Well, good luck.

## JANUARY 2012

Oh, how I dislike winters that are not real winters! Give me snow, freezing temperatures, when the air is bracingly cold, when cheeks become red, and the little hairs in one's nose stiffen. When sun is reflected in a million little mirrors of snowflakes and branches of trees glitter with rime. I love to walk in such weather, to hear the crunch of snow under my feet, to marvel at the beauty surrounding me. The winter in Ashland has no such days. Well, maybe one or two in several years. Most of the time the temperature is somewhere between 35 and 45 degrees Fahrenheit. It often rains, or is gray, foggy, miserable. And I feel gray, foggy, miserable, old.

Yes, those are the times when I feel my age, when all the things that are now necessarily relegated to the past hurt most, when I am very conscious of how much I have to give up. I so much loved dancing. It was always one of the biggest sources of joy for me. Now, I get so short of breath so fast that it has stopped being pleasant. I love good food yet it is still easy to gain weight, but very difficult if not impossible to lose it. So eating is limited, which also means cooking great, inventive food is limited too. And after years of cooking in Poland and the Soviet Union, when I had to cook with what was available and not what I would like to create, I finally live in a place where I am able to invent dishes to my heart's content. Then comes my cardiologist who says — limit this, forgo that, count calories, grams of fat, remember cholesterol, etc. I like the title of the as yet unwritten, memoir of a friend in her nineties, "Relinquish, relinquish, relinquish." Okay, I am being morbid. It's not as bad. A lot of so called healthy dishes can be a delight to eat. And spring will come soon. That is what happens here very early most of the time — the trees start to bloom at the end of February. So, patience my dear and stop complaining.

## NEXT DAY

The sun came out, I immediately feel better, and reading what I wrote about food yesterday I remembered one summer in Pluski and how I met the Storks, who, you may remember, later gave us the piece of land on which we were able to build our beloved Pluski house.

It was summer of 1958, Wojtek and I were not married yet, we both studied at the university and worked at "Express Wieczorny," an afternoon Warsaw newspaper. Not being able to live together yet wanting to spend time together, to sleep in one bed, whenever we didn't have to be in the city we would go to Pluski by train. The summer I am writing about we did just that. Train, the long walk from Stawiguda to the village, then once there, we rented a room at some farmer's house, which was very inexpensive. We fished and picked mushrooms and berries in the forest and sometimes stole a few potatoes from a field for our daily nourishment. The only expense was buying bread, milk and oil for frying the fish. We loved the lake, the forest, and last but definitely not least, sleeping together. After a week or two of this kind of life, there inevitably came a day when we absolutely had to go back to work. The train to Warsaw was leaving Stawiguda, the station closest to Pluski, late in the afternoon, so in the morning we went out on the lake to fish. The day was gorgeous, sunshine, slight breeze, the lake calm with just small ripples so the rowing was easy. We fished, and just for once the fish were coming in droves. Shortly, we had a bucketful of perch and pike. We swam, lazed in the sun, made love on the bottom of the boat, and of course came back to the shore a little on the late side. Then we had to hurry, clean and fry the fish, pack our backpacks and eat. Well, there were many fish, and when poor you want to eat everything available so nothing goes to waste. We did. Then in the afternoon heat we had to hurry to make the seven kilometers to the station in time for the train. Heavy backpacks, overfull stomachs do not help in a hurried march. At a certain point, maybe three or four kilometers on, I started to have an extreme pain in my side. Wojtek took my backpack but it didn't help much. I reached a point when I began to cry, then I lay down in a grassy ditch and begged Wojtek to go on without me. I just wanted to lie there and die. He was at a loss, he absolutely, if he wanted to keep his job, had to go, I was in no state to accompany him, yet leaving me was out of the question for him. All of a sudden, we heard horses and wheels on the road. A carriage with a pair of horses appeared. There was a man driving, a woman by his side. We knew them by sight as the richest farmers in the village by name of Stork. Mr. Stork seeing us by the side of the road stopped the horses and asked whether we would like a ride to Stawiguda. A heaven sent ride. Of course we accepted with gratitude. I was no more thinking of dying, we sat comfortably on soft seats and digested in peace our big fish feast.

It was also the beginning of a great friendship that lasted for years. As I wrote before, we were able to help them when Mrs. Stork got cancer and afterwards they were instrumental in our ability to build the Pluski house. Every summer vacation that we spent in the village we would spend a lot of evenings together. They had two children, Józef was my age, Hedwig was two years younger. Mrs. Stork jokingly called me her Schwiegertochter (daughter-in-law) and I called her in return my Schwiegermutter (mother-in-law). So much so that I don't remember her first name. She was always Schwiegermutti for us. Even years later when they emigrated to Germany we visited them in a little town near Dusseldorf and they visited us at our home in Podkowa. We kept up with Józef and Hedwig too, although that friendship slowly died out when the parents passed away.

## January 21, 2012

We saw a new opera today at the Tinseltown cinema broadcast live from the Metropolitan Opera. *The Enchanted Island* is a fantastic mixture of pieces of music by George Frideric Handel, Antonio Vivaldi and several other Baroque composers most of whom I have never heard of. The final composition was done by Jeremy Sams who advanced in my private opinion to the category of "genius." It is beautiful. The libretto, written also by Sams, is based on Shakespeare's *The Tempest* and *Midsummer's Dream* and is perfect for the kind of pastiche that Sams wanted to do. We liked it so much that we decided to come to the second showing of it in a month's time.

I am so happy about the technical development in our times. Just think, my grandmother was already an adult when she had her first radio. Up to that time the only music she could listen to was if somebody played an instrument or sang, or the few times a year when she would travel to a big city to go to a concert. Then, when I fell in love with the opera, it could be enjoyed at an opera house or on the radio, but radio doesn't show the staging, which I think in opera is not to be missed. Now, the live broadcasts from several operas and theaters go to big screen theaters all over the world. While Donnelly and I sat here and watched *The Enchanted* Island, Łucja and Fritz were enjoying it in Zurich and a friend of mine, Ewa, saw it in Kraków, Poland. The only inconvenience for us is that as it is broadcast live from a matinee show in New York, we get it at nine or ten a.m. here on the west coast. It was funny at first to go to the opera in the morning. Now it became normal. Europe has it better, they have it in the evening due to the fact that most countries are five or six hours in advance to the east coast of U.S.A.

# February 2012

A few days ago, we spent a fine day in the company of our dear friends Michael and Joe W. She was born and raised in Kentucky and most of her family still lives there. One of them is an aunt to whom Michael is very close. They often visit the old lady and as they, just like us, dislike flying and really enjoy long distance driving, they spend hours in their car. Like us they like the uninterrupted conversations, or listening to books or music. This is something that can only be experienced on such trips. The only other way of travelling that gives me similar pleasure is going long distances on a train. Preferably in a sleeper, when the two of us enclosed in a little compartment can observe the outside world passing by, but never intruding on our solitude.

My love of travelling led to the beginning of my interest in Wojtek. A few months after I met him, when I still just liked him but was not smitten, I was in bed with a bad flu and when Wojtek came to visit (of course with a nice bouquet) my mother allowed him to come into my room. At first I was quite upset. You know, being seen with a swollen red nose, hair messed up, sweaty and I suppose smelly. But he seemed to pay no attention to my looks and when he saw an atlas on my bed, he told me of his great dream to go around the world in a Polish truck. He thought that it would have been a great advertisement for trucks produced in our country and that there might be a chance to convince the Ministry of Heavy Industry to finance such an expedition. That made me forget about my disastrous looks. My eyes lit up. Yes! We could do it together. After all he would need a translator in many countries, as he spoke only Russian in addition to his native Polish, and I at that time was fluent in English, French, Arabic and Italian. We immediately started planning where and how we would go. He took it on himself to find out how much money we would have to have for traversing seas and oceans, for gas, and rudimentary nourishment. We decided we would forgo hotels, we could very well sleep in the back of the vehicle. By the time we finished talking about the whole enterprise it was late evening, I felt much better, and most of all I liked him much better.

Nothing came of it. When we approached the minister of the industry, he just laughed. He was a realist, he knew that the trucks Poland produced would break down after two or three days of travelling, that nobody in the world could repair them successfully, that we, together with the trucks would be the laughing stock. Okay, so our dream was not to be. But we did fall in love with each other and eventually married and had all those children. And Poland changed very much too. In the early seventies, the Poles bought the know-how from

Fiat and started producing the tiny Fiat 126. It was a good car although very small and the government wanted to not only motorize the country, but also to export the new product. How to convince others that things made in Poland were now high quality? Wojtek's dream resurfaced. We lived in Moscow then. We saw what a market the Soviet Union could be for our cars. There were so many Russians and they all were starved for automobiles. Wojtek went to Warsaw with a plan — we would take two new Fiats to travel with our five children. With tents and other camping stuff we could drive from Warsaw to Moscow and then south to Crimea, take a ferry to Georgia, traverse the Caucasus mountains into Armenia, visit Erevan and then back to Moscow and Warsaw. We would film the whole trip. Little Fiats filled with kids going merrily up high mountains. Little Fiats from which tents and sleeping bags were being unloaded. Camps set in awesome places, everybody happy — you know the ads we all see now on TVs. At that time in the so-called "communist" Poland or the Soviet Union advertisement was totally unknown. But it could whet appetites. It might even attract some western markets which we desperately needed for hard currency, if only to pay the Italians for the know-how. This time nobody in the Ministry laughed. Yes! Do it, was the verdict. They would pay for the whole expedition. They would even send an accompanying van with a mechanic and plenty of camping materials, as long as the van would never be shown on the film. The TV was only too happy to show the film and offer it to other countries.

Around the world it wasn't. But a long and fascinating trip it was. One car was driven by Wojtek with two kids, the other by me with three. Behind us in safe distance, so that nobody suspected them to be part of the convoy, a van with a mechanic, spare parts, reserves of filming utensils, food stuff in ice coolers, etc., etc. After all, those Fiats were really tiny and advertisement films are not expected to be honest.

In those days we had to have permits from the Russians to travel on very well-planned routes. One day, when we were all very tired and Iwonka became carsick, we drove off the main highway into a dirt road — just half a kilometer or so to get among some trees for shade. The kids were happy to run around, the grownups stretched and prepared some snacks and drinks. It all lasted maybe half an hour, maybe a tad longer. When we got back on the road we were stopped shortly by the police. Where had we vanished? What were we doing? Who did we meet? That's how we knew we were constantly monitored. No impromptu side trips in the future, we were told, or we'd have our permits cancelled. So we drove through Orel, Kursk, Kharkov straight to Crimea.

That was unpleasant. But a few days spent in Yalta bathing in the warm waters of the Black Sea and resting in a good hotel gave us the beginning of great enjoyment. We visited Livadia Palace, the place of the meeting of Churchill, Roosevelt, and Stalin in February 1945. Went for long walks through the town checking out all the places we read or heard about. In pre-revolution years, Crimea was a resort of choice for the rich. Several of the big, important families had their palaces here. Whoever could afford it had a *dacha*, or came to relax in hotels and boarding houses. After the revolution one of the good sides of socialism was that the right to a monthly vacation was given to every working person, and as the working people were not very well paid, the state took it on itself to provide free resorts or boarding houses to the vacationers. Even we in Poland benefitted from this attitude after the Second World War was over and the otherwise grim times of communist government came on. We did avail ourselves of free vacations in state-owned resorts while our kids spent their summers in well-run camps.

All those magnificent palaces in Yalta were changed to resorts for the upper echelon of the party, all the smaller palaces and villas were to accommodate the working classes. A magnificent youth camp, Artek, had been built in 1925, where children from the whole country, at least once in their young years, were feted for a month of their vacation time. At the time of our living in Moscow, it was said that twenty-seven thousand children enjoyed Artek every year. The kids, who in their families were often poorly nourished and housed in crowded apartments, here were fed a good, healthy diet, slept in beautiful dorms, swam in several pools or in the sea, had games, participated in filmmaking etc., etc. Even my kids, who definitely were not poor, on seeing it all, asked whether they could stay. Well, they couldn't, we were on a working holiday.

Relaxed, we took the ferry to Sochi, then drove on through the gorgeous Caucasus mountains east. Shortly, in one of the small Georgian villages I saw a little hut with a big pile of watermelons in front of it. We stopped and tried to buy one. We spoke Russian of course, and by that time our Russian was nearly perfect. An old man selling the fruit told me, "No watermelons." I pointed to the pile and asked him why he doesn't want to sell us one. "They no good" was his response. He was actually quite rude. At first I was surprised, then I thought I understood. "Sir," I said, "we came all the way from Poland, look at the registration on our cars. We always heard that Georgian fruit is the best in the world." The guy's face lit up in smiles. "Oh," he said "you no Russian, I give you best watermelon." He proceeded with picking up the nicest, ripest of the pile. Taught us how to knock on them and listen for a specific sound the knocking produced. He cut several just to show us for what sound we should look for when buying melons. He refused to take any money and in addition to an uncut fruit "for later," he fed us with the juiciest, most aromatic watermelons we had ever eaten.

Another meeting with simple Caucasian people was one night when seeing a lovely meadow in the mountains, we decided to spend the night there. It was late, the darkness falling fast, but luckily a full moon helped us. As usual, the kids, when let out of the cars, began running and playing games invented on the spot, and the men started to set sleeping bags on the soft grass. One of the guys from the van lit a bonfire. I was trying to prepare something to eat. We were rather short on water that evening, so when I saw two old men coming towards us with a big kettle I was enchanted thinking they are bringing us some water. The men were very friendly, in addition to the kettle they had some cups to drink from. But to our astonishment the liquid that came from the spout was wine, not water. Okay, so the kids had the remnants of our water, we partook of the wine, and I can tell you the evening was very merry.

In cities we stayed in hotels. The only chance to get a bath, to sleep in comfortable beds and to eat the absolutely delicious food of the region. Stalin's little town of Gori had a Stalin's Museum, but we were also shown an impressive citadel located on one side of a big hill, or small mountain if you prefer. We visited Stalin's birthplace home (he was born Iosif Vissarionovich Dzhugashvili; Stalin meaning "made of steel" was his revolutionary nickname), bought a book of his poems in Russian. Very good, sensitive poems I thought. Also, he as a young man studied to become a priest before becoming a revolutionary. It is fascinating to read his biography and see how youthful ideas about freedom and justice can slowly become the murderous acts of the older man. How true is the saying: "Power corrupts, absolute power corrupts absolutely."

The psychological changes in people as they go through life were and are of particular interest for me. Thus I read a lot of biographies, especially of those who made an impact in history, or scientific research.

In Tbilisi, the capital of Georgia, we contacted some journalists we had met in Moscow and they showed us how Georgians can enjoy life. Yes, Georgia was at that time part of the Soviet Union, yet when you talked to the people you didn't hear any fear in their voices. They cracked political jokes, they were positive about the good sides of socialism, negative, but in a constructive way, about the bad sides. We had three evenings, stretching into late nights of great meals, with outstanding Georgian wines (three come to mind: Khvanchkara and Kindzmarauli, both semi-sweet but owing to high level of tannin the sweetness is not pronounced; and Mukuzani, a dry dark red), and very enjoyable company. Maybe because of those evenings I don't have a clear memory of the city, except for a deep-seated remembrance of pleasure.

After Tbilisi we drove straight south to Erevan, the capital of Armenia. Here another great experience. We hardly ever read about Armenia. A small country somewhere between Russia and Iran. I had read of course, about the massacre of Armenians in Turkey in 1915. It was one of those things widely and well reported in the west, yet while it was going on, nobody did anything to stop it. It is supposed that around one and a half million Armenians died by Turkish hands. Once again, it was religion combined with Armenian talent for business and ensuing financial success that were at the bottom of it. Just like the genocide of Jews in Hitler's Germany twenty-something years later. Armenians are Christians. Their church is called Armenian Apostolics with their own leader, Catholicos of All Armenians. We visited an old center for their mother church, the Etchmiadzin Cathedral. It was originally built in 301 after Christianity became the official state religion. Through all the subsequent centuries it was many times partially destroyed or at least badly damaged by invading Persians and Turks, yet always restored after fighting had stopped. Even the Soviets, although they destroyed many churches in Russia and other Soviet States, didn't harm this one except for a certain diminishing of upkeep. Starting with the political thawing in 1950s after Khrushchev came to power, the cathedral regained its importance and magnificence.

In Erevan we were to contact the family of our doctor in Moscow, with whom we developed very friendly relations. After getting settled in a fine hotel in the center of the town we called the doctor's parents. I am sorry to say I do not remember their names, but I do remember very well the warmth with which they received us. First of all they wanted us to move to their little house, for which we thanked them but explained that we would be very uncomfortable with burdening them with five, not always calm and well-behaved children. But we'd be happy to spend time with them, get to know them well, and maybe use them for our guides around the city. Well, they did all that, and it was in their kitchen that I learned to cook some Armenian dishes, one of which, the Talma, became later our and our friends' beloved summer food. It is a big (necessarily, as it has to have lots of ingredients) pot filled with all kinds of vegetables and leaves stuffed with a mixture of ground meats (preferably beef, lamb, and pork, but I often make it just with beef) with rice, parsley, garlic (a lot of it), salt and pepper. The vegetables are most often zucchinis, tomatoes, and bell peppers (I know, I know they are fruit, not vegetable), cabbage leaves and grape vine leaves. All of it is covered with a good tomato sauce and baked in the oven. One eats it with crusty bread, or naan which is a best replacement of the Armenian lavash. Accompany it with red wine and you have a feast.

 I was grateful to the women for allowing me to accompany them in the kitchen. Nothing makes it easier to feel free, natural, open with each other as doing things together. We talked about our children, about our careers, about our men. The first two were similar. The men situation differed very much. Armenian men at that time, I don't know how it is now, were still stuck in the old tradition of "women should obey their husbands." I told them how I had learned in the first hour of being in Yerevan that the culture here is very different. It was the first day in the city. After we had registered at the hotel, I went out to a kiosk to buy a newspaper. It was a very hot day, I was wearing a dress with a halter top and totally bared back. Imagine my shock when literally a few steps outside a man stroked my back whispering something I didn't understand. I turned wildly and yelled at him in Russian. He quickly left my side but even before I reached my destination another one did the same. I rushed back to the hotel, complained to the lobby guard, who with a sly smile told me that here in Armenia only prostitutes dress like this. I did put away my summer dresses after that and had no more unpleasant meetings in the streets.

The men in my doctor's family were very nice and respectful. At a certain point after dinner they proposed a game of *Sheshbesh* (Backgammon). The invitation was addressed to Wojtek who did not know the game so he told them he doesn't play, but that I do. They were surprised — they did not like it I thought, but being good hosts they offered it to me. I love Backgammon. In Egypt it is a widely played game — there it is called *Taula*, and my father taught me and played with me so often that I became quite proficient. The father of my doctor friend sat down with a little sneer meaning: well, what does she think.... His sneer vanished shortly, I beat him nicely. He seemed to be quite nonplussed when I offered to give him a chance of revenge. We played, I beat him again. The women were quietly giggling in the corners, the men seemed astounded. To the end of our several days' long visit they treated me with great respect, but did not offer another game.

After our stay in Yerevan we travelled with just night stops back to Moscow, and Wojtek went to Warsaw with the films we made. The film was edited showing our whole trip as a documentary, but big chunks of it were later used for many commercials. Wojtek refused to be paid for the film, as we were on a working trip and the ministry paid for all our expenses, so the film became the property of Polish TV, to be used whenever and however needed. In one of the pieces shown on TV, my boys were filmed as they jumped out of the car and started fighting, with kicking and screaming. It was quite understandable, as they had been sitting for several hours in too small a space and were finally free to let the tension out. When they saw the piece they were very offended and angry at their father, but I think they did learn a lesson to behave always in a way that would not be embarrassing.

## MARCH 2012

Jan and Monika decided to get married at the end of June. They have lived together for ten years, worked together in their music business, built a lovely house in the suburbs of Warsaw, so it was high time to put an official stamp on the relationship. I am very happy for them. They obviously love each other and are pretty well suited to each other. Donnelly and I are, of course, going to be part of the ceremony. We'll go to Zurich late in May, transfer to Poland in June, spend two weeks in Pluski with Jarek and family, then move to Jan's new house for a few days before the wedding and ten days or so after the big day. The young couple decided not to go on a honeymoon, but to stay at home and visit with us and with Monika's parents. That will give both sets of parents the opportunity to get to know each other. We have already met her mother Barbara Kamińska, but haven't had the pleasure of meeting her father Waldemar. Jan speaks very highly of him, his intelligence, and sense of humor. He likes to spend Christmases and other holidays with them. Barbara and Waldemar live on an island north of Szczecin. I am looking forward to all this.

## APRIL 16, 2012

Had an appointment with Dr. Dauterman, the cardiologist. My heart seems to be fine. No need to do anything more than what I am already doing. Thank God for that.

## May 2012

What a very busy month! Knowing we'll be in Europe for nearly two months we had to find somebody to take care of Bucik the cat, of my house plants, of the garden. Luckily Chio May, our ex-housekeeper and now friend, isn't going anywhere so she agreed to do that. It'll cost us a pretty penny although she doesn't charge a lot compared to others. I am always sorry for the animals when we leave them for such a long time. After we come back home, Bucik is usually so offended that he doesn't want to be close to us at first, it takes a few days of cold shouldering us before the loving companionship is restored. We also wanted to see our friends before leaving so we had several dinners at our or their homes, and we went to a few concerts we didn't want to miss. We also had to take out of their frames eighteenth century prints by Chodowiecki, which have been in my family since the forties and which hung on the wall of our staircase first in Poland in the house my children grew in, then here in Ashland. I thought it would be a great wedding gift for Monika and Jan. He knew them well from his childhood, and being so old they are quite valuable. We did something funny — we copied them on our office copier and put the copies back on the wall. Jan will have the originals, and we won't miss the look of our staircase. Cunning isn't it? We also had a change of plans, decided not to go to Zurich. We'll see Łucja and Fritz when they come for the wedding, and we will go for a longer time to Pluski.

## June 2012

So once again in Pluski — relaxing and filling ourselves with the beauty, and peacefulness. Days are spent on the lake, in the forest or simply in the quiet of the house with a good book or with Donnelly's singing. As usual now, whenever we are here, Rudolf is visiting. Such an old, dear friend. I told Donnelly the story of Rudolf's childhood and it moved him so much that he wrote a poem about the man.

## RUDOLPH THE LOST
*(a dear old man in Pluski and close friend of family)*

*Life has swirled around him and through him*
*like an angry hurricane.*
*Caught in the storm of history,*
*his body washed upon the Pluski shore.*
*He found an island free of fear,*
*but the pain lingered on.*
*It trapped him, imprisoned him.*
*It stole away his youth.*
*And when he found himself again,*
*he'd lost the golden years.*
*So gently, firmly, once again,*
*he's gathered to himself*
*The simple pleasures left to him,*
*not taken by the storm.*
*He tends his rabbits and drinks his beer,*
*and walks his island home*
*With the ease of a lonely man*
*who has learned*
*That his fate*
*is not his own.*

I am glad that Donnelly likes him also. Although there is hardly any communication between the two without my translating, they seem to be comfortable with each other. We go wild strawberry picking together and it is such a calm, friendly time. I have made some confiture of the fruit. It has a taste and aroma incomparable to other fruity preserves. I made enough to give to all my kids and to be able to take some back home.

Tomorrow we'll go back to Warsaw as the wedding date is coming.

## July 2012

The wedding was absolutely magnificent. Money was not a problem for them, they could have as marvelous a day as they could only dream of. Monika is such a beautiful woman and like many young women she wanted her wedding to be spectacular. It was. A good dressmaker made a dress that fit her magnificently, a theatrical professional make-up specialist did her makeup, a fine hairdresser was there to see to it that not one hair spoiled the design. They had rented a historic car that in the early fifties was built specially for Stalin's visit, but was never used. The wedding itself was held at the Registry Office at the back of Royal Palace in gorgeous rooms furnished with antiques. Then we had drinks and snacks and photo-ops in the terraced gardens in the back of the palace, above the Vistula River. Hundreds of people were present, as both of them have many friends and acquaintances. The closest circle of family and friends, roughly some 150 people, were invited for dinner held in the evening in a restaurant in an old, very elegant palace, in the basement of which there was a nightclub rented out by the young couple for a whole night of dancing and drinking. My God, what a difference to Jan's siblings' weddings, or even his first, which were all held at the local town halls with a dinner for maybe sixteen guests at our old family home. *Tempora mutantur et nos mutamur in illis* (Times are changing and we change with them).

They had organized everything, even a chauffeured car that would take Donnelly and me back home after the ceremony to rest and change for the dinner party and the night of dancing. Same for Mr. and Mrs. Kamiński, Monika's parents. The dinner was delicious, and sitting at a table with all my children and grandchildren added to the pleasure. In the nightclub a fine band played rhythmic music for dancing, tables were set inside and on a terrace outside, and a buffet offered plenty of snacks just in case anybody got hungry in the early morning hours.

Both Donnelly and I love dancing and I am glad to report that we didn't tire until after two a.m.

On the whole, the wedding was something all the guests will remember for a long time. I do hope it proved to be what Jan and Monika wanted and they will remember it always with great pleasure.

## TWO WEEKS LATER, ASHLAND

As is often the case, coming back from Europe I am exhausted emotionally. This year, especially with the wedding and with constantly being surrounded by people, it was very difficult for me. When I am with people whose world views are very different from mine, yet whose attitude towards me matters, if only for Jan's sake, I try to curb my tongue, not to be the outspoken, opinionated usual me. And that is tiring. So here at home I try to lead a life as peaceful as possible. To be alone with Donnelly. To be alone with myself and my thoughts. And in such moments the dreams tend to come. It is as if my brain tried to go somewhere far away from the daily preoccupation with family, with problems. One such dream that I usually call "a film dream" came last night. I saw a late middle age couple in their living room. A room filled with overstuffed furniture with crocheted antimacassars on the armchairs, with a big TV and a lot of little knickknacks. The woman sat in an armchair knitting, her eyeglasses moved down to the middle of her nose so that she could look at her knitting or raise her eyes to watch her husband who was anxiously pacing the floor. And I heard their conversation:

*– You know Martha, I gave it a lot of thought, and I really don't see any reason to go into this kind of expense and trouble.*
*– What are you talking about? Now look, do you think this length of the sweater is going to be enough?*
*– Oh, stop that knitting for a minute and listen. We have to talk about it.*

*– About what? And anyway, I do pay attention when I am knitting. Well, tell me is it long enough?*
*– Yes it is. Now do you really think we need a bigger house?*
*– Yes, I do, but look, this length is not going to cover my hips. I suppose I'll have to knit some more.*
*– Oh, Martha, stop this darn knitting and pay attention! What do we need a bigger house for? There is just the two of us. Now, look, if I promise to watch less football, we won't need a separate TV room, and anyway I hate your stupid shows just as much as you hate football. It is ridiculous to change houses, pack, unpack, go to all the expense just because of a few football matches. MARTHA! Will you stop that knitting?! I am talking to you!*
*– Don't shout John, you are really being so unreasonable. I am paying attention, and it is not about football. At least not only. Remember the last time Susie visited with the kids? You constantly complained about how tired you were with the noise and all the toys lying underfoot? You finally went fishing, for what — six days, or was it even seven? We do need a bigger house. A TV room, maybe even a second guestroom…*
*– A second guestroom? Have you lost your senses woman? They come here so rarely!*
*– Well, I haven't told you yet, but you see, Susie and Tom are splitting…*
*– WHAT?!!*

## JULY 18, 2012, AT THE OCEAN

Yesterday, in an absolutely gorgeous sun, we were lying on the sand doing nothing. Slowly there came to me a realization that everything in me was pure sensual feeling without any words, any description, any formulated thinking. I was heavy with relaxed happiness, with an exquisite feeling of warmth on my skin, the ever so light touch of the ocean breeze, the smell of the salty water in my nostrils, the sound of gulls, a slight stirring of sexual longing.

It is only today that I've tried to put it in words. Then, my experience was purely physical although now when I write about it, I still feel the memory of those hours on the beach in a sensual way. How interesting to see the divisions in my brain, the different places for remembering words, stories and seemingly separate from them the sensing, the feelings. And the enormous amount of feelings — emotional like fear, anger, happiness, boredom, but also the purely sensual like heat, cold, tiredness, lust, hunger, taste, smell and so on, so on, seemingly ad infinitum.

It was so strong that I didn't want to speak about it, yet I must have mentioned something to Donnelly about the joy of doing nothing, because after we came back to the cabin, he wrote a poem. He allowed me to put it in here.

*AT THE OCEAN*
by Donnelly Fenn, July 2012

*What did you do at the ocean?*
*Nothing! Nothing but watch the waves,*
*Watch the white-caps lift and fall,*
*Their rhythm broken in conflict with the receding tide.*

*Nothing, but watch the easy, darting gulls,*
*Owning the breeze, slanting and slashing,*
*Ever searching for the ultimate morsel.*

*Nothing, but sit on a storm-tossed log,*
*Its once majestic grandeur laid out in horizontal stillness,*
*Still offering sweet repose and reflection.*

*Nothing, but marvel at the wind's*
*Patterned and ridged arrangements,*
*Sands blown in perfect symmetry.*

*Nothing, but wander among slicked stones,*
*Glistened smooth by relentless tides,*
*All free for the precious taking.*

*Nothing, but gather the memory*
*Of moments spent with my love,*
*Who makes small nothings everything.*

## JULY 29, 2012

Wojtek died today. It was expected. He was so sick for such a long time. Yet it hit me with an unexpected force. We were together for over thirty years. I could say we grew up together. After all when we met we were so young and naïve. We had good times and difficult times, for most of those thirty years we loved each other passionately. Yes, we also fought, and towards the end of our marriage I grew distant, feeling imprisoned in a relationship that was constraining. He behaved honorably when I asked for divorce. The year Donnelly and I spent in Poland he was very friendly towards us both, took us several times to the opera and theater. Visited, even brought sometimes fresh rolls and milk for our breakfast. I liked his visits very much, we got into our usual discussions about politics and economy. I liked his way of reasoning, yet I disliked, as in the years past, his disdain of politicians and how he thought he knew better than any of them how to run the country. Sorry to say he was often right. Yes, he was a difficult man, but such a good, honest man. And so wise in so many ways.

My last visit with him was just before we left Poland. He was coughing so much he could hardly speak, but in his usual way showed me that he was glad I came. He asked for a cup of tea. I made it for him, but did not pour a totally full cup. I suppose I didn't want to risk spilling it on the saucer. He looked sneeringly at the cup and asked "What, skimping on water?" And then, he who all his life was extremely private, told me and

Iwonka who was with us, a heartbreaking story of how, in an attack of coughing he wet his pants, so he went to the bedroom to change, sat on an armchair to put his fresh pants on and the next thing he knew — he was lying on the floor, shaking with cold and still holding the pants in his hands. "I must have lain there for a long time to get so cold. You can't imagine how humiliating it is this lack of control over your own body." He started to cry. I put my hand on his shoulder. He took it and kissed it. I asked him would he want me to stay in Poland longer to help him. No, he said, that would be even more humiliating. We talked a little longer, but seeing how tired he was I finally said goodbye. I knew it would be the last goodbye. I left with a heavy heart.

Today, when Jarek called to tell me, I just went to pieces. I cannot truly comprehend that Wojtek is no more. That this beautiful mind doesn't exist anymore, that all that love of life, of honesty, of his children vanished, is so irredeemably gone. Now also, this enormous portion of my life is definitely closed and I am the only repository of all those intimate memories of our life together. Now what I remember of my life with him is the official story, no one to contradict me.

No more changes in our relationship, no more new memories to be formed. I feel lonely in my past. Does that make any sense?

Oh, Wojtek — divorce or no, you were still a part of me.

## August 2012

Whatever I do, I think of Wojtek, of those years together, especially of the times that were good times before everything started to unravel. Today, a memory of another trip with him came to me. It was when I was pregnant with Łucja, when Jan was still in diapers and Jarek was just barely four. My sister Isia had her first child, a son Grzegorz. She and her husband lived in a studio apartment in Warsaw. It was a lovely studio with an enormous glass wall towards the south. Very pleasant in winter, but now at the end of a hot July, with a newborn it was hellish. One day she called with a proposition. If we would like to go somewhere to have a vacation without children she could move into our house in Podkowa and take care of our boys. While for her it would be a fine change to be in a house among the trees, with a biggish garden to be able to put her son to sleep out in the shade, in fresh air. Of course we would like to — was the answer. At that time we had a second-hand VW Beetle convertible, and the idea of using it to go south to Bulgaria to beaches on the shore of the Black Sea was just enchanting. I had a bare shoulders cotton dress wide enough to cover my already big belly (seventh month), packed a swimsuit I had sewn for myself with a nice bra-like top, a big bag for the aforementioned belly connected with a mini bikini panties, and a totally bare back. We decided to take a tent as we, as usual, had little money, and off we went. We stopped in Prague, then in Budapest for a day or two, and then we entered Yugoslavia. That was one country we had some monetary problems with as they had so-called hard currency, officially unavailable to us Poles. We did buy some on the black market to be able to buy gas, but as it was no more than three hundred miles from Hungary to Bulgarian border we knew we could do it in less than one day. Even through the mountains, even in the southern heat.

It was Friday, some sixty miles after passing Belgrade, when our car broke down. A nice, helpful policeman towed us to the nearest gas station and told us that they do repairs also. Fine, but we had no money, remember? I called our embassy in Belgrade hoping they could help us, but were told by a guard that the embassy was closed for the weekend. Evening was coming, the gas station people allowed us to put up our tent in the back, we had water and some snacks in the car, we went to sleep.

Next day Wojtek bought a glass of milk for his pregnant wife with the change he still had and we started worrying. But not much. Neither of us was a worrier. Then I saw a Volvo with Swedish registration, filled with five young men, coming in to pump gas. I approached the driver's window and asked whether they would consider towing us to Bulgaria. The driver started to laugh. Imagine such a request — towing a car for over two hundred miles through mountains and tunnels! And then he looked down and saw my belly. The laughter stuck in his throat. He became very serious and said yes. They all came out to examine the possibilities of how to tie us to them, commiserated with our dilemma, and after finding a piece of strong rope at the gas station we got connected and off we went.

It was the craziest trip I have ever had in my life. First of all, our new friend sometimes forgot about us and sped up to speeds unknown to poor Beetle. Then when we were going through a long tunnel the rope broke and we were left behind. Luckily they noticed, managed to come back, retie the damn cord and we continued. Oh, the nerves when we are young! Not for one moment did I panic. And when we reached Sofia, where — as the Bulgarians were in our Soviet bloc and thus we had all the money we needed — we invited our saviors to a big, sumptuous dinner at a fine restaurant which, as they said, would have been beyond their students' budget. We became friends and kept in touch for a long time exchanging letters and planning visits, which plans never came to fruition, sorry to say.

It was not the end of the adventure though. After the car was repaired and we finally got to the seashore we found there were no free places in hotels, motels, or campgrounds. Once again we were at our wits end what to do. Wojtek stopped by a little house where we saw a man tending his garden and asked whether he maybe knew of somebody with rooms to let. The man looked at us, thought for a minute, asked whether we had a tent, and hearing that yes we did, calmly started to pull out his tomato bushes. "You can set camp right here, I'll just even out the ground."

It was a memorable two restful weeks that we spent with him and his family. They allowed us to use their kitchen and bathroom, often invited us to join them for dinner, which we ate under a pergola covered with grape vines so the dessert was there right above our heads, and once again we had new friends, we talked history, aired our dislike of the Soviets, and drank good Bulgarian wine. Next year they came to Poland to visit us, so we were able to repay their hospitality.

I also had a very funny adventure while sunbathing on a beach. I usually dug a hole in the sand to put my belly in while sunning my back and reading a book. One day Wojtek went a little to the side to have a nap in the shade of trees, and a young, handsome man seeing me alone and obviously liking my back came over and started to flirt with me. I was in a very good mood that day, and seeing a possibility of playing a joke on the unsuspecting guy I led him on. Finally he proposed we go dancing, I smilingly agreed and started getting up. My belly slowly became visible as it extricated itself from the sand hole. The man gave a loud gasp, turned round and ran. And he did run fast. Was he afraid I would chase him?

When we came back home we found a slightly difficult situation. To make Isia's life easier I left her with our housekeeper Rózia. Rózia was not a very good housekeeper, and not always honest — I remember the time when I asked her to roast a chicken for our dinner and the chicken she served had only one leg. "Rózia, what happened to the other leg?" "It must have had only one," was the answer. Yet, she loved the boys and I could trust her with them while I was working, so we kept her even with some items missing from time to time.

I'd forgotten though how very intolerant Isia was. She was exacting about the housework that Rózia was supposed to do, and also inquired about those missing items (they were never anything big or expensive). Rózia got furious. They quarreled to the point that one day Rózia grabbed a frying pan and tried to hit Isia. Of course my sister immediately fired her. So now I came home two weeks before my delivery time and found that I didn't have a housekeeper. I was at a loss, what was I to do, who would take care of the children while I was at the hospital giving birth. I went to buy a newspaper, and while there at the newsstand I asked the sales girl if she knew of somebody looking for a housekeeping job.

A heavily pregnant woman was standing near and hearing what I said approached me to say that if I could wait a few days she could come. I looked meaningfully at her belly and she smiled. "I am due the day after tomorrow, your pregnancy is still quite high, so I think we would be okay if you would allow me to come to work with my baby." I did, she did, and for many years she was our beloved *pani* Zosia the housekeeper. Our babies for months slept together in the same crib. And later played in the same playpen. We became good friends. She still is in touch, visited Donnelly and me when we were in Poland.

## September 2012

The month started with a very interesting (as if sometimes they are uninteresting!) Elastic Mind meeting — a discussion on the psychology of owning guns. The room was full. It being Ashland, only one man was pro-gun ownership, and he even came with a gun strapped to his belt. For a moment, seeing this gun I was unsure whether to proceed. I remembered having read somewhere, I think it was in "The Second Coming" by WB Yeats: "The best lack conviction while the worst are full of passionate intensity." And the truth is that the most intelligent and thoughtful people have doubts, want to see everything from different points of view, are tolerant of other opinions. Which means we do not have to be afraid of them. It is so different with the fanatics — all those who firmly know what is right and what wrong, those who know how everybody should live their lives. It usually is this kind of a person who feels the necessity not only of owning guns, but also of being armed at all times. Well, I decided to go on, the discussion was lively, the gun owner was asked a lot of questions about why he feels he needs the gun. I am glad to report he made it absolutely clear that a person has to be illogical and very afraid, really paranoid to think that a gun in a modern society can ensure one's safety. He made quite a fool of himself. A dangerous fool. I am mighty glad he did not hate us all to the point of shooting.

Then on September 21 we had a big reunion at West High in Torrance, California. It was the fiftieth anniversary of this school's existence, and of Donnelly's beginning his work there as a music teacher and choir director. That part of his life was, and is, very important to me. Because of it I started to pay attention to him as a personality worthy of my interest. He had worked at West High for twenty-seven years, and he must have been a remarkably good teacher. To this day many of his ex-students love him enough to keep in close contact by e-mail and visits.

Shortly after I met Donnelly in 1989, when he still was one of several people I liked to spend my time with, he took me out to dinner. The server was a woman, but after appetizers I noticed that there was a change and a young man started taking care of our table, and what's more he kept trying to catch Donnelly's eye. It was nice that Donnelly paid so much attention to me that he didn't notice it, but the waiter's antics were so obvious that I told Donnelly to look at him. He did and both the men's faces lit up. They greeted each other with great joy. Donnelly got up and introduced the waiter to me as his ex-student, who in turn told me how important his music teacher had been, how he owes who he is to Donnelly, and so on, and so on. It was nice to hear but one swallow doesn't make a spring, as they say.

Within a month, though, I had experienced several such situations. Every person who had him as a teacher felt they had to tell me how important he was in their development. Well,

I started to really pay attention. He must have loved the kids and really tried to be much more than just a choir director. As he said once, he discovered how needy of attention and advice the teenagers were. He was also very unconventional — taking his choir to sing not only in usual venues like Disneyland, old people's homes, churches or hotels, but also to a meadow in Colorado that he had seen the previous year when hiking with his father. The meadow was so beautiful that on seeing it, he immediately decided to take a summer chorus of alumni and current then singers to this meadow one day to sing a beautiful song written to a poem by E. E. Cummings. And so he took the choir there, they stood in formation, they began to sing, and…they started to furiously swat themselves. It was boggy, marshy, their feet were slowly sinking into mud, mosquitoes had a feast…and the song's title was: "I Thank You God." Well, fate quite often is ironic. But I am sure everybody who was there still remembers the adventure.

The story that topped it all for me was how sometimes Donnelly even defied the law in defense of a kid. There was a boy who often showed up in school all black and blue, obviously beaten. Donnelly took him to a place they could talk quietly and learned that it was the boy's father. For some reason neither the young man nor his mother wanted to call the police, Donnelly asked whether there might be a family member with whom the abused boy could stay and learned that yes, but the nearest trustworthy cousin was in Idaho and the boy didn't have the money to go there. So what did the teacher do? Something absolutely forbidden — he gave the boy money for a bus ticket to run away. It was the right thing to do. The fully grown-up man now says that it saved his life as he had been close to com-mitting suicide. He is a fine, successful man now.

Back to now, to 2012. Donnelly had so many calls insisting he show up at the reunion that he felt he absolutely had to go. And where he goes I go, so while I was preparing for the trip, he prepared for a swan song of leading his ex-students in singing. He put out on the Internet a list of the folk songs that his choirs sang for fun over the years, asking everybody who planned to attend the reunion to vote which of them they would like to sing. Many, many did vote. The fifteen songs that got most votes were then, once again, on the Internet, put out for the willing to practice. Then Donnelly contacted some of his instrumentalists from long ago to find the necessary accompaniment. To make a long story short — at the reunion, after a football match, several hundred people assembled on the school lawn in front of a band shell. Donnelly and the instrumentalists went onto the stage and the music started. It was so emotional, so touching to see all these people singing. Many had tears in their eyes. You have to remember the dates. Some of those who attended that school at the beginning were now sixty-eight. Definitely not kids anymore. Others, the middle aged ones came together with their children, it was a very special hour. Once again I witnessed how those people loved him. The only thing I do not understand is how come his ego is not swollen out of proportion. How he manages to be such an easy person to live with.

The next four days were very busy with school celebrations, but also with visiting Louise, some friends, and finally with moving to the house of my ex-employers and now dear friends Ronald and Diana. We love being with them and of course it would have been impossible to be down in southern California and not stay with them.

When we returned from the reunion we learned that a very dear friend, Leon McFadden, had died. He had been for some time in hospice. He was ninety-two, so we knew we would lose him. Still it was with such sadness that we received the news. We do have a few of his paintings which were given to us as gifts, but I am sorry we never had enough space to hang more of the ones I admired so much — they were way too big for the size of our house. Both he and his wife Flannery were our closest friends for years. Together, or separately later on when they divorced and Flannery remarried. He was as close as possible to genius — a fine mathematician, with great knowledge of physics and history, a fascinating painter, and as unconventional a person as possible. A good, generous man. Very humble, although I sometimes suspected that it was put on, to hide his own feeling of being very special.

## October 2012

An art gallery in Yreka, where Leon had lived and to which he donated his art, organized an evening to celebrate his life, and created a show of his paintings and drawings. We bought one — a drawing of a nearly naked man, which Donnelly hung in his bathroom. Leon was a prolific painter and he worked in many styles, sometimes inventing ways of communicating with people through the kind of art he felt would be best at the time.

I remember when he did his mathematical art. Introducing mathematical symbols into paintings that were abstract yet very emotional. My granddaughter, little Łucja, was with us when we went to see his newest. She was nine or ten, stood in front of a row of these seemingly very abstract pictures and all of a sudden hugged me, and very seriously asked why was Leon so sad. Yes, it was at that time that his marriage to Flannery was in trouble and the child could feel the sadness in his painting. Both Donnelly and I will miss Leon.

## November 2012

When we moved to this new place I couldn't for quite some time get used to the smallness of the living-dining room. I thought that parties for more than eight were over. Two of us and four guests seemed the maximum of what we could do. Well, we had the traditional Thanksgiving for twelve. It's the same people who had come to our Thanksgiving dinners for around ten years now. I wouldn't know how to change the group. How do you tell people that some might still be part of the holiday and some are being dropped? No, it wouldn't do. So Donnelly took out into the garage the biggest, carved armchair, an enormous potted dieffenbachia, and my beloved Arabic coffee table, we put the dining table lengthwise in the room, stretched it to its full length and presto — there we had room for twelve. It was great joy to see that we can do it and everybody enjoyed the turkey with all that accompanies it.

## December 11, 2012
The autumn is unusually warm. Today we had to cut the last roses as the forecast says it will rain tomorrow. The bouquet is beautiful.

## A few days later
Once again part of the furniture goes to the garage to make space for a Christmas tree. I am slowly getting used to the smallness of our house. Several pieces have been put on rollers. During "normal" time the TV is pushed against the wall and the carved armchair stands in front of it, partially obscuring the ungainly machine and creating the feel of a small but cozy sitting room. In the evening if we decide to watch something, the chair is moved to the side, the cabinet with the TV is rolled out and we have a viewing room. I just have to remember why we downsized and everything becomes fine.

I constantly marvel at our good luck in finding each other. It must be rare to be able to be so compatible when meeting at a rather late time in life. I wrote a little poem about how good it is to wake every day at Donnelly's side:

## WAKING WITH YOU

*First morning light, first morning stir,*
*And then you smile through sleepy eyes.*
*Hazy lines of your face*
*Still blurred by my sleep*
*Form a promise, an invitation*
*To a day filled with joy,*
*To a day of calm surrender*
*That doesn't mean defeat.*

## JANUARY 19, 2013

I drove to Mt Shasta today. Had an unpleasant moment when a woman, obviously distracted by her cellular telephone, stepped right in front of my car. Luckily for both of us I was going quite slowly, and paying attention to the road in front of me, so by swerving and breaking hard I managed not to hit her. I was so shaken though, that I had to stop by the side of the street and wait for a good ten minutes to calm down.

While sitting there I remembered a near accident like this in Moscow. It was winter of 1972. Late evening, one of the main streets downtown Moscow, asphalt covered with slush, sleet falling from a dark sky, all four lanes packed with cars. I am driving in the left lane. From the front of the car to my right an old woman runs in front of me. I swerve left into a grassy center divider to avoid her and very nearly hit a policeman who is standing there. My car stops inches from him. He jumps to my door, yanks it open and begins yelling at me. I lose it. I get out of the car and scream obscenities about him, his mother, his brain, his country, political system, schools, etc. My yelling at the top of my voice stops the cars around us and produces an unexpected reaction in the policeman — he tries to push me back into my car, while trying to calm me at the same time — "calm down *dievochka* (a name given to young or young looking women), calm down, please…" I was too surprised by his reaction to shut up immediately. Somewhere deep inside me I was expecting handcuffs, a van carrying me off to Liubianka or some other godforsaken place of interrogation and torture. The softness of the policeman's voice, his obvious fear that if I go on he would have to do something about it, finally reached me. I allowed myself to be pushed into the driver's seat and though I was still shaking, I switched on my ignition and carefully eased into the traffic. From that time on I looked at Russian police in a very different way.

I learned a few valuable lessons that day. First was the realization that to be aggressive is sometimes a better behavior, contrary to how I was brought up. Then came the realization that in societies where people are growing up in fear, under a tyrannical rule, only strong, aggressive behavior is respected. "If she is yelling at me in such a way, obviously she has a right to do so." Same as the time I yelled at the policeman guarding our apartment building. It served me well for the rest of my six years spent in the Soviet Union. Last, but not least, it was a lesson to expect the unexpected while driving.

## A FEW DAYS LATER

If I were to compare my life to a novel, it would have to be a multivolume saga. Something like *The Forsythe Saga*. Each volume set in a different place, different time, mostly different culture. Even the fact that it all would have been about me, wouldn't necessarily unify it. The me in each of these volumes would differ so much from the previous one, from the following one. Luckily for me — if it were always about the same person, it would have meant that I never learned, never grew, never diminished, changed.

## February 2013

Such a blunder! We were invited to a Sunday dinner at Sean and Mary's. We like them very much, the evenings spent with them are always fine, interesting and tasty as they are great cooks and know about food. Yet, we totally forgot. Had a lazy day of newspaper reading, talking, a walk and a quick dinner. We were just settling ourselves for a TV evening when the telephone rang. Sean asked why weren't we there at their house. "The food is ready, where are you?" We were mortified, promised to be at their place in a few minutes, rushed out of the house, never told them that we already ate and partook of a second dinner with gusto.

Donnelly was quite frightened that it was the beginning of forgetfulness of old age so I had to calm him down with a memory of another of my blunders, this one when I was in my thirties. No fear of senility then.

It was in Moscow. A woman professor, I forget of what, from University of Warsaw, attended some international conference in the city. Wojtek wanted to do an interview with her as she was considered one of the very best in her field and was to give a lecture at the conference. To facilitate things, he invited her for lunch at our house on a Friday. Well, the previous night some twenty foreign journalists descended on our house after a political meeting at the Foreign Affairs Ministry. Both Wojtek and I were known to be pretty easy and always-ready-for- some-fun hosts, so people felt free to come when they felt a need to unwind. We had some snacks, lots of drinks, we danced and enjoyed ourselves mightily until early morning hours, by which time the main rooms of the apartment were covered with dirty dishes, overflowing ash trays, spilled drinks, etc. A pigsty.

In the morning I got up to get the kids out to school and immediately afterwards fell back into bed and into a deep sleep. At around noon we woke. Still in our dressing gowns we managed to make some coffee, and bleary-eyed sat down to drink it, looking dispiritedly at the battlefield around us. Then—a jolt

— a doorbell. Who the hell... Wojtek went to the door. It was the woman professor with a bouquet of flowers in her hand and a nice smile on her face... Oh, my God! You can imagine how mortified we were, how embarrassed. We did invite her in, we did try to explain, we were cringing in our chagrin. I am happy to report that our guest proved to be a fine person, she gave a hand in putting the room in order, drank her coffee while we splashed our faces and got dressed. I made some pretty good omelets, a salad which was a rarity in Moscow, and we had a fine lunch, after which Wojtek and she repaired to his office and worked on the interview. I am sorry I do not remember her name although I do remember her face and magnificent composure. So, it does happen to young people too. No need to worry about senility encroaching on us. Or maybe we should...?

## March 6, 2013

The last three months of Elastic Mind meetings were dedicated to hidden reality. We looked at it from different points of view — in January the discussion was based on the book by that title by Brian Greene, a theoretical physicist and strong proponent of the string theory. His book has a very telling subtitle — *Parallel Universes and the Deep Laws of the Cosmos*. It is too complicated to write in detail about it here, but the main idea is that if our universe is infinite, then there are infinite possibilities of combinations of particles and thus there must be more universes in which identical combinations occurred. And if so, then there must be more such intricate combinations of particles, could we call them medleys (?), like those that create you or me. Hence the idea of parallel universes. Yes, humans, do not think that you are IT. That you are unreplicable (my computer says there is no such word, but I think if there isn't there should be, so I'll use it), that in seven days long ago a God created you in the image of himself. Unless of course he is infinite and thus his creation is also such and Brian Greene is absolutely right.

Then in February we added to the same theme, books by Eagleman (*Incognito*) and Gozzaniga (*Human*) and in March we stretched it still to the philosophers' perspective. My, oh my, was it interesting to hear what different people think of it! Some were admiring the logic of the argument, some tried to convince everybody that it has to be nonsense as we all know that God created us as very special, some were dubious about everything. The discussion was fascinating, and I am glad to report, very civilized.

## April, 2013

A month ago, both Donnelly and I entered a poetry competition, today the winners were announced and prizes distributed. I am glad to report that both of us won with our poems. I had previously had some recognition for my Polish verses. I read at an art gallery in Los Angeles to a Polish audience and the reception of my poetry was very touching with some women in tears, and some laughter in appropriate places. Then a Polish newspaper in New York (*Nowy Dziennik*), with circulation of a million copies, printed at first two of the five poems I sent them, then a few months later the remaining three. I was very proud then as my work was on the same page as a poem by Wisława Szymborska who later won the Nobel prize for poetry.

The only time I read my English poems was in June of 2000 in New Orleans at a poetry convention. It was a queer experience. When I came up to the podium and opened my mouth to read the first poem only some kind of an ugly, squawky, raspy rattle came out. I lost my voice. I panicked. What embarrassment, what was I to do? I saw Donnelly rise in the auditorium, he was ready to come to the rescue. It's then that I felt I needed to explain to all those gathered — so barely able to speak, I rasped, "I normally have a voice. I must be terrified of all of you...."

The whole room convulsed with laughter. And that was the turning point. I saw the funniness of it and regained my voice. I thanked the listeners and read my poetry to a big applause.

It was my second visit to New Orleans, which I had visited previously on my momentous Greyhound bus ride, and I absolutely fell in love with the city and its loud, joyful streets. We walked a lot, visited many of the famous places that I had no time for during my first visit, danced in the streets to fine little bands and we promised ourselves to come again. We also bought our first big possession — a still life by Alvar. As we were passing an art gallery I saw with my peripheral vision a picture that appealed to me. I stopped and proposed, "How about buying something to remember our visit here?" Oh no, Donnelly answered. I asked why and he told me he was very much against those mugs or ashtrays with the names of visited places…. Well, I showed him the painting that caught my eye. He started laughing in relief, "Oh, I forgot who I am with" he mumbled. We went into the shop and the picture is hanging to this day in our living room. We still love looking at it. By now Alvar (whose full name is Alvar Sunol Munoz-Ramos) is a very well-known artist with his works hanging in the biggest museums. He lives in the outskirts of Barcelona. I am sorry we didn't know it when we were there. It would have been fun to visit his studio and maybe buy another lithograph of his. Ah, as if we didn't have enough pictures. I am so greedy for beauty!

## May 2, 2013

Big day — the last meeting of Elastic Mind. I'd been thinking about ending it for quite some time. I am tired of having to find and then read, or at least carefully peruse, several nonfiction books every month. I would like to have time to read some mystery or other light fiction without feeling guilty that I should do something more serious. And then there is my writing. I would so much like to be able to give it my full attention. But every time I was near to throwing in the towel, not literally of course, I would see how people enjoyed the meetings and I pushed my resolve away. Now I've done it.

That last meeting was devoted to the book by Richard Wolff, *Democracy at Work: a Cure for Capitalism*. The theme "Do We Have to Change the System to Revive the American Dream?" The room was full, discussion animated, and then people told me how sorry they were to lose the EM, tried to convince me to go on, the library came up with flowers, cookies, a lovely letter of thanks for all the years I put in. I was surprised when I discovered that I led the discussions for seven years. They even created a bronze plaque with my name to be put on a book shelf in the nonfiction section of the library. I was very moved, but at the same time happy with regaining my freedom. Afterwards the most faithful of attendees came home with me to have lunch. We had Armenian *talma*, we had wine, beer and coffee with cake that JoAnn baked for the occasion.

Will I miss doing something important outside of my home? Time will show.

## May 4, 2013

The local newspaper, *The Daily Tidings*, sent a journalist to write an interview with the "famous" Elastic Mind leader. A lovely young lady, Angela Decker, came to our house and over tea and sweets talked to me. She was very thorough in her job and in addition to questions about the group asked also about my writings. I showed her a short story or two and a few poems. She seemed to like them all, asked more questions about my life, proved to be very professional. I would like to get to know her better. She is married, has two boys, and reminds me of myself at that stage in life when I tried to combine work and family and to be positive about the combination. She is somewhere in her thirties I think, so we'll see whether she'll find it interesting to visit an old person. Not everybody young does. I will try to invite her for another cuppa sometime soon.

## END OF JUNE, 2013

We had a very mixed, feelings wise, trip to Portland, Seattle and the Olympic Peninsula. In Portland we stayed with Howard and Linda and, as usual, had a great time with talking and catching up on things. I told them about my writing and asked Linda to please read and tell me truthfully what she thought about the first sixty pages that I brought with me. She read dutifully and then had a tepid reaction, praising and telling me to go on, but I felt that it was just that she wanted to be nice. That hurt. Howard didn't even ask to see the pages. We saw Laurie and David, went for a lovely long walk in the Forest Park, took them out to breakfast and generally enjoyed the time with them. The really important event in Portland was an interview I had at the immigration offices. Two months ago I applied for American citizenship. Now that an officer has talked to me, asked a lot of very personal questions, I am to wait for the final confirmation and a swearing in ceremony.

In Seattle we stayed with Marcia and Marshall Baker, my dear friends from the times we spent in Moscow. Oh, how I love those two. Marshall, as usual, was pretty busy with his writings, Marcia spent her time freely with us and then in the evenings we all had nice dinners and fascinating conversations. Marcia read what I wrote and as we were sitting together while she was reading I saw her face light up with interest to the point that I treated it as the best compliment I could have gotten. Donnelly took a picture of that, I have it now in my study and it serves as an encouragement in my writing. Then we went to the Olympic Peninsula. I very much wanted to see it, to hike in the famous forests, to stay on the beaches, and relax. Well, it wasn't to be. It rained cats and dogs all the time. We never even saw the mountains, couldn't go into the forests, and the one time we went for a beach walk we got soaked to the skin even in our raincoats. So after three days we left for home and drove in miserable weather most of the time.

## July 17, 2013

Some more plans from Łucja and Fritz that involve Donnelly and me. Last year they had spent their vacation in New Orleans and fell in love with the city and its people. They had stayed at a bed and breakfast place owned and run by two men — Matt Harring and Lynn Stetzer. The kids were so happy there that this year they want to go there again, but this time both Łucja and Fritzie want us to join them for three weeks in such a way that we would be together for Donnelly's birthday on the fifteenth of September and for Łucja's birthday on the twenty-ninth. What's more, Fritz wants to have a taste of the American way of vacationing in a big RV for part of the time. And to really know what it's like, he wants it to be the biggest of RVs. To help him in the arrangements he asked Donnelly to find a place in Louisiana to rent it, to talk to the rental company, etc. So now Donnelly is busy with the RV and I with maps and decisions as to which way to go to New Orleans, as we decided to drive there. I am pretty sure that as we do not want to tire ourselves too much, and we do want to see places, we'll have to set a week for the travel. Oh, I am looking forward to the whole experience.

## August 20, 2013

Well, the date has been set, we are leaving the house for NOLA on the sixth of September and arriving there on the twelfth. Łucja is going to be there waiting for us, Fritz will join us two days later.

I looked through my calendar to see why I haven't written anything for over a month and, imagine this, I was actually surprised at the amount of theater dates, concerts, visits to friends and their coming to us. Somehow, when it is just day to day I never am conscious of how much entertainment we cram into our weeks. They say that in old age separating oneself from social occasions, from outside of home interests, is dangerous, leads to senility. If so, neither Donnelly nor I are in any danger.

In two days Diana and Ronald are coming for a week. We'll go to the theater, we'll talk, talk, talk. But at a certain point, we'll have to leave them and go to Portland as I have been notified that my swearing in ceremony is going to be on the twenty-seventh. They do understand that it is extremely important to us to be there.

## August 28, 2013
I am an American citizen! Hurray!

## August 30, 2013
We were invited to a pair of dear friends, Marcia and Jerry Simon's, for supper. Imagine my delight when I saw that it was a surprise party to honor my becoming a citizen! Many of our common friends were there waiting for us. Marcia and Jerry baked a rectangular cake covered with white, red and blue icing in the shape of the American flag, and Jerry wrote words to the melody of "You are a grand old flag" that speak of me as a grand old gal, and praising me in a way I have never been praised, at least not in song. Pictures were taken, everybody present sang the new version of the old song, I cried with emotion. Oh my, what good friends I have!

Now I have to start preparing the house, garden, cat for the long absence. Then the decision what to take with us, after all it's going to be over a month. Donnelly will take care of the car of course. In this we are a traditional family — old fashioned male and female roles.

## September 6, 2013

Today in the morning we started our big trip/adventure. It has become a ritual by now to put on a CD by Neil Diamond at the start of driving. Right from the beginning, his "Sweet Caroline" puts us in a good mood. The rhythm, which I like to beat on my thighs by the way, makes us feel more energetic, more prepared for what is to come. Then comes "The Cracklin' Rose," "Song Sung Blue," my beloved "Play Me," and a song that is especially dear to me, "Shilo." In this one he speaks about loneliness in childhood and about a friend he imagined. "Shilo when I was young, I used to call your name. When no one else would come, Shilo you always came, and we'd play...." When I was a child in the time of war, I had an imagined friend too — Pan Krzesło (Mr. Chair). When I felt especially lonely, when everybody was preoccupied with their stuff, I would sit on the floor, in a corner of the room, pulling a chair to shield me. Then I would talk to him, this Pan Krzesło, and he always understood me, he always answered me the way I needed to be answered. He also told me many stories. My own private Shilo. On the whole, this CD, because of its role in the many trips we've taken, means the onset of an out-of-usual life, of unbounded joy.

After the whole CD we usually need some peace and quiet, some thinking time, some exchange of thoughts. Only later we go back to either The Limelighters or John Denver — two other of our regular driving CDs, or to the radio.

Today's trip started this way too. There is some magic, some superstitious feeling that all is going to be fine after this beginning. And I who usually pooh-pooh at all the nonsense of believing in talismans, amulets, rituals, here I am following this uncharacteristic behavior. But all the same it does feel good.

Now we are at a motel in Los Banos. Tomorrow to the border between California and Arizona on Interstate 10. Next day to Phoenix where we'll visit with a family of one of Donnelly's ex-students. I don't know them, have no wish to spend time with people I know nothing about, but Donnelly wants it, so I agreed. Then in the evening we'll go further, for as long as we'll have strength to go.

## September 8, 2013

What a fantastic surprise! I was quite resigned to be bored, to try to survive a visit I didn't look forward to, yet from the minute they opened their door I liked them, the natural way they greeted and invited us into their home. They have several children, some of them adopted. The wife and mother comes from Hungary, the man is an American by birth. The conversation was animated, interesting, encompassing many subjects. Just like I always want a conversation to be. They took us to an Italian restaurant, where at a table for, if I remember correctly, ten people as the children joined us, we resembled an Italian family, with the loud talking and laughing.

## September 11, 2013

After Tucson we entered an America people know little about. Poverty, depressing poverty. Little towns with boarded up shops and businesses, with run down homes, nonexistent gardens or parks. It is shocking to see, to experience firsthand the enormous difference between what we usually think of as America, the average West Coast cities and villages for instance, and what we were driving through here. Why the people living in that part of New Mexico and Texas do not take care of their own surroundings? What is the difference? Is it because they had been raised in a different culture, with different needs? Or is it that poverty and lack of hope, just seeps away all energy? Why do I feel that this could never be a place I could live in, that these are people I would never feel comfortable with? Is it so deep in me, that general mistrust of those who differ from us in their culture, their life style? If so, I am ashamed of my own feelings.

I do know about the differences between white and black cultures, longer settled Americans and new arrivals from our southern neighbors, or from Asia for that matter. I do understand the human mistrust of those whose lifestyle differs from ours, who seem to adhere to other values than ours. I understand why people do not want these newcomers to move into their neighborhoods, change the atmosphere, the kind of noises, smells that they are accustomed having around them. Understand, yes. But am I okay with it? A big NO. The proof of it is that I feel ashamed when I find similar feelings in myself. Why do I feel such shame? Because it is an inhumane attitude and to top it, it is unrealistic, it leads only to disasters. As we see in history people have always moved. Be it fleeing from war, or from famine, or from natural disasters. Long, long ago there were still uninhabited places in the world, places one could go and settle in peace. But through thousands of years now the new arrivals either had to assimilate to the cultures found or conquer them brutally, destroying the native culture, and at some times, annihilating the people they conquered. Assimilation is often hard if not impossible because of the attitude of migrants on one hand and those whom the migrants want to merge with on the other. We have many examples of such behaviors. Assimilation — the Mongols in China, Tatars in Europe, Turks in the Middle East. Destruction of native culture, life style — we don't have to look far, isn't this what was done by the Europeans here in America and what led to the creation of one of the most powerful countries? Total annihilation of a nation — an example of which would be The Germanic Teutonic Order, calling themselves The Order of the Cross — who either murdered the old, ethnic Prussian people or forcibly Germanized them and called themselves Prussians, which eventually had disastrous consequences for the whole of Europe. It was here in the Germanized old Prussia that the militarization of Germany started. Today on Internet we can find funny (?) disparity of information about the history of the Prussian people. The sources with visibly German names speak of Prussia as a German land, unjustly taken from them after the first and second world wars, forgetting anything that happened before 1700. *The Encyclopedia Britannica* on the other hand speaks of the old Prussians being related to Lithuanians. The encyclopedia says they were conquered by the above mentioned Knights of Teutonic Order, who annihilated the natives and their language, brought in German settlers and eventually, although for a long time a fiefdom of the Polish-Lithuanian Commonwealth, Prussia became the cradle of German militarism. Once again — history as people want it to be. Quite often so far from truth.

In Europe, in the U.S.A. we have managed to develop a civilization of relative ease of life, which necessitates certain conventions as to how we live, how we relate to others, how we behave. We try not to see the very poor, which, after all, in these countries are in the minority. We think, however fallaciously, of our culture as mainly middle class. We think we have a superior justice system, an honest democracy. And then we are faced with an influx of others, be it the people freed from slavery or coming from Latin America, or in the case of Europe mainly from Africa, and we feel in danger of losing that comfort of "let's pretend we are the best in the world."

It is slightly different for me. I chose to change my country, but basically although I am still in the same culture, I have no deep roots here. But for people who have lived in America all their lives? Whose parents, grandparents created this country?

It must be very difficult to see the unkempt houses, overgrown with weeds yards, run down towns.

We often hear that the poor are poor because they are lazy. But isn't it the other way round? Aren't they not doing much to their surroundings because they are poor and tired, and because they feel hopelessness of their situation? Look at what the lack of opportunities does now to the young, even middleclass young — drink, drugs, isn't it a way to escape reality, hide from the feeling of helplessness?

So it wasn't pleasant to go through the south of New Mexico, and part of Texas. But then we came to San Antonio. A lovely town bustling with life, with new construction, with the River Walk and its restaurants and shops. We stayed at a fine hotel. What a relief from the motel of the previous night. We enjoyed the river, had a long walk which was very much needed after hours in the car, had a fine dinner and felt relaxed and happy. As if we had never been depressed by the sight of those poor little towns. Out of sight out of mind. And I call myself a realist!

And now we are in Lake Charles, already in Louisiana, another fine town with a good hotel. After settling in our room we went for a walk at the shore of the lake. Not only was it very pretty, with a lovely park, but also we saw a very moving memorial to the victims of 9/11. Today, as it is an anniversary of this tragedy there were flags and something that touched me deeply — a tee shirt of a fireman from New York was displayed on the monument. Both Donnelly and I felt the need to stay there for some time and think about all those who perished. We sat on a stone bench, remembered the terrible day, remembered the dead, but also talked about the aftermath, about the wars in Afghanistan and Iraq. The criminal, in our opinion, decisions made by George W. Bush, Dick Cheney, and Donald Rumsfeld. Those decisions that killed far more Americans than the terrorists did, that destabilized the whole Middle East and made the world much less safe. And this without even mentioning all the innocent Afghanis and Iraqis who died in the result of these three men's unrealistic goals of spreading "democracy." As if one can play with people's beliefs, culture, history. I remember when I heard about the decision of attacking Iraq, how horrified I was. In my humble opinion it would have been better to give Saddam Hussein money for building schools and hospitals.

Yes, a big chunk of that money would go into building a few more palaces or padding his own accounts, but some would have had to be used for legitimate purposes, if only for show. And Iraqis would know about the gift, they would love America. As it was later proved Saddam never did help the terrorists in the first place. And as much as he was a tyrant, we have to remember that he created a secular state, and that under his rule the women were not barred from education or careers. Yes, people were rather poor and had no political freedom. Yet it was up to their decision whether to oppose and risk their lives or not. Now they have no say in where or when they might lose that life in a terrorist bombing. We would have saved a lot of money and what is much more important, so many lives of our soldiers. In the end the region would not have descended into murderous chaos, as it has. Revenge, war, jingoism — it has never led nations into happiness and prosperity. But those are opinions of a retired teacher and a housewife from Ashland, Oregon. We do not care for the oil profits, we do not have a need of proving to ourselves that we are powerful. We know we aren't on any big scale, we know that we are on a small, small personal scale. No people die because of our decisions. And that is a good knowledge.

But life goes on, so we had dinner and now I am going to take a long bath and do my hair. Tomorrow we arrive at the B&B where Łucja is already waiting for us.

## September 15, 2013

Donnelly's birthday. Today he is seventy-nine. He doesn't look it, it hasn't diminished his mental abilities, he still knows how to love and enjoy life. What more can you ask?

On Saturday, Fritzie came as planned. The B&B that Łucja has praised so much lived up to her opinion of it. It is very peaceful and comfortable. Nicely appointed rooms and bathrooms. In the common room, which is part living room, part kitchenette we have great armchairs, shelves with books and board games, a dining table and chairs, and a very well-filled fridge for our breakfasts and snacks. But the most beautiful and inviting is a little garden behind the house. A marvelously composed jungle of trees, bushes and flowers with a gazebo furnished with table and chairs, some lovely ornaments and, what is great in the stuffy heat of New Orleans, a strong fan under its roof. Łucja, Donnelly and I did some food shopping, so when Fritz arrived we spent the whole evening relaxing in the gazebo with good food and wine.

Today we invited the kiddies to a fine restaurant to celebrate the day, and went for a long trek over the French Quarter. Tomorrow more sightseeing. "And so to bed," as my beloved diarist Samuel Pepys used to say.

## A FEW DAYS LATER

We walk a lot, over the Mississippi, in the French Quarter, in parks and cemeteries. We learn the history of the city, we learn about the disaster of Katrina, we eat, listen to jazz and dance in the streets. There is one big disappointment though — and that is the famous Bourbon Street. The last time Donnelly and I were here, for the poetry convention in 1990, we enjoyed that street very much. It had plenty of restaurants and bars and in each of them jazz bands were playing. Mostly traditional New Orleans jazz. We also heard some fine singers of the blues and spirituals. As we walked along the street we would stop at places with music that was particularly appealing to us, have a bite to eat, or just a drink and then continue on to the next place that caught our attention. I still remember how I liked Bourbon Street.

This time what we experienced was very different. First of all no jazz, just a blaring kind of music, the main attribute of which is its loudness, deafening loudness. Well, times change, businesses have to attract younger clients who are obviously not into jazz anymore. Okay, but the whole street had changed into, what I would call, an open bordello. The amount of prostitutes, the state of their undress bordering on nudity, the youth of those girls shocked us. Some of them seemed to be in their early teens. And I must say we are not easily shocked. And we both enjoy seeing pretty young girls on streets and beaches, but after a third or fourth girl tried to offer her services to Donnelly, and quite aggressively at that, although as we walked he held my arm, we decided to leave Bourbon Street and never return to it. What a pity. Luckily it was only this one street. The other parts of the French Quarter were still fine, with jazz, with art galleries, with places to stop without being accosted by unsavory types.

## Next day, late evening

I always thought that the way I prepare shrimp with lots of garlic, fresh marjoram, lemon, and a sauce made with white wine and a good homemade broth, is absolutely the tastiest shrimp possible. My friends also tell me so. Well, Dooky Chase's Shrimp Clemenceau is better. Oh, Dooky Chase, you fed us superbly tonight. What is this Dooky Chase? It is a restaurant originally opened in 1941 by Edgar "Dooky" Chase and his wife, then expanded by his son Chase Jr. and daughter-in-law Leah who made it into a fine restaurant which soon became a political hub for black voters, a place where blacks and whites could meet, and this, combined with Leah's culinary talents, elevated Dooky Chase's to international celebrity. Among the people who ate there were Ella Fitzgerald, Lena Horn, Ray Charles, George W. Bush, Barak Obama, just to mention a few. The place is beautifully appointed with fine art on the walls, spotless white table cloths, crystal and silver, and food that is absolutely superb. I even bought their cookbook, and Leah herself wrote a dedication and signed it. She is a lovely old dame and still supervises the kitchen. We came out so full that we felt an absolute need of a little walk. Most of the homes around were already rebuilt after the hurricane Katrina that devastated them in 2005. We were told that the whole of that neighborhood came together to help restore the famous restaurant, which had sustained severe damage in the flood. A few of the houses in the neighborhood were not as yet restored so we could see for ourselves the seriousness of damages. One man working on his little house told us that the biggest problem now is trying to find the owners of some of the damaged buildings. "Maybe they died, or moved away and do not want to return," he said. Let's hope the city will be able to repossess those and rebuild them, for now they are an eyesore.

Tomorrow we are picking up the RV and going southwest to Houma, where we'll stay for two days and go on a tour of the swamps and marshes. Then Grand Isle and its beaches where we shall park our vehicles in a camping place on the beach for a few days of total relaxation, grilling fresh shrimp bought from fishermen, and enjoying peaceful evenings of conversation and board games.

## September 28, 2013

What a week! We began with staying at an RV camping site in Houma, which for all of us was a first. We got slowly acclimated to sleeping in the vehicle, washing in its tiny bathroom, making breakfast in the kitchenette, etc. The kiddies gave us the use of the bedroom, which had a big comfortable bed and plenty of storage, while they slept on the sofabed in the living room part of the RV. Łucja was very knowledgeable about cooking in the small space of the kitchenette, and organizing the foods and pots and pans in a sensible way. My daughter! Fritzie was in his element mastering the driving and maneuvering of this behemoth of a vehicle.

Next morning, we had an unforgettable experience of a several hours long tour of the swamp. The captain of our little boat was everything one might want to have for such an excursion. He was born and raised on the bayou. His mother, who must have been a very adventurous woman as she had started the tours business in addition to being a local pilot of small planes, had taught her son everything he needed to know. On retiring she passed the whole business to him. We fed an alligator, which came to our boat when the captain called him! We admired the plants, trees and flowers, listened to quite a lot of history and biology of the region. I even learned for the first time the difference between marshes and swamps. The former do not have trees, only reeds and grasses, the latter support growth of trees and woody brush. Wild nature, yet tame alligators, and cellular phones!

At a certain point when rain came, our pilot moved the boat under an overpass and called his wife to see what the weather service said about the length of the rain. She checked our position, then a moving map of the precipitation, and told him that in around fifteen minutes we should be free to go on. The pilot used the idle time to tell us about his life and about his mother. Then, just as promised, in fifteen minutes we left the shelter of the bridge and continued our trip.

In the evening, as we were looking for a place to have dinner, we lucked out on a local eatery with good food and a lively band of musicians who played Cajun music. What fun. We ate well and danced until late.

The next day we finally reached our destination — the beach on Grand Isle. Camping on a beach is for me the most desirable camping of all. The closeness to the water, the sound of the waves, and long walks on the sand, combined with the eating of freshly caught seafood, is close to second best to spending time in Pluski. We have to add to this the pleasure of long evenings in the company of Łucja and Fritz. They have taught us, new for Donnelly and me, a card game called Ligretto. We liked it from the start, even though the young ones beat us mercilessly.

It is a game showing who has the faster reactions. Of course, age is not a benefit here. So be it.

Now we are back in our B&B in New Orleans. Tomorrow is Łucja's birthday, which, as I wrote before, I consider to be my special day too.

## September 29, 2013

My little girl is forty-seven today. It seems like just a few years ago she was such a little girl. Forty-seven years ago during my labor, when I moaned with pain, a young male doctor told me to stop, saying it didn't hurt that bad. I asked him how did he know, how many times did he give birth to a child. He took his revenge on me after she was born, and he told me I have a daughter. I was surprised. I even said "Oh, no, it's impossible." I was so sure that after my two boys I would have a third one. The doctor then quipped, "Madam, I studied medicine for seven years, I know the difference between a boy and a girl." I laughed until my insides hurt.

Now she is such a lovely, accomplished woman, well educated, well read, fluent in four languages and able to communicate in two more. Happy and lovely to be with. We had a great celebration in the back garden of the B&B. Łucja grilled a whole big whitefish, we made a salad and brought good wine, the owners, Lynn and Matt came with a big, richly decorated cake and we all had a fine evening.

Tomorrow we leave for our trip home. It is going to take longer, as we want to go on side roads, as much as possible.

We'll explore parts of the country neither of us has seen before.

## October 2, 2013

Oklahoma was always connected, in my mind, with the dust bowl, with the poor, haggard Okies migrating with their whole families into California. Everything I ever read about

Oklahoma in history books, in Steinbeck novels, or saw in films spoke, about the dust storms and tragedies of the people who lived there. It was even part of the Fenn family story. Donnelly's mother told me that when he was a baby the family lived in Flagler, Colorado, which was also affected by the dust storms. On stormy days she had to cover both his and his twin sister's cribs with wet sheets to stop the dust getting into the babies' lungs. And, she said, she had to wash the sheets several times a day. What a difference with what we see today while travelling through Oklahoma state. It is mostly green and well cared for. We have found a beautiful, peaceful ranch, breeding cattle, horses, sheep, and zebras. The ranch has also a few cabins for vacationers. They were empty now, so we were given the one we liked best, which is situated over a big pond, far from civilization, among the hilly pastures. It is near the small town of Antlers. We decided to stay here for two days to relax, sleep, and read. I will think of Oklahoma differently now.

## October 6, 2013

Another longer than expected stay. This time in Santa Fe. Such a gorgeous place, magnificent weather with plenty of sunshine and a rather cool breeze. I have often admired the paintings of Georgia O'Keefe, but have never before seen an original one. Only reproductions, and only of the most famous ones. Here, in her museum, I fell in love with her work. It is not a big museum, but we have spent quite a long time in it. So many of her drawings and paintings had to be seen a second, or sometimes even third time. We found so much beauty and sensitivity in her work. Donnelly bought a reproduction of her oil painting of cottonwoods to hang in his bathroom.

On one of our walks through town we stopped at a gallery that caught our eye with drawings of nudes. We went in and met the owner, Mr. Shropshire, a charming man with whom we talked for a long time. He told us that by profession he'd been a nuclear engineer, had worked in Alamo, in Vienna, in Johannesburg, Tokyo, and New York, but after retiring he opened this gallery and named it for his late son Justin Robert. He had loved art all his life and while working in Vienna he met a Czech artist, Tomas Hrivnač. He liked Hrivnač's work very much and bought a lot of it. In his gallery now, what we see is the biggest in the world collection of Hrivnač's art. Well, we admired the pictures and sculptures, but we told Mr. Shropshire we could not afford to buy any. He said it did not matter, he liked to show art to people who appreciated it, and anyway, there didn't seem to be crowds in his gallery, so it was a pleasure for him to talk to us. It most definitely was a pleasure for us too. The art was mostly nudes. They were done in such a way that, I suppose, even the biggest prude wouldn't protest. In addition to nudes, Hrivnač painted flamenco dancers and drew animals. Finally, we were satiated with art, tired and hungry, so we said our goodbyes and went looking for a restaurant.

When we were planning the trip, we decided to stop at the Petrified Forest and the Grand Canyon, but as our good-for-nothing Congress managed to shut down the government, all the National Parks are closed so we'll just head home tomorrow or the day after.

## October 10, 2013

Home, sweet home. As usual we are happy to be home. The house is small and without any architectural charm, yet we had managed to create quite a lovely and comfortable interior. And of course sleeping in our own bed is very appreciated.

Also, Ashland is so colorful in October. The trees present a riot of reds, yellows, oranges, and the gardens are still filled with flowers. Our roses in the backyard are covered with an abundance of blooms.

## December, 2013

There was a bad train accident in New York. A commuter train going towards Manhattan derailed. There are four confirmed deaths and sixty wounded. My thoughts went to the survivors and those who lost their family members and friends. I know — I should be most sorry for those who died. Somehow I feel more for the ones that are left with the pain of loss, or in case of survivors with the haunting memories. I was in such an accident, it stays in my memory as vividly as if it happened yesterday. Yet it was in 1963 or 1964.

It was summer, I lived in Warsaw, Wojtek was in Poznań attending a big international fair and I was supposed to join him for a few days. A big event for me, as Jarek was one or two years old, which meant my being tied to the apartment for most of the time. I remember that I often felt I'd been sentenced to house arrest. I felt confined, often unhappy, resentful, as if an armed guard stood in front of my house. I had liked to be alone before. But there is alone of your own choice and a different alone when tied to this little creature, totally dependent on you, yet giving little in return. Babies are for me just an extended digestive tract. You put food into one end and you clean the other. I had always heard how cute little babies are. I couldn't see it. Bad mother, I suppose. I think I only started to like my children when they began to speak, to show some intelligence. I liked them especially when they asked questions. But that was still in the future for me as a mother.

Are those the unpleasant sides of women's education? Through the years at the university, work, and earning my own money I got used to a sense of freedom, of being in control of my time and movement. I loved being among grownups; as I wrote before, to this day I enjoy conversations, especially with people who are either more intelligent or better educated, or simply had or have a different kind of life. Life of a kind that I know little about.

Although theoretically I wanted to have children, I was obviously not prepared to cope with daily duties, with the lack of freedom, lack of company of adults. The limitations that were even more painful when I compared my duties with Wojtek's kind of work. As a journalist, he travelled, talked to different people, had a fascinating life, while the poor me was spending my days in washing nappies, cooking, or at best walking with a stroller. Of course in this kind of pity party I used to forget the amount of time I was spending reading books, the lack of daily stress of a job, or the benefits of all those walks. In hindsight I see those days as very enjoyable. Hindsight! How different from what we feel at the moment.

Anyway, I became deliriously happy when my mother offered to stay with Jarek for a week, enabling me to join Wojtek. A whole week! The first free week since the little one was born! I prepared myself well, no cost spared. A visit to a beautician, hairdresser, masseuse, pedicurist, manicurist; if I could have thought of anything else, I would have done it. A new silk dress. A mini — very fashionable in Poland just then. A pair of atrociously high heeled shoes. And then the taxi, the train, and pure joy. I could have sung out. I could have kissed bystanders.

I found my place in the train. The other five passengers in my compartment were young army officers. Handsome, dressed in well-pressed uniforms, vibrantly healthy, in other words very attractive. They immediately started to flirt with me, and when I managed to steer the conversation towards a more serious topic, we really enjoyed each other's company. We relaxed, we talked, laughed a lot. And then came the jolt. It felt as if the train hit a wall. The suitcases from the rack above our heads flew into us, the carriage screeched, wobbled, leaned to one side and fell with an enormous crash of broken glass and mangled metal. A moment of total silence, then eruption of crying, yelling, moaning, pleas for help.... My officers showed their mettle then. One of them climbed up to the side window, which now was an opening in the new ceiling and checked whether the electric cables were lying on the train, which luckily they were not. Then one of those down in the compartment grabbed me around my knees and lifted me up, while the one on top pulled me out and helped to get down to earth. Only then the rest of them came out and immediately began organizing help. Those were days way before cellular telephones, so someone ran to some houses visible in the distance. Then we all, with the help of other survivors, started pulling out those who couldn't do it on their own. My companions employed me to take care of children while they were helping their mothers, grandmothers and a very badly hurt father. I remember that my new dress had a long and flowing silk sash for a belt; well it came in handy tying a piece of wood to a visibly broken limb of a young girl. Finally, finally, after an hour or so the first ambulances arrived. We had doctors, we had nurses, we had bandages, and most important we had transportation to hospitals for those in the worst shape. I was not needed anymore.

Somebody, one of those unhurt, organized a group who wanted to go in search of a highway so we could get out of there. I joined the walk through fields. Not easy in my high heels. After what seemed like an interminable trek we came to a road. Shortly after, a big truck appeared. It couldn't take everybody as its bed was half filled with metal pipes, but those who wanted to sit on top of those pipes were welcomed by the driver. I managed to get on there. Okay, we were being driven to Poznań, we would get to our destination, our troubles were over.

Well, not so fast. As bad luck goes, on that hot, oppressive day, we were to endure another calamity. A thunderstorm! Not something one would want to go through while sitting on a pile of metal pipes. Not in the open when rain and then hail were beating on us, as if all hell broke loose. I've always liked thunderstorms. The lightning, the noise of thunder, the torrential rains that, quite often, accompany a storm, were always fascinating for me. Yes, when I was sitting in a calm house, by a window shielding me from it all. Now, on this truck, with the rain pouring, with twigs from wind-torn trees falling on us and dead leaves being plastered onto our faces, when the hail bruised us and made us shiver with cold, it was a very different storm adventure. Well, all's well that ends well. Nobody got killed by a lightning bolt and the truck driver delivered us to the center of the city.

I was a wreck, my lovely hairdo was no more, my silk dress clung to my shivering body in tatters, one of my fashionable stiletto heels was missing, my makeup had run, creating queer maps on my face. I entered the hotel where Wojtek was staying, a very elegant hotel. Immediately a porter appeared and tried to get me to go back out. They could not allow a terrible street person to damage their image, could they?

Only after my big pleas, after my absolute obstinacy in trying to get back in, some kind of a manager appeared and led me to an office in the back to hear me out. I told him who I was, but as my handbag had been lost I had no ID. He did allow me though to make a call. I knew a guy in the biggest local newspaper, Romek Polanski (no, not the famous, or to some, infamous film director). In the past, we had had good times with him and his wife. He and Wojtek had made several journalistic trips together. I found the paper's offices number in a telephone book. I called and was relieved that he was there. He said he couldn't come as he was operating a line for field reporters who were calling from the site of the train wreck, but first he told me that Wojtek was beside himself with worry, running around the hospitals looking for me. And then he talked to the hotel guy, explained everything, and told him to please give me the key to Wojtek's room. Which the man did. Within minutes I was lying in a hot bath, waiting for my husband to come and join me. It finally happened. All was well. Not for everybody though. The next day we learned that more than thirty people died, and many were severely injured.

## JANUARY 18, 2014

Magda came three days ago, for a two months or longer stay with us. I am very upset about the shape she is in. I know her as a cheerful, optimistic, hardworking, down to earth woman. I love her. She is such a good, loving and honest person. Yet the woman that we see today is a very depressed wreck of her previous self. She says that she doesn't want to go back to Poland. Ever. She wants to make a life for herself here in America. She says she has me as a role model.

So we started to ask how she wants to achieve this. We know that a work visa can be obtained if the petitioner has a promise of a job from an employer who cannot find candidates among legal residents. A fine engineer comes to mind. But Magda has no profession. Of course I know that it can be manipulated, just like Howard's lawyer did with my case. But for this she would have to start working and be successful and liked enough so that the employer would want to go to all that trouble. What kind of jobs are there for which people have a hard time finding a reliable person who speaks pretty good English? Well, the care of an elderly or a sick person would be one, taking care of a baby, or small child would be another. Magda says that she couldn't emotionally cope with a senile or sick man or woman. She also pointed out that she has no experience with babies. When her children were born, a grandmother of hers lived with her and Jan, and took care of the babies. What she would like to do is to work in a restaurant as she is a very good cook, and she loves the work. I don't think that she could get a work permit to do this. Then she said maybe she could go to a culinary school and was very upset when she learned that all her savings couldn't pay for even one year of such a school. After discussing all other possibilities, I realized that she is so different from the Magda we knew, that there must be something very much wrong with her general health. We won't be able financially to provide her with healthcare here in the U.S., yet she desperately needs a good doctor. The only thing we can do is to take as good care of her as it is possible while she is with us, to at least make her calmer and stronger, so that she understands the need of going back home. After all, she has free or nearly free access to doctors in Poland. Oh, how I want to help her, to see again the lovely woman she is deep down.

## MARCH 22, 2014

Magda left yesterday. We are flying to Poland on the tenth of April. If need be I can help her there. Even if only to take her to doctors, to see that she gets good care. I am also anxious to see what is wrong and how serious it is.

## APRIL 23, 2014

We are now here in my old home. The house which I designed, which I furnished, organized, in which I lived for twelve years, in which I raised my kids until they were strong and independent enough to leave home, to test their own waters. Now Jarek, Jagoda and the two little ones, Mieszko and Martynka, live in it. I knew it wouldn't be easy. The memories that are connected to the rooms, the furniture, the art on the walls, even the garden in which lilacs and mock orange that I planted as small seedlings are now enormous. It all assailed me with great force. It is now my son's family home to organize the way they see fit. I knew that my quite emotional reactions shouldn't be shown to them, that I should not in any way criticize or speak about how it had been. It took me a good week to get used to the reality, to calm down. The fact that the four of them are so loving and so tender towards both of us helped a lot. Jagoda is the best daughter-in-law I could ever want. Jarek, who is now a stay-at-home dad, proved to be very good in this role. The kids are very well taken care of, both physically and, what is even more important, mentally and emotionally. They are happy, obedient, and play together without quarrels. Mieszko seems to be more scientifically minded, Martyna has a very creative mind and while they play she tells a lot of invented stories. She's got great imagination, that girl. She reminds me of how I made up fantastic stories when I was her age.

We had a lovely Easter. In addition to the six of us, Jagoda's sister came from London where she lives, and Jan and Monika visited. Then on Easter Monday Isia, who is in a wheelchair, was brought by her husband Stanisław. Isia's daughter Marta, her man Marek and son Achim came with them to dinner, after which Magda and Oskar came too. It was such a good Easter. Magda told us how grateful she is that we insisted on her coming back to Poland to see a good doctor. She was diagnosed with diabetes and thyroid problems so serious that the doctors insisted on treatment ASAP. Although it is less than a month since she was first seen at the clinic, she is visibly improving. Hallelujah. She is still very pale and thin, but her spirit is on the mend.

On the twenty-seventh, we shall go by train to Berlin where Łucja and Fritz will be singing Verdi's Requiem with their choir. I haven't been to Berlin since Germany became reunited, and Donnelly has never seen it before, so we are both looking forward to a lot of sightseeing. Olaf is going to be there too and, as he knows the city pretty well, he wants to be our guide. The kids have rented a three-bedroom apartment so we should be quite comfortable.

## May 6, 2014

So we are back in Podkowa, back at the house with Jarek and Jagoda and the kiddies. We are treated here as if we totally belong, not as guests. I enjoy picking up Mieszko from school and sitting by his side when he is busy with homework. I love evenings spent talking with the grown-ups, or playing Ligretto, although Jarek is so competitive and so good that nobody else can win a game, which often upsets Jagoda. When he was a child he played backgammon with me and could not understand that I was happy both when I won and when he did. He remembers to this day my explanation that I am happy to win of course, but when he wins I am happy that I have such a bright son.

The Berlin trip was pure joy. The first three days Łucja and Fritz were busy with rehearsals, and Donnelly and I spent the time seeing the city. Berlin is beautiful, the way Germans rebuilt the eastern part is impressive. The amount of greenery surpasses anything I ever saw in other cities. A single park, the Tiergarten, which covers 1996 square miles (Central Park in New York covers 1317) and has fourteen miles of walking paths, is awe inspiring. And there are many more parks and tree-lined streets. We visited all the important sights: The Branderburg Gate, the Reichstag, the Jewish Museum; we took a long boat ride on the river Spree, from which we admired very modern structures housing the government. So we really enjoyed Berlin, but for me the biggest happiness came from the fact that all this was shown to us by Olaf. He knows the city as he had spent quite a bit of time there as part of his medical studies, and for him to choose being with his grandparents instead of visiting friends really showed how he feels about us. I even had an evening alone with him when Donnelly wanted to go to a rehearsal with the singers.

The concert was beautiful, couldn't be any better. It was two choirs combined, the Berlin and the Zurich. After the concert, many of the singers met at a local restaurant and we had the pleasure to meet and talk to colleagues of Łucja and Fritz. Hearing that Donnelly is also a singer, people asked him to sing. He sang an aria from Tosca and got big bravos. That warmed the atmosphere even more, and we had a very enjoyable evening. Then came the days of the five of us gallivanting around town, visiting museums and taking the aforementioned river trip. As you can see, we think the city well worth spending time in, I wouldn't mind going there again. The general atmosphere is so different from American cities. We never felt any tension. So many people ride bicycles. I even saw several times small children riding with their parents or older siblings, right there on busy streets. Plenty of *biergartens* and restaurants on the sidewalks, no feeling of "hurry, hurry, work, work" that you have in New York and so many other U.S. cities for instance. Oh, Europeans, you know how to enjoy life!

## May 10, 2014

Yesterday I had such a great pleasure — a dinner with Iwonka and her children. Ula came with her boyfriend Piotr, and Marcin was accompanied by his fiancé Kasia. We do not see Iwona often enough. She works so much that we usually see her only two or three times during our stay. Same with Ula and Marcin. This time Donnelly and I invited all of them to a Greek restaurant with an outdoor seating. We all love the food, and the staff of this restaurant are friends of Ula. She has spent several of her summer vacations in Greece, speaks fluent Greek and English, and on the whole is a lovely young woman. She works in a bank now and seems to be successful in what she is doing. It was such a pleasure to be able to talk to her and observe her in action with other people. Marcin is a criminal psychologist and is very satisfied with the work he does in the justice system. Kasia has just graduated from a law school. They plan to marry soon. I found her very interesting.

When I talked to Iwonka I asked her whether she still remembers how to count in the seven languages that she knew how to count to ten when she was a child. She laughed and started — in Polish, Russian, German, English, French, Italian and Arabic. Her kids were astonished and asked where did it come from. I laughed and told the story. When Iwonka was nine she was diagnosed with scoliosis. It was pretty severe and the doctor prescribed for her a set of exercises that she was supposed to do every morning for half an hour. Normally the children were getting up at seven in the morning, which meant that both I and she had to get up at least half an hour earlier. No child likes to get out of bed at half past six. She hated the exercises, she was envious that the others were allowed to sleep longer, she cried. That was when I invented counting the repetitions in different languages. The game was how soon she could remember those numbers from one to ten. How soon, after counting together with me, would she be able to count on her own. The challenge made her forgo the pity party and start enjoying the process. And was she proud when she could impress her siblings with all those unknown to them words. I am happy that she still remembers them to this day.

## MAY 24, 2014
I had a fine Name Day. Like in the old times, my friends came with lilacs and chocolates. Stanisław brought Isia. I was treated once more as somebody very special, which of course I like. A Name Day is such a nice tradition. The twenty-fourth of May is my patron's, St. Joan of Arc's day so everybody who knows me as Joanna knows it is my day. Birthdays are usually known only to family and closest friends, on a Name Day one sees how many people care enough to celebrate with one.

## MAY 28, 2014
We had a phone call from Chio Mei, that our cat Bucik died. Our beloved cat, such a friend. I cried myself silly. What a sad homecoming it is going to be!

## JUNE 2, 2014
At home. It is so empty without Bucik and all the rituals we had with him. We buried him in the garden. I don't want to have any more animals. It is too sad to lose them.

## June 20, 2014

A few days ago I read in *The New Yorker* a write-up on a book: *In the Light of What We Know* by Zia Haider Rahman. It so grabbed my attention that I immediately went to my Kindle and ordered a sample, read it, felt even more interested, drove downtown to our local bookstore and bought it. For the next three days I couldn't tear myself from reading. It is absolutely fascinating. On all fronts. The story — two guys, friends from Oxford University, mathematicians, meet after several years of not seeing each other and start talking. One of them acts in the book as a narrator telling us of those conversations and later on about the notebooks of the other one (by name of Zafar), relating everything that happened to him in the years of not being in touch with the narrator, who remains unnamed throughout the book. Some conversations are told in a regular "he said, and then the other responded" way, some are just remembered by the narrator. Anyway, we are privy to how and what they talk about. And they talk and tell stories through the whole book, all 497 pages. And how they talk! And what stories they tell us! To put it all in a few words, we learn about their lives — one is from Bangladesh, the other from Pakistan — but also about the history of Bangladesh, of war in Afghanistan, mathematics, finances in the 2000s, with good explanation of the crash of 2008, race relations in Britain and U.S., class divisions in England, a mixed race and class love affair, and quite a few other themes. Mainly, I would say, we learn many things, but, what is more important we are made aware of the role of education and class divisions in the life of people. I never thought that a person from a lower class, or an immigrant from a very different culture, might be feeling estranged from their peers their whole life. So what if he/she may achieve a great education, a fine position in the society, financial ease — there are always the little differences in a world outlook, in manners, in things remembered from childhood, that will create a barrier. A barrier felt by both sides. The person who came into a new country or entered a higher class through education, money or marriage, will always feel deficient, not having had the experiences of his/her peers; those who surround him/her also are aware of the newly arrived person's gaucheness at the table, different sense of humor, lack of ease in knowing how to dress for what occasion, or simply in remembering childhood books and fairy tales. All this separates them whether they are conscious of it or not. It is so important for everybody to be part of a group that gives them the comfort of belonging. And we feel it mainly through a lot of small traits, memories, nearly automatic reactions, behaviors. Does that mean that I am against stepping out of our class or culture? Oh, no. We just have to be mentally and emotionally prepared for the difficulties.

In Rahman's book, we are pulled into the workings of two brilliant minds, their ideas and opinions. We are exposed to a rich language. What else could one want in a book? I am near to the end and am sure that it is one of the best books I've ever read, if not the best. Oh, how happy I am. How lucky we are that all the time there are people who write such books. How lucky that as soon as we finish something interesting, we find there are more books to read and enjoy. I love books that make me think and rethink, that give me a possibility of constant growth. I haven't been able to stop myself from reading passages to Donnelly, so now he is impatient to get it in his hands. More reason to finish it fast, but I already know that after he is done with it I'll want to read it a second time, much slower, paying more attention to the language and ideas.

There is something about the beauty of the English language that is often seen in books written by people for whom English is a second language. It started, as far as I know, with Joseph Conrad (his name was Józef Konrad Korzeniowski, but the difficulty of pronouncing this name was such that after he started writing he changed it to Joseph Conrad). Then came many others. To name just a few who I like to read — Jhumpa Lahiri, Khaled Hosseini, Chitra Banerjee Divakaruni. All those authors write in English, but it happens in other languages too — for instance there is Andrei Makine, a Russian born in the Soviet Union who writes in French and who with his first book *Le Testament Francais* won the very respected prizes Prix Goncourt and Medicis (in 1995). Are they more attuned to the words, to grammar, because they learned it after their own tongue, or because it comes second, the learner has a chance of comparing the two, enriching the way they speak with the sensibilities of a different culture?

Well, so I am looking forward to rereading. When I already know the plot, I can concentrate on how the book is written and am more alert to the beauty of the prose.

## A FEW DAYS LATER

I finished *In the Light of What We Know* and now Googled the author — it seems that the main character of the whole work is based on the author, Zia Haidar Rahman. Both Zafar and Zia are Bangladeshi, both were brought to England as children by their parents, who are uneducated people from a small village in Bangladesh. Both studied mathematics in Oxford, both worked on Wall Street making great money and later became lawyers working in the international human rights movement. The narrator is a totally different person who, although from a Pakistani family, was born in England and grew up in an affluent and intellectual home. He is portrayed in such a way that though we hear that he was a successful student, but not as good as Zafar, we understand that a lot of his achievements came from belonging to his successful family. We are made to see clearly the difference in how they are received in society, and think how many brilliant kids are never able to develop their potential, satisfy their innate curiosity, and how many mediocre intellects are nurtured to become people in power. George W. Bush comes to mind, doesn't he? There is also a question of the title — *In The Light Of What We Know*. It implies that we do not know everything, and the words "in the light of" suggest that what we know might not be enough. We can speak of things we know, we can think we know what there is to be known, both about the world around us and about ourselves, but what percentage of reality is it? The very idea of enlightenment, of seeing, brings immediately the understanding that there is a lot in the dark. We think we know our parents, siblings, friends, but isn't it true that we only know our own representations of them? First of all, they don't reveal everything that is in them, but also we do not want to see the parts that would belie our story of who they are, what they represent to us. And what about the interactions with ourselves? Isn't it true that we carry a representation of who we are in our minds, a story that is comfortable, convenient? How else could we surprise ourselves, or sometimes even disgust ourselves? How else could we react with, "I don't know why I did this," or "I am sorry I did it, I didn't think...." That whole idea of reality being beyond our reach boggles my mind. Once again I hear my father's words — "don't lie to yourself" — and I realize how difficult that is. And I see how "in the light of" relates to my own memories and thoughts.

## July 22, 2014

Aunt Helena died yesterday at the age of ninety-eight. Everybody's dream of an old age and death. She retained her full mental faculties and physical abilities until last week, when she suffered a stroke and got pneumonia. A few days in a hospital and then she died in her sleep. Donnelly and I visited her in May. She prepared a lovely lunch for us, declined any help with carrying plates from the kitchen to the dining room, shooed me out of the kitchen when I wanted to help with the dishes.

In conversations she was lively, interesting, and interested in what we had to say. The only complaint we heard was that hot weather, especially damp heat, was becoming very tiring, to the point that she had to go for her daily walk pretty early in the morning. The day of her stroke was very hot with a thunderstorm in the afternoon.

She was the last of the generation of my parents. There isn't anybody now who would remember me as a child or a teenager. Now I am the oldest in the family. This realization sends shivers down my spine.

## July 23, 2014

Aunt Helena's death has struck me deeply. I am constantly thinking about her and how important she had been to me. She was everything my own mother wasn't. Strong, hard working, seemingly always knowing what she wanted and where she wanted to be in her life. Even her marriage to Tolek (our pet name for Antoni) was unconventional to a high degree — my father used to joke that instead of rearing animals she reared a very useful bull for a husband. Most of the time he didn't work. By profession he was an engineer, she taught him to do technical dentistry. He loved working with machines or gardening. She kept him home to just do that or had him help in her surgery. So that nobody else could influence him? So that he didn't meet other women? Who knows. Compared to my mother's dependence on my father, her adoration of everything he did, thought, said, Helena's attitude to Antoni was very refreshing for a young girl. Her behavior showed that women can be stronger than men, that instead of being used, we are capable of using. And then I started to think about my mother — why had I always considered her weak. Her death should have opened my eyes to a very different side of her. In her early seventies she started to become quite senile, by the middle of her eighties she was totally divorced from reality. Finally, when she was eighty-eight she decided one day that she didn't want to get out of bed. My sister Isia called me asking what she should do — make her get up, call a doctor, although Mother seemed to be healthy, or let her stay in bed. We discussed its repercussions, the fact that she might not be able to get up after a prolonged bed rest, the danger of pneumonia etc. I asked Isia whether I should come. She told me that as far as Mother was concerned it was not necessary as just the other day her sister, our Aunt Helena, visited and Mother was very happy being sure that it was me. Asking how long did I plan to stay in Poland, and whether life in America was still good for me. Auntie did not disabuse her sister of that belief. Isia and I agreed that were we in such a condition we wouldn't want anybody to contradict us. Most probably she was tired of life, of the limited life she was leading. Let her do what she wants, was our decision. In a few days mother refused to eat, slept most of the time. Then refused to drink, fell into a coma. One day, as my son Jarek was there helping Isia change bedclothes for his grandmother, she opened her eyes, and according to what both Isia and Jarek told me, a look of great happiness came to her face. She smiled a big joyous smile and died. Is that the death of a weak person?

## August 25, 2014

We went to the theater yesterday. Saw *Into the Woods*, a musical written and composed by Stephen Sondheim. Fine performance, as usual, at our local Shakespeare Festival theater. The first part lively, fun to watch, reminded us of all the fairy tales from our childhoods. The second, rather grim, depressing, showing the weaknesses and evil of human nature. Of course we, the audience, could not get left with such ruminations on the fallibility of our nature, so the last scene is an uplifting story, a song telling us that nobody is alone, that everything is going to be fine. Sweet, melodic song, actors loving each other, willing to help, and all that false crap. Nauseating optimism.

On our way out we passed an old woman whose back was bent 90 degrees in the area of her waist. She walked leaning heavily on a walker lowered as much as possible. Her hair was coiffed nicely, she wore a longish skirt and a good quality sweater, she talked animatedly with another woman, obviously having enjoyed the play. Why did I use a past tense? She was still enjoying herself, the companion, the evening. Yes, that is what I love about America — that people with such disabilities have the drive to enjoy, to participate. That nobody seems to say, "this is not for me, I'll just spend my time in an armchair feeling sorry for myself." Well, at least I think "nobody," but the truth could be that those in the armchairs are simply not visible.

## SEPTEMBER 2014

Donnelly and his twin sister Dorothy became eighty years old on the fifteenth. We drove to Seattle for the occasion. Dorothy is not in good health and travelling is rather out of the question, so we went there to be with her and her family (her son Andy Pearson, his wife Robin, and their four lovely teenage children). Laurie and David, Donnelly's kids, joined us there too. It was quite a celebration, everything went smoothly and we all were happy visiting. To relax after such an emotional week, Donnelly and I went to spend a few days at a lodge over Odell Lake. A beautiful, peaceful place with great walking in the forest, fine food, and plenty of time to read and talk. And then, totally unexpectedly, after coming home I started to feel very weak. It progressed to the point that I went to my doctor. He ordered tests, they did not show what's wrong, yet I am weaker and weaker. I cannot walk for longer than ten minutes; I feel comfortable only lying down. I am worried.

## DECEMBER 20, 2014

All that time was terrible for me. The doctors didn't know what was wrong. The tests were inconclusive. Finally, on December 6, in despair that he could not diagnose me, my cardiologist decided I should stop taking Crestor, a statin medication I had been taking for several years. Within days I started to feel better. I am not back to my old self yet, but it is obvious that it all was a side effect of that damned Crestor. What a waste of time for me! I was too weak to even read or enjoy my normal life. The older I get the more precious every day is. I don't have the luxury of a big future, do I? Another poem tied to all these sad thoughts that assail me lately:

### WHEN I DIE

*And when I die cremate my remains,*
*Spread the ashes over meadow green.*
*I'll live in the grasses, flowering herbs,*
*The sun will be mine and the wind.*
*I'll exist in a billion of cells dispersed,*
*In plants, animals, people.*
*I'll fertilize, feed, remain for ages*
*The usefulness, particle, I am now.*

I do feel I have been useful most of my life, I do not have many regrets about how I have used the time that was given me. What more could one wish for?

## JANUARY 2015

I was thinking today about beauty. I am pretty sensitive to it, sometimes I feel I cannot live without it. And it doesn't matter whether it is visual, auditory, or intellectual. But how do I define beauty? St. Augustine wondered whether things are beautiful because they give delight, or whether they give delight because they are beautiful. Yes, the typical problem of what came first — the egg or the chicken. It seems to me that evolution would be the best explanation — something pleases us when it is beneficial to our survival, to our health or reproductive needs. It would fit with the hundreds of years of considering rosy cheeks, full breasts, and wide hips in women to be the requirement for feminine beauty. But then how about today, when the attractiveness of a woman has been reduced to her resembling a young boy? Is it because there are too many people in the world? Is that the reason for so many same-sex couples? Nature trying to improve the situation?

But back to beauty, classical conceptions of it spoke about perfect arrangement of integral parts into a coherent whole. And by coherent what was usually meant was proportional, harmonious, often symmetrical. The evolutionary development of the idea of beauty would make sense, when we consider such great differences in perception of beauty in different parts of the world. A beautiful day for us is a sunny day, yet I can bet such a day is not seen pleasurably in Sahara. On the other hand, if we translate our enchantment with greenery, with flowers, with fields and orchards as a natural reaction to the promise of food, how can we explain the love for rocky, dry, sometimes menacing mountains? Or why do we admire the dead, twisted tree trunks thrown haphazardly on the ocean beach? As usual I have more questions than answers. And all because of the pleasure I had seeing the shapes of leafless, winter trees I watched while walking.

## NEXT DAY

In my "previous life," the life before coming to America, I was enchanted with politics and politicians. On one side there was the Soviet Union, on the other Poland with its need for freedom, for independence. While living in Moscow Wojtek and I became good friends with, among others, Mihail Kapica, who, if I remember correctly, was at that time a deputy prime minister, a specialist of Soviet-China relations. We had spent many an evening together with him and his wife. My children should remember him, as he liked to play with them. He was very tall and often would grab a kid and, holding him/her upside down, had them "walk" with their feet touching the ceiling. Those evenings I remember as opening my eyes to how an important international power acts in the interest of their own country. How people in power think differently about the scale of importance, about the lives and needs of individuals. How it is possible to totally disregard the value of soldiers' lives and their families. All in the idea of "country" and its standing in the world. In Poland we had several politicians as, maybe not friends, but at least good acquaintances. That meant my participation in many decision makings, which so often happened at a dinner table. Our dinner table included. Often, between compliments about the food, I would also be asked my opinion. Some of those men (yes, there were no women) seemed to be really interested in my thoughts. Especially Tadeusz Wrzaszczyk, the Minister of Heavy Industry and later Deputy Prime Minister. He became Wojtek's and my good friend, and always asked for my opinion. At least once it made a difference — after asking me what I thought about Poland buying the know-how for production of cars from Renault or from Fiat. He listened attentively to my argument for the latter. He decided in favor of Fiat. Was I proud!

I thought about it today after reading what I wrote yesterday about beauty. How does this tie in with my increasing need for beauty? Well, with years I gained a distaste for what I saw as corrupted politicians. Were they always so, but I was too naïve to see it? Were only the honest ones attracted to Wojtek and me, so that we had known only those? I suppose that to think otherwise would be disingenuous. There must have been the idiots, the corrupted ones always, only I didn't see them. Anyway, now when I look at politics, it disgusts me to the point of separating myself from that life, even to the point of not wanting to read about it. I decided to spend the rest of my life, what is still going to be given to me, on enjoying the beauty of the world. The music, the poetry, the literature, the people who have that beauty of brain and spirit, and of course nature, which is a constant source of happiness for me. Luckily we live in Ashland, and it is so easy to immerse ourselves in all those aspects of beauty. There are not many small towns with five professional theaters, a university, a fine library, that are surrounded within walking distance by mountains, forests and lakes. Will I be able to change my interest in what is happening in the world of politics? Or will I go back to reading the news and then get furious?

## March 15, 2015
I am a great grandmother! My lovely granddaughter Little Łucja, Jan and Magda's daughter, gave birth to a little boy. She lives in London now with the father of her child, who is a British citizen of Colombian origin, so the little one is half Polish, half Colombian, and a British citizen. That is part of the globalization that we constantly hear about, isn't it? I am very moved and sorry we are so far from each other. They are naming him Indigo Angelo Gonzales Kubicki. The little blue angel, I wonder how he is going to shorten that name in his future? My father would have been enchanted, now there are citizens of Poland, USA, Germany, Switzerland, and Britain among his descendants. I am happy — I always felt I was a citizen of the world, and this brings me even closer to that, doesn't it?

## April 10, 2015
People are born, people die. Basia, Aunt Helena's daughter, died today. She was fifteen years younger than me. Nobody in the family knew that she had cancer. She hid it very well. One thing is good, her mother died before her. It would have been the biggest tragedy of Aunt Helena's long life had she known about the cancer. It is a sobering feeling that I have because of all those

deaths so close to me. *Memento mori*. How could I forget that I too am mortal, that I do not know the day or the hour. That I have to be grateful to fate that I still live, and enjoy my life, and try to live to the fullest. Try? I think I do live to the fullest. There is a Polish song about the joy of life, sung beautifully by Anna Jantar, who herself died in her twenty-ninth year in 1980 in a plane crash. There is a line in it: "I really know how to live." I have always identified with this song, and now even though I am (no need to kid myself) closer, so much closer to the end, I still feel that I know how to live. But all these deaths around me fill me with profound sadness of missing.

## April 27, 2015

Donnelly and I attended the live broadcast of Metropolitan performance of *Cavalleria Rusticana* by Pietro Mascagni, followed by *I Pagliacci* by Ruggero Leoncavallo. Those are two relatively short operas usually produced together. *Cavalleria* came first. I didn't like the staging which was, as I call such productions, "original for originality's sake." Dark, simple, empty stage, its center rotating slowly, filled with chairs. A multitude of chairs. Everybody was dressed in black or dark clothes. The choir had a lot to do with moving those chairs in, out of, or simply around the stage. No sense to it whatsoever. After we came back home I went to my computer and watched pieces of Cavalleria on YouTube. A production from Zurich, the famous film by Franco Zeffirelli, something from La Scala. It all proved I was right in my disappointment. In those other productions the voices were better, the scenes on an Easter morning more logical — people dressed up, the scene colorful, with flowers, with fruit sellers, with happy children. One could believe it was Easter in an Italian village. It is supposed to be "verismo" — truth. This production was far from it. The voice of main actress (here Eva-Maria Westbroek) I did not like to the point of my wondering how was I going to stand her for the whole time.

Luckily I did like all the other voices, and especially Marcelo Alvarez who starred in both *Cavalleria* and *Pagliacci*. And here I come to the main reason why I write about that morning at the opera. *Pagliacci*, as I mentioned before, was the first opera I ever saw. I was with my father. The La Scala production was fantastic, or so I felt. My father told me what the story was about — love, betrayal, vengeance, murder. He told me to listen for an aria that he thought was the most beautiful — "ridi pagliaccio," which as he explained means "laugh clown, when your heart is breaking." He was moved when he spoke about it. I, of course, couldn't understand the sung words. It was in Italian which at that time was totally unknown to me. Yet I saw my father's emotional response. I saw tears in his eyes. I was very moved by his reaction. I did not understand it at all. Yes, the music was great, yes the man on the stage was visibly upset while he sang, but there were also many funny scenes with the clowns. It definitely did not move me to tears. Now when I am over seventy it did move me tremendously. Not only because I felt for Canio, the clown, but also, or should I say mainly, because I at last understood my father's emotion. Now when I know love, when I understand the pain of having to hide despair under laughter, under small talk, I understand what was going on in his heart. You see, at that time I didn't know that he was madly in love with a young woman, Hanne-Lore. He was so much in love that he wanted a divorce and a new marriage.

I learned about his affair a few months later. We were already in Egypt when one evening he took me on his lap and told me that most probably my mother and he would divorce. And then he asked me whether I would agree to live with him and Hanne-Lore. I was incensed. I was furious. My whole ten-year-old world was on the verge of being destroyed. Here I was in peace and stability for the first time in my life, and he wanted to break it all up. I remember jumping off his lap, yelling NO!

I will not stay with you. He sadly asked — so you prefer to live with your mother? NO, NO, NO was my answer. I don't want either of you, I'll run away, I'll find a way to live on my own. Well, just as stupid as my old wish to run away when I was two. But just as strong.

My parents did not divorce. The thing was never mentioned again. I calmed down. I forgot eventually about the possibility of the rupture in our family. Only now, watching *Pagliacci*, I understood why he was near tears when we watched the opera. I finally understood that my father gave up his happiness for me. For his duty towards his children. He was never fully happy afterwards. Yet, he did love my mother in his way. I never heard them quarrel, I saw many shows of tenderness between them. When finally both his girls were on their own, married, he then asked my mother for a divorce. She agreed. They remained friends and he took good care of her until his death.

Shortly after the divorce he remarried, which proved to be a mistake. He was very unhappy with a woman raised in a strongly Catholic family, who, although brilliant and a great conversationalist, was one of those "all for show, for how people see us" women. And a terrible snob. Which was an anathema for my father who disliked all artificiality. Well, when they were "dating" he saw only the beauty, intelligence, ease of conversation. He saw what she wanted him to see. Her name was Maria Konarska. I actually came to like her. I got to know her life and understand where those airs came from. I was sorry for her. Raised in a fairly well off family of landowners, quite beautiful and bright, she had been engaged to be married to a very handsome man, son of our Polish prime minister. A man of great future, it was believed. Soon after the engagement in 1939 the war started, and her fiancé died in one of the battles. Then came the devastation of their estate, the usual poverty and hardship of the German occupation. They coped, the father and a younger brother tried to rebuild, to run their farms, to survive.

They succeeded. Yet as soon as the Soviets came the first thing the new government did was confiscate privately owned land of more than fifty hectares (125 acres). They kicked the owners out, allowing them to take only few possessions. Roughly what could be put on a horse cart. From their lovely manor, they were able to take two pieces of furniture — Maria's lady's desk (I described it when writing about my father's room), and a curio cabinet. They did manage to salvage the silver cutlery and the best china and crystal, which I later admired very much when visiting. The father of the family became deeply depressed. This later developed into a persecution mania.

Maria was twenty-five at that time, her brother sixteen. She was the only person who could get a job. She did. For years she earned the money to keep her parents and brother, to allow him to go to a university. She studied in the evenings, graduated, studied more, advanced in her job. She was thirty-five when her father died, forty when she met my father, forty-two when they got married. Around fifty when menopause hit, with all the bad sides — hot flashes, hysterical tantrums with crying and shouting, I was really sorry for her, but even more for my father. He didn't expect such development. Wasn't used to feminine instability. My mother was a very calm person, I never heard raised voices in our home. Now, at the age of nearly sixty he was at a loss how to cope. Drank heavily. Once when he was visiting us, and I saw him relaxed and enjoying his time with his grandchildren, I invited him to stay for good. Our house was big enough so that he could have a separate little apartment. He became very somber and said, "I made my bed, now I have to sleep in it." He went back. When in his seventies he got cancer of the throat, she became his angel, took exceptionally good care of him, and he did duly appreciate her help. It was after his death that Maria and my mother became friends.

## May 23, 2015

In something I read lately I happened to see a quotation from Voltaire that made me think about that pet peeve of mine: manipulation. He said, "Those who can make you believe absurdities, can make you commit atrocities." And so many historical facts come to mind. One of them is how we perceive presidents, governments. We know deep down that their main role is to protect, help develop their own countries. Each and every one of them has a different country, a different culture to contend with. So Hitler for instance brought ruin not only to Europe but also, or should I say mainly, to his own Germany and is considered to be an evil ruler. But take Stalin who committed mind boggling atrocities, and whom we consider to have been evil, yet he is still glorified by many in Russia. In the seventies, during the Brezhnev era, I heard many times from Russian acquaintances that they respected Stalin because he made the most powerful countries afraid of Russia. "He made us great," I was told. And Gorbachev whom we think of as great, because he helped to dissolve the USSR, is reviled in today's Russia. So much depends on the history of a nation. The U.S.A. was created as a democracy, but Russia, and for that matter Middle Eastern countries, have never had such a political system. It is an absurdity to believe that we can install democracy in such places, and, yes, it leads to atrocities that began because of the absurd goals of the Bush administration. It would be wise to stop reviling Putin and speaking of him as an evil person. He seems to be good for his country, which is giving a better life to the citizens, and which allows them to have freedom of religion, and although limited from our point of view, but quite astonishing for the average Russian, access to information and arts. We just should watch him very carefully as he is a sly politician. I like to compare him to a great chess player — always thinking of future moves and having goals reaching far ahead. How do I know it? I do watch the Russian news from time to time. In Russian. And marvel at our own distortion of facts. It is only when one has access to different countries' propaganda that one sees how everybody bends the facts to their own needs. We all should have more humility and knowledge of history when judging others.

## July 10, 2015

When my children were small, and I was so often very tired, I read mainly detective stories. Agatha Christie, Simenon, Earl Stanley Gardner were my way of relaxation. The so-called mysteries were not very mysterious and did not create much tension. You know, none of the contemporary blood-curdling violence and fear-inducing thrillers. My beloved detectives were Miss Marple, Poirot, and Maigret. Then as I started to sleep better, as the children took less of my time, I went back to reading more serious novels and a lot of nonfiction. The culmination came with Elastic Mind. Those were the years of reading mainly books that dealt with serious matters. After seven years of leading this group I again craved lighter stuff. I discovered Donna Leon. She writes detective stories based in Venice where she has lived for many years. Her protagonist Guido Brunetti is a man I would like to be friends with. Both he and his wife, a professor of English literature at the local university, are people I would gladly spend time with. As usual with me, if I like an author I try to read everything he or she wrote. So it was with Donna Leon. I only stopped when I had read all of her twenty books, and am waiting impatiently for more. Then came Andrea Camilieri with his Sicily-based policeman Montalbano, and finally I discovered Louise Penny, a Canadian writer who manages to create great plots, interesting characters, and psychological portraits that grabbed me totally. A fantastic mixture of mystery and deep thoughts about humanity. Again I read all she wrote and can't wait for more.

This thing with reading everything a writer wrote sometimes leads to very unexpected results. Shortly after I met Donnelly he told me about Toni Morrison. He was reading her *Beloved* at the time. I went to a used bookstore and bought six or seven of her novels. At first it was hard for me to understand the language used by the African-American subculture, after all my English came from a British school and reading mainly British literature. After around one hundred pages though, I got it and enjoyed it to the max. There came though a moment after reading her fifth or sixth book when I began to feel that Toni Morrison was taking over my brain. I felt that I was looking at the world, at people, from her perspective, that my mind was not mine anymore. I got frightened. I had never had such an experience in my whole life. I put away her books and asked Donnelly, with whom I shared a house by then, to not allow me to read any more Toni Morrison. It took me several years before I could go back to her books. Luckily for me other writers do not have such influence on my thinking.

I could name several books that early on influenced me in a lasting way, but one seems most prominent: *Essays* by Michel de Montaigne. It was during that first trip with my father that in one of the hotels he told me not to read the book he left on his bedside table as it was a book for grown-ups. It was in French, my French was rather simple at that time, but after, I don't know, fifty or so pages (of course I got into the book as soon as I was left alone) I started to understand and enjoy what I read. *Essays* spoke to me with a strength I never knew before. Of course, a lot was beyond my ability to comprehend, but it showed me what I should be looking for, thinking about. All my life I've always had a copy of that book with me. It and Samuel Pepys's *Diaries* were the first books I bought when I came to America.

*Essays* is a constant joy to me. You might have noticed that I began this book with a citation from it. Now I think it would be appropriate to end with a citation from the note "To the Reader" that Michel de Montaigne wrote in his famous work:

"Reader, this is an honest book... I have given no consideration in it either to your service or to my glory. My powers are not capable of such an aim... If I had intended to seek the favor of the world, I should have adorned myself better and should have presented myself in a studied bearing. I wish to be seen in my simple, natural, and ordinary fashion, without effort or artifice, for it is myself that I portray... So farewell, from Montaigne, this first day of March, fifteen hundred and eighty."

Montaigne speaks for me across all those years — first in my childhood, and now near the end of that great arc of life. After all, it was in the *Essays* that I saw for the first time: "The value of life lies not in the length of days, but in the use we make of them." And so, like him, I want to say: Farewell from Joanna, this tenth day of July, two thousand fifteen.

Made in the USA
Monee, IL
22 May 2021